LITERARY
CONVERSATION

Thinking, Talking, and Writing about Literature

PATSY CALLAGHAN
CENTRAL WASHINGTON UNIVERSITY

ANN DOBYNS
JOHN CARROLL UNIVERSITY

ALLYN AND BACON
BOSTON LONDON TORONTO SYDNEY TOKYO SINGAPORE

Vice President: Eben W. Ludlow
Editorial Assistant: Morgan Lance
Manufacturing Buyer: Aloka Rathnam
Marketing Manager: Lisa Kimball
Editorial-Production Service: Electronic Publishing Services Inc.
Cover Administrator: Suzanne Harbison

Copyright © 1996 by Allyn & Bacon
A Simon & Schuster Company
Needham Heights, Massachusetts 02194

Library of Congress Cataloging-in-Publication Data
Callaghan, Patsy.
  Literary conversation : thinking, talking, and writing about literature / Patsy Callaghan, Ann Dobyns.
    p. cm.
  Includes bibliographical references and index.
  ISBN 0–205–16897–3 1. English language—Rhetoric—Problems, exercises, etc. 2. Criticism—Authorship—Problems, exercises, etc. 3. Literature—History and criticism—Theory, etc. 4. Critical thinking—Problems, exercises, etc. 5. Discussion—Problems, exercises, etc. I. Dobyns, Ann, 1946– . II. Title.
PE1479.C7C35   1995
807'.6—dc20   95–34155
                                                                                      CIP

Printed in the United States of America

10 9 8 7 6 5 4 3 2 1   99 98 97 96 95

Text credits are found in the Acknowledgments (pp. 253–54), which should be considered extensions of the copyright page.

For our parents

Contents

P r e f a c e

Learning to Love the Search

"I like to read, but I don't really like analyzing the details."

"I didn't say anything because I disagreed with what was being said."

"Every teacher wants something different. Can't you just tell us what you want?"

"Sometimes I like my papers; sometimes they just feel phony or mechanical."

"I don't know what to write about until I go read the critics in the library."

"I know what I think, but I can't prove it."

We wrote this book for any reader who has ever said these things or felt like saying them, and we wrote it for any instructor who has listened with concern as capable students make such comments. We see several key questions underlying the students' words, questions not limited to novice readers but central to current scholarly discussions about interpretation, rhetoric, and pedagogy. What is interpretation? What do we do when we interpret? How are our interpretations influenced by our lives, our membership in communities and cultures, and our knowledge of literary traditions, conventions, and practices? And who are *we*, anyway?

As we asked ourselves these questions as teachers, readers, and writers, we began to see the power in a metaphor that has become familiar in scholarly studies focusing on language, thought, and culture: the conversation.

Every day, readers make sense of their experience through the interpretation required by conversation. We want readers to interact with literature in ways as natural, complex, challenging, and gratifying as those they employ in everyday interactions with others, motivated by the desire to understand and to be understood.

This text invites readers to join widening and concentric circles of conversation, beginning with the interaction of the reader with the voice or voices in the literary work, and expanding to include the contributions of other readers, the dialogues of the disciplinary community permitted by the shared language of literary conventions, and finally the voices of other experienced readers available through published works of criticism. Within each circle of conversation, students are given opportunities to explore their observations and generalizations through private reflections in reading notebooks, through the collaborative dialogues of reading groups, and through public, finished essays that ask them to look at a work from a sequence of progressively complicated positions: students write responses to, analyses of, critical arguments about, and research essays on literary works.

Because the number of works we can teach in a term or a semester is limited, we developed a process of interacting with literature that would enable our students to take authority over their learning away from us, allowing them to become informed readers and to see us less as answer-givers and more as colleagues. We believe that students learn best when they participate in a community of diverse learners who share observations, question each others' assertions, value each others' differences, and look for common understandings. As Wayne Booth says, good college teaching "leads students to want to continue work in the given subject and to be able to, because they have the necessary intellectual equipment to continue work at a more advanced level." Maya Angelou, too, advocates this way of approaching literary texts: "I'd like my students to learn how to learn, to be involved in the process of teaching themselves. And to make commitments—not to be in love with the position, but to be in love with the search."

Our intent in sharing this text with you is to support your efforts to help students take responsibility for their own searches, constructing their own questions and answers, and participating in the kind of conversation that leads to discovery and new knowledge. In introductory courses, where readers encounter a range of literary works, they can gain confidence in their critical abilities by accepting the invitations to engage, reflect, respond, analyze, generalize, and interpret that appear regularly throughout each chapter. In upper division courses, readers can work with this text on their own or together, expanding their repertoire of interpretive strategies and increasing their knowledge of options, conventions, and traditions.

Acknowledgments

As you experiment with this text, we hope you will talk about your ideas, suggestions, and experiences with your colleagues, exploring together your students' questions about interpretation and writing. We certainly have been the beneficiaries of such dialogues, in which our mentors and colleagues have generously shared their theories and practices. Our indebtedness to the transformative scholarship of Wayne Booth, Kenneth Burke, Mikhail Bakhtin, Louise Rosenblatt, John Gage, Ann Berthoff, Lawrence Green, and Henry Giroux is apparent throughout the text. We are also grateful to our colleagues, Bobby Cummings, Sally Joranko, David Klooster, Christine Sutphin, and Eileen Turoff, who taught the manuscript in draft and offered responses; to those who read it and offered suggestions at various stages, including Patricia Bloem, Linda Bensel-Meyers, and Tom Conley; and to Caron Knapp, whose advice about disks and e-mail accelerated our process considerably. Essential to the development of the text were the comments of our reviewers, Stephen C. Behrendt, University of Nebraska; L. Bensel-Meyers, University of Tennessee–Knoxville; Tom Erskine, Salisbury State University; Cheryl Glenn, Oregon State University; George Otte, Baruch College (CUNY). Finally, to Chuck, Sarah, Jeff, Kevin, Ian, and Ellen go our thanks for their intelligence, good humor, and patience.

Please include us in your literary conversations as you think, talk, and write about literature.

Patsy Callaghan
English Department
Central Washington University
Ellensburg; WA 98926
E-Mail: callaghp@cwu.edu

Ann Dobyns
English Department
John Carroll University
University Heights, OH 44118
adobyns@jcvaxa.jcu.edu

Interpretation as Conversation

The Reader, the Writer, the Work

INTERPRETATION AS A NATURAL ACTIVITY

We all interpret, every day. Imagine this: as you walk down a busy street, you see an acquaintance across the way. You wave. She does not wave back. You try again. No reply. What goes through your mind? She didn't see you. (But she was looking right your way!) She didn't recognize you. (But last time you met, you spoke for nearly an hour about a job possibility!) Did you say something during that visit that offended her? On the other hand, is she near-sighted? Or maybe she's just being rude. Or . . .

Depending on your skills as an interpreter, you could go on and on. The example shows two things about interpreting: it's natural, and it's an attempt to make meaningful an ambiguous event, moment, or observation by identifying or connecting with it. You may be attempting to understand something you didn't predict, or make the unfamiliar familiar, but in either case, you may find yourself frustrated when you try to interpret something without knowing enough. In the scenario described above, you don't have enough information, nor are you particularly conscious of the ways in which you are reflecting on the situation. Imagination runs freely. However, you are thinking in predictable, nameable ways about your experience. You check the "story sequence" to see if your expectations are reasonable. You check your perceptions: were you not seen, or were you seen and ignored? You investigate, haphazardly but in some detail, both possibilities: if you were seen but ignored, is there an explanation in your mutual history? In your personality? In the other person's position or character? If not seen, is there an explanation in your or her personal experience that could account for the difference between perception and reality?

Our point is not that you should scrutinize every detail of your daily encounters. (If you did, there would be a reason for your friends and acquaintances to avoid you!) Our intent, rather, is to illustrate briefly and simply how adept we all are at the kinds of thinking involved in interpreting, and how the motive to interpret is the same as the desire to understand ourselves, each other, and the world we inhabit. This chapter defines interpretation as a natural human activity, as natural as conversation. We are all interpreters, and practicing the art of interpretation can help us confront and take pleasure in the complexities of living together in the world.

INTERPRETATION AS CONVERSATION

Consider the ways you go about meeting people. Encountering someone new, you make observations and generalizations based on your assumptions, your needs, and your expectations. If you are speaking to someone you are unlikely to meet again, you may respond superficially and mechanically. However, suppose you find a person engaging and can imagine a continuing association, even a friendship. Eye contact, voice, manner, mood, style, opinions, stories: these details take on significance as you ask yourself, "What is this person like? What do we have in common? How are we different?" And most of all, "Am I likely to want to connect with this person again?" These questions inform your way of seeing and valuing the other person as you reflect, react, and respond.

You may begin, quite automatically and subconsciously, to look for significance in details and patterns that complicate your first impressions: "She's about my age, comes from a small town and is having the same kind of difficulty I am getting oriented to this new place." You may even try testing your generalizations: you might, for example, mention your high school graduation date, the ages of your brothers or sisters or children, or the last concert you attended, or you might call attention to a difference between your new place of residence and where you grew up, or tell a story about some trouble you just had dealing with your new circumstances, to see if these facts strike a chord or establish a common pattern between you. You may also reach conclusions about the other person based on her response to your efforts to connect: "She'd like to make the effort to get to know me better," or "She's waiting for someone and is being polite."

These statements and conclusions are interpretations based on observations and motivated by the desire to understand and be understood by others. The metaphor of conversation enables us to describe this interpretive process as natural and familiar, complicated and challenging, and well worth the effort, all at the same time. During a conversation we are sending messages based on our own experiences and backgrounds. We are responding emotionally and imaginatively to the messages we are being sent, analyzing the information we are given, looking for significance and patterns in the details, and drawing and redrawing conclusions as we accumulate relevant information.

Conversing naturally with others depends on several abilities. First, it depends on our skill at engaging and responding: we need to find a way to relate personally with the people and the subject. Second, effective conversation depends on how well we know and use the conventions and patterns which guide it: people who are difficult to talk to often violate the unspoken rules of conversation and set us off balance or make us uncomfortable by the content or manner of their contributions. Third, effective conversation depends on whether or not the participants discover or identify shared understandings that can provide a common ground for discussion: though their conclusions may be different, the participants have the same understanding of the issue and can thus talk about the relative merits of their reasoning. Fourth, it depends on our ability to listen to others and our willingness to change our minds when new knowledge or new circumstances warrant a change.

The conditions and abilities, as well as the complications, that characterize conversation also characterize literary interpretation. Good readers observe the language of the work, noting its features and details and reflecting on their relationship and significance. Good readers listen to the voice or voices of the work, engaging with its perspective, or sometimes varied perspectives. Good readers also pay attention to their own responses, positive or negative, and inquire about them, asking what features of the work and what factors in their personal lives or values might have caused the responses. Good readers can make up their minds about what a work means, but they also can revise their interpretations when new experience or new knowledge warrants a change of mind. When readers do all these carefully, they are reading responsibly. The process of reading responsibly can help us move beyond first impressions or preconceived notions to considered, reasonable understandings and positions.

In the following chapters of this book, we invite you to practice the arts of literary conversation, building on your natural inclinations to respond emotionally and imaginatively to new situations, to make sense of details and observations, to establish common ground that will enable you to understand other people and their ideas, and to find significance in your interactions with others who are like, and not like, you. Literary conversations happen inside of literary works, when characters interact with each other or with their social or cultural environments. There is also a kind of conversation between the writer's voice and the reader, as we try to connect with the persona in the work, asking ourselves about the person or persons telling us the story. Another kind of literary conversation happens when we talk to other readers about a work we have shared, during which we reveal, discover, and connect our thoughts in the process of making the work meaningful together. Yet another kind happens when we seek out other readers who have written about a work we are interested in; literary critics, too, are involved in conversations in writing with each other, conversations we can join when we want to, validating, challenging, or broadening our own interpretive ideas.

INTERPRETATION AS A DESIRE TO CONNECT WITH OTHERS

Think back to a time when you received a grade that surprised or confused you. Which interpretations of the event did you try out in your mind? Did you wonder whether the teacher had misread your answer? Did you wonder whether you misread the directions or the criteria? Did you try to figure out why your sense of the quality of the work was so different from that of the teacher? The interpretive questions you ask yourself will depend on who you are and what you assume about your abilities, your instructor's character and skill, your experiences with similar tasks, and your criteria for judging the value of the assignment. To clarify the confusion, you would need to talk to the instructor and inquire about those assumptions, trying to locate the source of the misunderstanding. What would motivate that conversation? Your desire not to be misunderstood. You may or may not feel comfortable enough to seek out an explanation, but without shared assumptions, there will be no understanding. One assumption of the art of interpretation is that we *care* to address incomplete or mistaken understandings. And yet, so many factors inhibit or limit understanding. Personality, culture, experiences, gender, upbringing, economic status, desires, and fears all can influence our response to others, and can influence their responses to us.

Because of our differences and because language itself is full of ambiguities and possibilities for confusion, the skill of interpretation is necessary to make conversation, and therefore interpersonal connection, possible. Interpretation is more than scientific analysis of the data of the language. When interpretation stops seeming connected to an emotional experience evoked by the literature, it loses the pleasure of the potential connection, and often, therefore, its significance for us as readers. Interpretation must be inspired by the human desire to engage with a question regarding an event, person, or experience that we care to understand.

The "pleasure" we talk about in literary interpretation is the same as the feeling we get in good conversation. We say "I get it," or "I see what you mean," or "We seem to be on the same wavelength." We also often take pleasure in saying "I see where you're coming from, but let me explain how I'm seeing it differently." All those moments in conversation—when we're agreeing familiarly, or when we're disagreeing discerningly and respectfully—provide a sense of achievement that comes from bridging, if only tentatively, a gap in understanding.

Most human beings desire to understand what is going on around them and to be understood within the context of their world, even when that world is as small as the dialogue between two people. But understanding is not always easy. The world's complications can be dangerous to us; differences, uncertainties and ambiguities remind us of our separateness and make us fear, hate, dismiss, or demean things and people unlike us or incomprehensible to us or not predicted by us. But responsible, informed interpreting can ease fears, bring solutions, offer possibilities, promote empathy, and create the possibility for mutual understanding. On the other hand, many of the world's complications—from interpersonal to global interaction—are exacerbated by irresponsible, uninformed interpretations. Humans will make meaning of experience, but sometimes that meaning fails to account for differences, fails to take into account assumptions and premises that provide a context for their reasonableness, fails to consider possibilities at least as probable as the ones that first occur to us.

We'd like to share with you a poem that raises interpretive questions about conversing and interpreting as a way of knowing who we are. The poet, Jeremy Cronin, is a South African who was arrested in 1976 for having assisted the African National Congress; in this poem, from a collection called *Inside*, Cronin shares an image from his prison experiences. Read the poem at least twice, and then write out some informal reflections on the questions that follow.

JEREMY CRONIN

A Person Is a Person Because of Other People
(Motho Ke Motho Ka Batho Babang)

By holding my mirror out of the window I see
Clear to the end of the passage.
There's a person down there.

A prisoner polishing a door handle.
In the mirror I see him see
My face in the mirror,
I see the fingertips of his free hand
Bunch together, as if to make
An object the size of a badge
Which travels up to his forehead
The place of an imaginary cap.
    (This means: A warder.)
Two fingers are extended in a vee
And wiggle like two antennae.
    (He's being watched.)
A finger of his free hand makes a watch-hand's arc
On the wrist of his polishing arm without
Disrupting the slow-slow rhythm of his work.
    (Later. Maybe, later we can speak.)
Hey! Wat maak jy daar?*
    —a voice from around the corner.
No. Just polishing baas.**
He turns his back to me, now watch
His free hand, the talkative one,
Slips quietly behind
    —Strength brother, it says,
In my mirror,
    A black fist.

* What are you doing?
**boss

EXERCISE 1.1. LITERATURE AS CONVERSATION

Reflect on the following questions in writing. Discuss your answers with others.

1. Summarize the situation in the poem. If there is conversation in this poem, who is talking to whom? What is said?

2. Whom do you identify with in the poem? What do you know about him? Why does he do what he does? What

does he want? What does he get? Why is it important to him?

3. How do you react to the poem? What does it make you feel? Have you felt that way before? In what situation?

4. What connections can you make between this poem and the first three subheadings in this chapter: Interpretation as a Natural Activity, Interpretation as Conversation, Interpretation as a Desire to Connect with Others.

5. What do you believe is meant by the title of the poem? How does the title fit the poem? Do you believe the assertion the title makes? Why?

Interpretation as a Conversation with a Writer

For practicing reader-interpreters, the analogy of conversation requires an imaginative leap. Reflecting on Cronin's poem, we can imagine the prisoner as a reader, the symbols reflected in the mirror as a poem, and the man whose hand shapes the message as a writer. But if we shift our perspective and focus on our experience of the poem, *we* are the readers, and Jeremy Cronin is the writer who shapes the symbols to share a message with us. In both instances, the work is made up of shared symbols through which readers and writers communicate, or converse.

The writer may not be present in a work as a participant, but the literary work presents an experience carefully crafted by a writer to be shared by a reader. The reader enters the work speculatively, motivated by a desire to inhabit, temporarily, the world constructed by the writer, in order to see something in a new way. Readers will never know for sure if their perceptions match those the writer intended for them to share. However, it matters that readers regard literary works as constructed purposefully, by a person who hoped to be understood, in the manner of one conversing with another.

A poet speaking in a literature class recently about her own poetry was asked by a reader, "What would you feel like if we read one of your works in a way that differed from your intentions?" "That would be fine," she replied. "When I finish a poem, it takes on a life of its own. But," she added, "I really hope you would find *me* in it somewhere." Her two answers are not contradictory—the poem will always include more than her intentions, both because of the ambiguities of language and because each reader brings his or her own contributions to the reading experience; however, the poem also offers evidence of her careful, purposeful choices, and attending to those choices can help us perceive what might be called an "informing voice," or persona, with whom we converse as we read.

A reader may imagine this writer-persona as one who challenges, disrupts, mentors, identifies, validates, informs, angers. After all, we have relationships with people who function in these different ways. But to accept this relationship, to take the risk of pursuing understanding, requires the desire to look at the world the way the work presents it and to identify, if only tentatively, with that perspective in order to see how it relates to or changes our own. Such practice has many values, particularly when you seek relationships with works that extend or challenge your own experiences and background. These relationships require that you become aware of your own expectations, principles, and values in order to compare them to ones you witness. They require that you make sense of a writer's choices or a character's actions in terms that previously you may not have considered. Therefore, they equip you to connect with difference, to confront and comprehend ambiguity in the world, to form relationships where you perceived only separation, and to replace fear or distance with understanding and connection.

As you converse with the work and with other readers about the work, you often come to understand yourself and others better in terms of your conversation. In microcosm, group discussions about the ideas, events, people, and world views in literature offer a way to practice the art of creating shared understandings about the world we live in.

EXERCISE 1.2. CONVERSING WITH THE POEM

1. In the last exercise, you reflected on the conversation taking place inside the poem, the one between the two prisoners. Now we'd like to invite you to consider an imaginative conversation with the prisoner. If you could talk to him, what would you say? What would you ask? How do you imagine him responding?

2. Imagine a conversation with the warder. You don't know much about him, so for the purposes of inquiry, think of him as a good man who believes in the rules. He works hard; his position and his property rights are threatened by political change. He has a job to do, and his work is dangerous. Ask him what he thinks of the poem. Imagine his resistances, and persuade him that he might find a way to understand it, despite the cultural and situational differences between his station and the prisoner's.

3. Imagine a conversation with Cronin, who chose to share this scene with you, who made specific writer's choices that influenced, even shaped, your response to the situation. If you had the opportunity, what would you tell him? What would you ask? How do you imagine he would respond?

4. If possible, try out the conversations described in Exercises 1, 2, and 3 with friends. Role play interviewer and interviewee, and note interesting observations that come up as you talk. What questions take on significance?

INTERPRETATION AS CULTURAL CONVERSATION: SEEING OUR BIASES, SHAPING OUR VALUES

We live in a world of interpretations, of differing and changing perspectives, expectations, and norms. To live in it positively and hopefully, we must be able to reflect on those differences and changes and still make decisions and judgments about what we think and believe. Practicing literary interpretation can help us reflect on what we know and learn, make decisions in a world where facts aren't always enough, and communicate our understandings to each other. By interpreting together, we both find and make the world we live in more comprehensible, more our own. When we interpret, we press ourselves beyond our own perceptions and observations in order to see something a new way, make reasoned judgments, assign values, and render informed opinions.

Sometimes, though, you have brought your experiences, your knowledge, and your training to bear, and you find yourself resisting the experience the work offers: "I just can't get into it. I can't relate." At those moments you can discover the powers and pleasures of reflecting on what it is that *prevents* you from engaging. The question "Why don't I like this?" can lead to discoveries about the literature, about yourself, and about your culture or the culture of the work that are as interesting and challenging as those prompted by any other question.

Literature reflects, through its assumptions and characterizations, a version of reality. The way we "understand" a literary work is, in a sense, the way we come to make friends out of acquaintances. We try to perceive and understand the way they see things, their version of reality. To come to terms with a literary work, we must assent to its assumptions enough to imagine ourselves within that world. Once we have done so, we can identify the way the world is, or is not, validated or challenged by our own experiences and knowledge. The point of writing out your resistances is not to prove a work wrong or right, but to identify differences that are significant, differences that tell us something about what we value, whom we value, what we assume, whom we believe, and whose vision is privileged over what other possibilities.

In the following poem, William Shakespeare sets up a distinction that seems simple but, as the subsequent student comments illustrate, is riddled with ambiguities. We invite you to read the poem, and then review what our students had to say.

WILLIAM SHAKESPEARE
Two Loves I Have of Comfort and Despair
(Sonnet 144)

Two loves I have of comfort and despair,
Which like two spirits do suggest me still;
The better angel is a man right fair,
The worser spirit a woman, color'd ill.
To win me soon to hell, my female evil
Tempteth my better angel from my side,
And would corrupt my saint to be a devil,
Wooing his purity with her foul pride.
And whether that my angel be turned fiend
Suspect I may, but not directly tell
But being both from me, both to each friend,
I guess one angel in another's hell:
Yet this shall I ne'er know, but live in doubt,
Till my bad angel fire my good one out.

EXERCISE 1.3. HOW DISCUSSION CHANGES RESPONSE

The students' summaries and responses were written before and after their reading group discussed Sonnet 144. They were asked to record their initial impressions and responses, and after group discussion, to record how their ideas had evolved.

1. Read the initial summaries and responses, and speculate in writing about the assumptions they reveal about literature,

Shakespeare, and gender. What are the initial questions and concerns of each writer?

2. Read the post-discussion summaries and responses, and compare them with the students' initial comments. How have their comments changed? Is there evidence that they have heard each other, or that they have listened to the persona or voice in the work in a new way?

INITIAL SUMMARIES AND RESPONSES

JACK: Although Shakespeare's language is a problem for me (I always have to read several times just to get a handle on the story), I think Shakespeare is reflecting on a previous relationship that has gone bad. I understand the feelings here, because I have had them about some of the women who have hurt me in my life. She was evil, he fell for her, and he got hurt.

NORMA: In "Two Loves I Have," my difficulty is understanding the connections Shakespeare has made between the two angels. How could they share one another's "hell"? It was obvious to me that he saw the woman as the evil spirit, but the ambiguity in the last few lines leaves me wondering. Evil wins?

MIKE: I'm not satisfied with my reactions, but I can't really connect with this poem. The angels, the spirits, it's all too fantastical to me. I like poems more that are grounded in real experience. The narrator is working something out on a plane I don't visit very often.

JENNY: I'm confused. I'm not sure what Shakespeare is trying to get across and I'm not sure I want to know. Because I am taking a women's literature class I am sensitive to the fact that Shakespeare made the "worser" spirit a woman, connecting evil inclinations and behaviors with women. There's been enough of that in the culture since the Adam and Eve story for me to be put off by it here. But I have a question: which angel is he talking about near the end? I got confused about which was good and which was bad.

TONI: There is some kind of struggle going on between good and evil, but all of the flimsy words like "doubt," "guess," and "not directly tell" lets me know the sides are not clear. The last three lines dumbfound me. I can't connect them to the rest of the poem.

They, and the title, seem to contradict the evil/good polarity
in the poem.

POST-DISCUSSION SUMMARIES AND RESPONSES

JACK: The person in Sonnet 144 is caught. Whatever caused him to
feel trapped between his reactions, the trap is causing him pain. He
wants to escape the despair but if he does, he'll lose the comfort
which he could have by being in love. He feels he must suffer
between living with a heart broken by love, or live with a heart
void of love. He knows he'll choose to be in love, though it brings
despair, because he loves the feelings it allows him to have.

NORMA: I believe the angels are both part of him, and his struggle
is internal. I read the lines "But being both from me, both to each a
friend/I guess one in another's hell," as saying that the angels
share intimate knowledge of each other. Each of them is in the
others' hell when the situation favors the other, and the narrator
feels helpless, or unable, or unwilling (?) to take responsibility for
his destiny, as if he is a simple pawn in the angels' arguments with
each other.

MIKE: The group discussion has made me wonder if the poem were
written not about things that are fantastic, but things the persona
felt and was going through personally. I began to tie the poem into
ways I think and feel about people, and especially pressures, in my
own life. Sometimes the factors surrounding everyday decisions
feel so large and distant that you can almost give them names, as if
they were not part of you. Sometimes what you need and what you
get are so different and so connected that you can feel pulled apart
by them.

JENNY: Maybe the female spirit isn't so evil after all. Maybe the narrator liked the female spirit better than the other, even if he isn't
pleased with himself for preferring her. The woman spirit is a part
of his own soul, as is the "fair man." The narrator's conscience,
then, is neither pure nor evil, but a combination of the two. Still, I
can't quite rid myself of the impression, in the language, that the
female spirit is disruptive, or the resistance to his connection of evil
with the female gender.

TONI: Whereas I'd seen this as a struggle for the good angel to
withstand the assaults of the bad, I now see it as a justification of

the inevitability of what he's calling evil. This person is drawn, at least at times, to the dark side, and his sensible (male) side warns him not to go there. And he loves and generally listens to that good angel. However, he also loves that dark side. And in the last three lines, it appears he will not be able to fully experience that alluring dark side until the good angel (light?) is flushed out.

RESPONSIBLE INTERPRETATION: SHARED UNDERSTANDINGS DEPEND ON SHARED SYMBOLS AND CONVENTIONS

The two prisoners in the poem "A Person Is a Person Because of Other People" could communicate because they shared a set of symbols: the shapes created by the prisoner's fingertips and reflected in a mirror became a kind of literary work, significant and powerful to a reader who understood their meaning. Those symbols become significant and powerful for us, as readers, when another messenger, the poet, translates them for us parenthetically in the poem. By sharing the symbols, we are joined in common understanding and are changed by our new affiliation.

The readers of "Two Loves I Have of Comfort and Despair" saw different possibilities in the poem, differences that affected their responses. Though the conversation about the poem relied on the readers' shared understandings—angel, spirit, saint, and hell, for example, referred to a symbol system these students were familiar with—there were many questions relating to the meaning or significance of specific language conventions and writer's choices. Discussions of possible answers to these questions also rely on a system of shared understandings about language and language conventions.

Within any area of interest, be it music, economics, medicine, or literature, particular methods of interpretation develop as nameable patterns that allow for more and more sophisticated analyses of observations and inquiries. As we use these strategies and methods to inquire about meaning, we acquire language that allows us to see features precisely and to communicate with each other more specifically. In addition, we develop sets of expectations—about causes and results, actions and reactions, intentions and fulfillment. These expectations, which might be called "norms," become the common knowledge of the area of study. In the area of literature study, this "language about language" is usually the primary subject of books about reading. In this book, we introduce methods and terms as they help us talk about what we see in order to answer questions the works raise for us. This "language about language" serves our need to understand and to communicate our understandings to others.

To help you integrate this "language about language" into your conversations about literature, we have included at the end of the book a section designed to link **style** to meaning. The Appendix, Coming to Terms: Literary Language and Its Uses, offers a list of literary terms, definitions, and examples that are intended to help you fit words to your observations and names to your ideas. It is divided into two sections. Part A includes descriptions of four kinds of terms and the questions they help you ask; these categories include Shape, Language, Participants, and Situations. Part B offers an alphabetical glossary of specific terms used in literary discussions. Terms that appear in boldface in this book are defined in the glossary.

Think about the Appendix as the kind of information Cronin offered you in the parentheses in "A Person Is a Person Because of Other People": he was translating the language of shared **symbols** for you so that you, too, could find their power and significance, so that you could be part of the conversation.

EXERCISE 1.4. EXPLORING THE APPENDIX

Read the entries on **sonnet, tone, critical approaches: feminist criticism**, and **values** in the alphabetized glossary, Part B of the Appendix.

1. Does the description of how the **sonnet** form usually works help you to understand the development of Shakespeare's Sonnet 144?

2. Speculate about the **tone** of Sonnet 144. Is it despairing? Is it comfortable? Is it fearful? Is it funny? What seems to be the speaker's attitude about his dilemma?

3. How might a feminist critic prioritize the questions at issue in Sonnet 144? What **values** govern feminist readings?

INTERPRETATION AS CLASSROOM CONVERSATION

How do we learn? When we need to know facts, we can consult authorities. When we need background information, we can consult people knowledgeable about the subject. Often, though, what we consider facts are really conclusions that a group of people have agreed on, given the information available. When the facts aren't enough or ready information doesn't resolve our questions, we try—as a jury does—to reach common understandings based on the information we have. As learners, we often come to know and understand collaboratively, by conversing with each other. As we pool information and share ideas, our knowledge is reshaped and refined.

Courses in literature are unique in presenting opportunities for you to practice the art of the cultural conversation and participate in the experience of collaborative interpretation, confronting issues of human values unresolvable by presentations of facts or applications of ready knowledge. Literary works are the territory in which we are best able to cultivate in ourselves the qualities that others have associated with the experienced or mature person: openness to genuine dialogue about differences of opinion; awareness of the relationship of our own views to our particular time, circumstance, and **culture**; the ability to inquire responsibly and ethically about opinions and beliefs; a willingness to change our minds when good reasons dictate that change is warranted. Literary works exemplify the whole range of human possibility, encouraging the kind of self-reflection and cultural awareness required of the experienced person.

Thus, although this work presents information and ideas that assist you in expanding your ability to see meaning and significance in literature, it also assumes that, rather than passive recipients of literary meaning, you are active participants in shaping literary meaning. You are invited to converse about literature formally and informally in several ways, through reading and writing groups, as well as through informal and formal writing. The following descriptions should help you understand how such group conversations can effectively contribute to your reading experiences. If you are currently in a literature course, it may employ these strategies for encouraging collaborative interpretation, but if not, you can organize or employ those which are most helpful to you as you think, talk, and write about literature. Think of the exercises throughout each chapter as suggestive of ways to incorporate these strategies into your reading and writing processes; in many cases, the group exercises can be modified to work as individual explorations, and the individual explorations can be augmented by a discussion with others.

Reading Notebooks

Many people are confused by literature because they think they should "get it" on a first reading. Actually, because you are reading not just to find information but also to make meaning, your first reading is an orientation that helps you engage with the work, as well as reflect on your reading to find your questions at issue, articulate your emotional responses and explore them, and take note of what seems significant. Some readers like to keep a notebook informally, simply making comments or asking questions as they think of them. Others have found it helpful to have some framework for beginning and organizing this reflection process.

Some readers like to write on blank paper and collect their reflections in a folder. Others like the "journal entry" format allowed by a bound notebook. The writer and critic Ann Berthoff suggested the "Double Entry Notebook" as a tool for encouraging reflection. She suggests we use notebook paper, dividing each page in two with a line from top to bottom. On the left side, we record direct quotations and summaries. On the right side, we comment on and ask ourselves questions about our notes. What's important about it? What does it remind me of? What does it connect to? What does it conflict with? What else does it seem to explain? It helps to leave room to explore tentative answers to our questions.

Another strategy for reflecting in a reading notebook is to begin by retelling, or summarizing, the work as if to a friend you respect who has asked you "What is it about?" Next, record your emotional and imaginative responses to the story, thinking about how you reacted and what in your makeup or history might influence your reactions. Then write about the **point of view**, thinking about whose perspective has been presented, what you know about the person or persons who tell the story, and to what extent you can trust the perspectives they offer. This way of responding is especially good when you can follow your reflection with group discussion. Because readers respond differently, they summarize differently: their responses partially determine how they see and assign significance to the details of the work. Sharing these reflections helps you expose and explore divergent ideas, which will challenge and enrich your reading experience.

There is no right way to record your reflections; the suggestions above are tools, not rules. The minute you decide to write questions, comments will come to you. The minute you decide to record a running commentary, questions will pop out. The important thing is to reflect: to pay attention to the signals being sent to you, and to be conscious of your effort to connect and comprehend them.

Reading Groups

Any group, no matter the size, whose members read the same works and set aside time to talk about them is a reading group. We know many people who are not in college, many who never had the chance to go, who take the time to be in a reading group. One builder we know sees his bimonthly reading discussions as a natural evolution of storytelling around the fire. Though we realize that the group discussion opportunities for readers of this text will take place mostly in classrooms with desks, we would like to keep our builder's storytelling image in mind. In addition to the invitations we make for in-class group discussions, therefore, we hope you will have opportunities to talk together about your reading in environments less conditioned by hourly bells and quarterly grades.

In this text, we refer to reading groups in exercises that encourage sharing opinions, reactions, and questions toward the end of clarifying and enriching everyone's understanding. Groups go wrong when one member dominates, when the belief in "right answers" prohibits the expression of alternate views, when the goal seems unclear and the conversation shifts to other topics, or when pressure to come up with consensus by 10:55 inhibits free exchange. Reading groups work when members know they are to articulate and focus questions at issue, raise and complicate possible answers, and look for patterns of significance that could elicit not one but multiple interpretations, each supportable with reasoned explanations based on experience, knowledge, and observations. Much of this text is designed to assist in the development of this ability to reach shared understandings about literature; we think the process is working when it refuses to end at 10:55 but spills into hallways and malls and dinner conversations.

Practicing the art of reading together can strengthen our ability to imagine ourselves beyond ourselves when we are reading alone, to include in our own reflections possibilities beyond our first impressions, and to construct meanings that take into account other orientations and perspectives.

Writing Groups

Involvement in a writing group is a good way to help you see how informal and formal writing, often seen as the individual product of learning, are also the products of dialogue—with authors, other readers, and literary critics, as well as the internal dialogues of personal reflection. Writing is a process of coming to know what it is you think, and your thinking is refined and clarified when considered by others. Understanding a literary work requires you to enter the world of that work through the imagination, the emotions, and the intellect. In the same way, your readers must find a way to enter the world of your paper, and because they can tell you when your purpose seems clear and your reasons seem acceptable, you know you have succeeded in your effort to be understood.

Writing groups work when the members are clear on both the question at issue and the writer's proposed answer to that question, and they read the writing in light of the writer's purpose. Members listen to the writer's concerns, examining the strength of the central focus, the way the paper engages the reader, the design of the argument, the development of key points, and the clarity of the presentation. In the best cases, both the writers and the readers leave the conversation changed: the readers have come to understand the work in a new way through the papers they have read, and the writers have acquired a clearer understanding of their interpretive statements, as well as specific suggestions for making them understandable, reasonable, and acceptable to their readers.

Writing groups are useful when group members have writing to share; the tasks of the groups will be determined by the writers themselves, in response to particular assignments and needs. However, we want you to be aware from this beginning chapter that your writing deserves the same kind of attention and critical review as the works of others, so at the end of each chapter, following one of the invitations to write, we have included suggestions for writing group activities that will help you reread your writing with others in ways that may help you clarify and express your ideas.

SUMMARY

The purpose of sharing interpretations is not just to develop our own appreciation of a literary work; literature acts on us and changes us. We become who we are, at least in part, through interaction with other people, and literature abounds with characters, situations, and language that can help us understand ourselves and our relationships with others. Thinking about our interaction with a literary work as a conversation enables us to keep in mind the goal of the shared experience. Getting to know the **persona** or informing consciousness, the "voice" in the work, can help us understand ourselves and our worlds, validating, challenging, or modifying our attitudes, beliefs, perceptions, and ideas.

The philosopher and literary critic Kenneth Burke offers us a way to consider the significance of our individual contributions to the literary conversation by imagining ourselves at a parlor gathering:

> You come late. When you arrive, others have long preceded you, and they are engaged in a heated discussion, a discussion too heated for them to pause and tell you exactly what it is about. In fact, the discussion had already begun long before any of them got there, so that no one present is qualified to retrace for you all the steps that had gone before. You listen for a while, until you decide that you have caught the tenor of the argument; then you put in your oar. Someone answers; you answer him; another comes to your defense; another aligns himself against you, to either the embarrassment or gratification of your opponent, depending upon the quality of your ally's assistance. However, the discussion is interminable.

The hour grows late, you must depart. And you do depart, with the dis-cussion still vigorously in progress.

In literary studies, as in other academic disciplines, we go to the party, arriving late and eventually leaving—with some old questions tentatively answered and even more new questions articulated. Why do we go? To understand ourselves among others, to reinforce old relationships and form new ones, to fit in and hang out, to assert our individuality and to discover our connections, and to challenge ourselves with new ideas and knowledge that may affect the way we see ourselves and others. Sometimes the conversations take familiar turns; at other times they surprise, frustrate, or confuse, particularly when others express opinions we've never considered before, opinions that seem foreign to our experience or prior knowledge. Some people seem to have an easier time than others finding a way to enter and contribute to the conversation with a sense of engagement and satisfaction. We hope this text will help you know how to work the room with comfort and pleasure.

An Invitation to Write: Using a Reading Notebook to Reflect on Reader, Writer, and Work

As described in this chapter, the reading notebook is a tool, not a rule. It is helpful to try out a variety of strategies for noting your reactions and questions. Then make a habit out of what works for you. To begin your exploration of reading notebook uses, we invite you to use the following questions to explore a literary work chosen by you or your instructor. These questions ask you to reflect on the work by summarizing it, on your responses to the work by recording your reactions and feelings and speculating on possible reasons for them, and on your sense of the perspective offered on the world by the writer or narrator by considering what **points of view** are conveyed. Not all of the questions will elicit good insights for all readers, but whatever you discover will add to a diverse set of ideas that you can then discuss with other readers.

After you have read a literary work of your or your instructor's choosing, reflect on and write about the work in three ways.

1. Summarize the work, as if you were answering a respected friend who asked "What's it about?"

2. Describe the **point of view** presented in the work. Whose perspective do we have? Does it belong to a **character** inside or an observer

outside the work? If inside, what do we know about that character? How does he or she see the world, and others in it? Can he or she be trusted? If outside, do you perceive that he or she has a particular attitude toward the characters or events? Are there clues as to how we are to regard the characters or events, if we are to share the perspective of the observer?

3. Respond to the work. Were you easily engaged? What did you empathize with? What did you relate to? Was connecting with the work difficult? If so, what seems to be the cause of your resistance? Features of the writing? Experiences or ideas of your own?

4. After you have written about the work in the above ways, reflect on the writing you have done. What does it reveal about you as a reader? What features of the work seemed most significant to you? Where in your writing are there reflections of your experiences or values? What questions about your experiences or values emerge in your writing?

Writing Group Activity

If you have a writing group, compare your three responses with those of others who have read and responded to the same work. Which of the three kinds of responses was most difficult for you? What kinds of questions arose when you were writing? How do your summaries differ? How do your observations about point of view differ? How do your responses differ? For each kind of response, what did you focus on? What did you ignore? What in your backgrounds or in the work seemed to cause different responses? Do you see patterns of response which point to issues in the work worth discussing further?

Sample Writing: Reading Notebook Entry on "A Person Is a Person Because of Other People"

Your reading notebook is a log of your contributions to and reflections on the literary conversation. In this sample, a student uses the summary/point of view/response structure to help him think about Jeremy Cronin's poem, which appears earlier in this chapter. Which of his comments do you find most intriguing? Why? What kinds of questions does this student seem to be asking himself?

Summary: It helped to know that the speaker of the poem is in prison. Apparently prisoners are not allowed to communicate with each other. And yet they do. In this poem, one prisoner communicates with another through hand gestures reflected in a mirror. They can't talk. They can't even see each other. What the speaker sees is just a reflection of a part of a person trying to communicate. They don't talk, and yet they do. They couldn't, except that they understand the same hand gestures in the same way. The speaker says his free hand is "talkative." Every time he sends a message, he sends it with his "free hand," meaning the one that's not polishing, but also the one that's "free" because it can communicate. That's interesting to me because it shows the speaker is aware of the way their communication is "talk," and because the talking is associated with being "free." It's like when his two fingers are compared to "antennae," which receive and send radio or TV signals. (This image also makes me think of ants in an anthill.) What little communication they have overcomes walls and rules and politics; in fact, from a South African poet in prison, it could even be a statement about how the desire to communicate can overcome any artificial boundaries, including apartheid.

Point of view: The speaker, first person, is telling his own story, getting a message and translating it for us. He is a prisoner, a criminal, but he is human in that he is alone, and he wants to connect with others. He is vulnerable to the power of the "baas," and his communication with the other prisoner, who signals "Strength," is important to him because it reminds him of who he is. The poem ends with "A black fist," and that is a symbol which gives him, both of them, a common identity and purpose.

Response: This poem makes me think about how much we take for granted—our permission to speak freely, our right to talk to anyone we want. And the poem identifies that freedom as a kind of "strength." I hadn't thought of that connection before. I also hadn't thought of one of the consequences of prison as restricted communication, and although prisoners in our country, unless they are in "solitary," can presumably talk to each other, they cannot speak freely, nor can they talk anytime they want to whomever they want. So part of our strength is our freedom of speech. Emotionally, I feel a kind of desperation in the poem, the guy reaching out the bars with a mirror to get a reflected glimpse of someone he can relate to. Even the few Afrikaner words contribute to my experience of isolation and effort. It's a powerful thing. It occurs to me, too, probably because of our discussion about poetry and conversation, that the guy sending the signals is a kind of poet himself, and the prisoner with the mirror is reading those messages. It must be worth the effort, even when you have to reach through bars and despite the fact that what you see is no more than a partial reflection of the whole picture.

Extra Practice: Additional Writing Invitations

1. Write about something you have recently read as if your relationship with it is one of friendship. (Keep in mind that there are many kinds of friends.) What kind of friendship is it? Is this relationship an easy or difficult one? Does this friendship validate you? Does it challenge or change you? Is this friend a mentor, an equal, a companion, a respected foe? What might you say to this friend if you had the opportunity?

2. Write about a book you tried to read but couldn't. If you can conceive of your effort to read the book as an attempted conversation, what about the book made you decide not to bother? What barrier to appreciation or understanding did you not care or feel able to cross? Why?

Chapter 2

Interpretation as Shared Inquiry
Finding Questions, Examining Answers

CONVERSING WITH THE WORK

Asking and Answering Questions

Does this statement sound familiar? "I read for answers, but all I find are questions. I'm just not getting it." If you read literature the way you read other texts, you will get discouraged quickly. Often, student readers come to their literature texts directly from readings in other subjects, and unless they consciously change strategies, they will read for information, attempting to outline key points or look for main ideas. These are all good habits of mind; they're just not very helpful for reading literature. You read literature initially for questions, not for answers, and if you find questions that engage your interest and your imagination, then you *are* getting it.

When we use the word "reading" to talk about literature, we are talking about a special habit of mind that involves several ways of thinking. Good readers find ways to engage with literature through their imaginations and senses. They know how to reflect on the work, observing both their own reactions and the questions the work calls to mind. They analyze their observations, collecting ideas and details that can provide the basis for sound generalizations. They know how to use their generalizations to interpret the work in a way that both clarifies their own thinking and contributes to others' understanding.

Good readers don't necessarily know everything there is to know about a particular work, but they will have listened well enough to the writer and to other readers to be able to enter a conversation about the reading and to contribute to that conversation in a satisfying way. In this chapter you will find samples of informal writing that exemplify several ways of thinking about literature. By writing in these ways, you can participate in a "conversation" about literary works in several senses: with yourself, reflecting on your own experiences and the way they support or challenge your perception of the work; with others, contrasting and synthesizing their observations and responses with your own; with the writer of the work, observing the choices of form and language that help evoke or that challenge your responses; and with other writers, texts, and ideas that provide a variety of contexts lending meaning and significance to the literature. In later chapters, you will learn how to shape your new knowledge into interpretive statements about the work's meaning and significance. No matter what statement you make, it will have been influenced by what others in these conversations have had to say.

Engaging with the Work

The first kind of thinking about literature, which we call engaging with the work, has to do with the way you enter the world of literature through your senses and your imagination. Writers explore emotions or experiences from particular points of view. The gap between us and a work of literature might be temporal (a different time), linguistic (different language conventions), or cultural (different customs, expectations, beliefs, and **values**). In any case, a literary work will always reflect a way of envisioning the world different from what we have experienced before, if only because the world is being described by someone else. Part of the writer's job is to invite us into a new experience and to shape that experience in ways that help us bridge the gap between our old knowledge and the literary world we are to enter. The better we are at naming and understanding the connections and distances works can present, the easier it will be consciously to appreciate the ways literature can encourage self awareness, *and* the easier it will be to respond to works that present worlds very different from our own.

Most readers have to read a number of pages of a **novel** before they orient themselves, or read a poem several times to begin engaging with it in a satisfying way. You will engage more easily if you look carefully for the way your knowledge or experience relates to the experience literature offers. It helps to ask questions about times you felt or understood something similar to what a work evokes in you. You might ask:

- What does this situation or person or place remind me of?
- Is the feeling created by the work one I've experienced before? When?
- What is similar about the two experiences?
- What is the source or cause of the connection?

If no associations come to mind, you might ask:

- How is it different from what I already know or have experienced?
- What do I like, or not like, about it?
- What in the work makes me uncomfortable, and why?

This list of questions comes from our observations of the kinds of associations, connections, differences, similarities, and resistances readers often find as they interact with a work. Although we believe that such questions emerge naturally in the process of reflection, our students have convinced us that when they are conscious of engagement questions, they are better able to generate responses to works, and that such questions help motivate further reflection and inquiry.

EXERCISE 2.1. ENGAGING WITH THE WORK

The students who commented on Shakespeare's Sonnet 144 in Chapter 1 discovered associations, connections, differences, similarities, and resistances in their initial summaries and reactions.

1. Look again at their comments, and compare them to the list of questions above. Where have the students asked or attempted to answer these kinds of questions as they found a way to respond to the work?

2. Look again at your reading notebook notes on the works in Chapter 1. Which of the engagement questions did you naturally ask yourself?

Reflecting on the Work to Identify Questions the Work Raises

If the ideas and experiences of literature were easy to understand, they wouldn't require the artful crafting that characterizes literature. Questions worth asking are not often easy to answer, and literature worth reading is not often easy to grasp. Most readers see details or features in a work that raise questions in their minds: How does that connect? What does that mean? Why does that seem important? Reflective readers are conscious, deliberate inquirers. They know what kinds of questions are worth asking, and they know that asking these questions will lead to discoveries about meaning. Reflective reading is often helped by reflective writing, jotting notes, probing ideas, and asking about conflicts, relationships, and changes.

What do we reflect on? Student readers often are taught to observe **character** types, functions of **setting**, kinds of sound and rhythmic patterns, types of **figurative language**, kinds and levels of **diction**, forms and designs and punctuation and divisions. All of these, and other, elements of literary language help us learn to look and answer. But they didn't always help us learn to *ask*. Problem finding is a skill distinct from and additional to problem solving. Literary language helps us label and explain answers to questions, but until we learn to find our own issues and express them, literary language offers only limited help.

Our students have found that three questions help them find and articulate problems that interest them. These questions are "generic": they can generate specific inquiries regarding the forms and functions of literary elements alone or in combination, or they can be used to inquire about relationships between readers and works or between works and **cultures**. As you read, you might ask:

What works against what?

*Inquire about perceived conflicts—for example, between **characters**, between characters and **settings**, between sound and sense, between **image** and idea, between reader assumptions and a work's **point of view**.*

What relates to what?

*Inquire about possible relationships and connections—for example, between a **metaphor** and the **plot**, between the social setting and a character's actions, between the sound and the emotion evoked, between the **stanza form** and the **mood**.*

What changes?

*Inquire about modulations through the piece—for example, how the **style** changes as the ideas evolve, how the attitudes of people inside or outside the work are affected by the events or the reading, how the **tone** gradually conveys a change of mind, how changes in the **setting** convey changes in **character**.*

Throughout these chapters, literary elements (like those listed as examples above) that might reveal conflicts or relationships or changes will be introduced or reinforced as you practice the art of interpretation. In addition, Parts A and B of the Appendix, Coming to Terms: Literary Language and Its

Uses, show how specific elements of form and language reveal conflicts, relationships, and changes that can become meaningful as you form generalizations. The value of knowledge about literary language for explaining and justifying your readings will become evident as you begin to analyze and evaluate the ways in which writer choices help shape reader responses.

Using the three questions above can help you focus your observations about language and form and make interesting connections between **style** and meaning; relating your observations to each other in specific ways will help you when you begin to answer the fourth essential question:

So What?

Your specific answer to the fourth question, "So what?," will be an *interpretive thesis statement* that takes into account your own experience, the way the work is constructed, and the significance or **value** of the work as it contributes to your understanding of yourself or your world.

EXERCISE 2.2. REFLECTING ON THE WORK

On your own, or as a part of a reading group discussion, you can brainstorm questions about a literary work using the generic questions above. It isn't likely (or desirable) that all of your questions will fit neatly into one type or another; the generic questions are meant to help move your inquiry process along, not restrict it to certain kinds of questions or limit their complexity.

Using the generic questions above, reading groups discussing Sonnet 144 in Chapter 1 came up with the following list of specific questions for class discussion. Consider what *kinds* of questions are at issue: where are they asking what works against what? What relates to what? What changes? So what? Which questions suggest more than one kind of inquiry? Which questions seem to you to be most promising for further reflection?

1. Does he like comfort? Does he like being in despair? Does he like one more than the other? Does he identify with one angel more than the other? Does he love one more?

2. How do comfort and despair relate to each other in terms of "better" and "worser," good and evil? Do those definitions change in the poem? Could it be that worse or evil is actually comfortable and that good/better brings about despair?

3. Why does Shakespeare refer to a good angel and a bad angel rather than an angel and a devil?

4. Is the conflict internal? If so, is it a conflict of good and evil? Of personality traits? Or is it external, representing actual events in the author's life? Or could it be both?

5. Why are the sides of the conflict characterized as male and female? What characteristics are we to assume are "male" or "female" in the poem? Does this show how the sides of the conflict are also related?

6. In line 4, does "coloured ill" suggest that the female angel is sickly? If dark, does that mean black, or suggest a dark personality? Could it mean painted, as in a painted lady, a temptress from the red light district?

7. In line 11, does "from" mean "away from" or "coming from"? Or both?

8. What is meant by "I guess one angel in another's hell"? How does this add to the ongoing development of the relationship between the angels?

9. What is he living in doubt about? Why does the poem end with the assumption (or hope?) that the bad angel will win out and drive away the good angel?

10. Are the lines between good and evil, masculine and feminine, blurred? How does the author use the friendship between good and evil to illustrate the confusion within himself?

11. What happens to change the narrator's view of fate, his role in the choices he can/cannot make? Does the poem make it easy or hard to believe in the possibility of the last line, that the "good angel" will win out?

12. Does humanity have a need for temptation? Can comfort and despair live simultaneously within one person? What is the value of the dark side?

13. If we can say he has a feminine and a masculine side, how are they related? Is he afraid of his feminine side? Is he being seduced by his feminine side? Does he want his feminine side to win?

14. Is the poem related to the Adam and Eve story? How would the creation story inform the relationship between comfort and despair?

Analyzing the Work to Perceive Patterns and Connections

Recall a time when you were looking at a collection of parts of something prior to assembling them: a puzzle, an engine, a kit for building a barbecue grill. You know the separate pieces are important; some other "arranger" has included them. The longer you look, the more connections you begin to see, the more systems of parts or relationships between parts begin to be evident. We often call that process, with a machine metaphor, "getting our bearings." When we ask ourselves "What's this?," we want to identify a category or a use for it, or make a connection between it and other pieces or parts.

Literary analysis, too, involves "getting your bearings," and is characterized by that state of mind in which you begin to see things as related to each other in specific ways. You begin to understand what you are responding to in relation to the world the work presents. This perception of coherence comes and goes during your reading of literature; in fact, it is important to remember not to let your first observations control your reading. Even if your thoughts begin to take shape and urge you toward generalizations, continue to test them against new observations or revised perceptions.

Analyzing is the process of generating and considering the strength of answers that make sense in connection with each other. While your own background and experience will in some ways shape your perception, having a repertoire of reflective reading strategies and methods can help you expand the range of possible meanings you can perceive. Sorting out and evaluating these possibilities requires that you test how well they hold up in the context of your personal response, against evidence in the work itself, and in relation to each other.

We don't want to give the impression that in practice you can neatly separate thinking called "reflection" from thinking called "analysis." It is nearly impossible to begin asking questions and not be compelled to analyze details that suggest possible answers, just as it is nearly impossible to engage with a work and not begin asking questions. We name these two mental processes simply to encourage sustained reflection as a reading "habit of mind" that will change the way you observe the features of the work, making analysis richer and more interesting. These skills are not stages but components of a reading process that takes into account your response, the questions the work invites, and your desire to answer those questions in reasoned, considered ways.

EXERCISE 2.3. ANALYZING THE WORK

Read the poem "Filling Station" by Elizabeth Bishop.

1. As you read, record in your reading notebook your initial responses, associations, and resistances. Use the questions in the section on "Engaging with the Work" if you need help getting started.

2. Reflect on the writer's choices, using the four main questions described in the section on "Reflecting" to facilitate your inquiry. Divide your paper into two columns. On one side, write down all the questions that occur to you. For example, ask of particular images "How do they *relate* to or *conflict* with each other?" Ask about words and phrases and punctuation "What is the *relationship* of these choices to the development of the poem?" Ask about the **persona** of the poem, "Does the way she sees the filling station *change* as the poem progresses?" Because you are practicing problem finding, think of as many questions as you can.

3. On the other half of your paper, note possible answers to your questions as you begin to get your bearings and notice how the parts fit the whole. Jot down details or ideas that seem significant. If general statements about the poem's purpose or significance occur to you, write them down for later consideration.

4. Share the questions and answers with your reading group. How many times did readers ask the same questions? How often did new answers emerge from a combination of responses offered by group members? What differences of opinion were expressed? What readings or ways of answering particular questions modified your own observations? Why?

ELIZABETH BISHOP

Filling Station

Oh, but it is dirty!
—this little filling station,
oil-soaked, oil-permeated

to a disturbing, over-all
black translucency.
Be careful with that match!

Father wears a dirty,
oil-soaked monkey-suit
that cuts him under the arms,
and several quick and saucy
and greasy sons assist him
(it's a family filling station),
all quite thoroughly dirty.

Do they live in the station?
It has a cement porch
behind the pumps, and on it
a set of crushed and grease-
impregnated wickerwork;
on the wicker sofa
a dirty dog, quite comfy.

Some comic books provide
the only note of color—
of certain color. They lie
upon a big dim doily
draping a taboret
(part of the set), beside
a big hirsute begonia.

Why the extraneous plant?
Why the taboret?
Why, oh why, the doily?
(Embroidered in daisy stitch
with marguerites, I think,
and heavy with gray crochet.)

Somebody embroidered the doily.
Somebody waters the plant,
or oils it, maybe. Somebody
arranges the rows of cans

so that they softly say:
ESSO—SO—SO—SO
to high-strung automobiles.
Somebody loves us all.

CONVERSING WITH OTHERS ABOUT THE WORK

One of the most effective and important ways to practice exploring beyond your own original perceptions is to read with others. Reading a work together challenges you to recognize and go beyond your preconceived ideas or first impressions. It encourages you to rethink your ideas, revising them in light of good reasons, or strengthening them when they sustain scrutiny. In addition, it provides practice in the kind of conversation that promotes responsible interpretation. In Chapter 1, we argued that interpretation implies conversation, which always involves clarifying or resolving ambiguities in order to create understanding. Public conversation about literary ideas also strengthens the quality of interpretation, as we revise and reconsider our observations and thoughts for their logic, their believability, or their genuineness: Does it make sense? Ring true? Feel right? As a reader, you are conversing with a work; as a participant in a reading group, you are conversing with others in your community, constructing meaning together.

The following literary conversation about the poem you considered in the last exercise, Elizabeth Bishop's "Filling Station," reproduces the comments of a group of readers, and despite their own protests that the transcript doesn't always sound like them ("Sometimes we sound smart, sometimes we sound dumb"), we think it illustrates the kinds of questioning, responding, agreeing, and disagreeing that can result in insightful and productive public exploration.

EXERCISE 2.4. LISTENING IN ON LITERARY CONVERSATION

Imagine you are in on this conversation. What might you add? Where might you agree or disagree? What kinds of questions does the teacher ask the student readers? What kinds do the students ask of themselves? When are they finding ways to engage personally, taking into account their own experiences? When are they reflecting or analyzing, asking and answering questions about the particulars of the work? When are they considering the context—evaluating the work within a perceived pattern or set of ideas or expectations in which the poem makes a particular kind of meaning?

TEACHER: What in the poem reminded anyone of a place or an event?

ANDY: Well, it's not like the poem, really, but I used to work in a little gas station in my hometown. Meyer's Texaco, two small, round-top pumps.

TEACHER: The place sounds similar—why do you say it's not like the poem?

ANDY: I liked that gas station. This person is pretty put off. She's disgusted.

JANE: Yeah. But I kind of know what that's about. I offered a friend a ride home one weekend, and to get to her house we took a narrow two-lane highway through the woods. After I dropped her off, I was really hungry, and I stopped at a diner. I got in there, and wished I hadn't gone in. But I stayed, and the food was OK. I just thought I didn't belong there. The place made me nervous.

TEACHER: What in the poem reminded you of your station, Andy?

ANDY: The group of guys, I guess, and the comic book, and the plant—we had a plant in the office. It always looked like it was going to die, but last I saw, it was still hanging in there. It was kind of like a pet.

TEACHER: And what reminded you of the diner, Jane?

JANE: Well, not the place really, although it was kind of dirty, I mean compared with fast-food places. It was more her feelings—her way of looking around, of feeling a little frightened. Words like "be careful" and "disturbing." But she doesn't leave. She's kind of interested.

LYNN: Interested, but cautious, and judgmental, too. She thinks she's better than they are.

TEACHER: Describe what you see happening in the first stanza.

ANDY: Somebody comes into this gas station—can I say she?

TEACHER: Good question. Is the narrator a woman?

LYNN: I read the poem from a woman's point of view. I don't see anything that would require that, though,

Notice how the teacher begins by asking a personal engagement question.

Now see how they locate their different responses in details of the poem. Note how their conversation naturally identifies conflicts, relationships, and changes.

Now they begin reflecting on details, asking and attempting to answer questions the poem raises.

except the author's name. I think I might have assumed, though, that women are more likely than men to be uncomfortable in gas stations, and that men are more comfortable with cars and grease, right?

Their answers incorporate reflection on their own expectations and assumptions.

ANDY: I might have wanted to use "she" because I saw the narrator as different from me. You see the narrator as like you. Anyway, the narrator comes into this place and doesn't like it. It's dirty, with an exclamation point.

TEACHER: Why the dashes, after the exclamation mark?

ANDY: It's like she doesn't turn away, she stares at it, even though she doesn't get it. And it all bothers her and kind of scares her, like in "Be careful with that match!" She's kind of scared, and tense.

JANE: Tense and uncomfortable. She looks at father in his monkey suit, and says it "cuts him under the arms."

They explore possible, multiple meanings of words and sounds by bringing their own experience and knowledge to the word in context.

TEACHER: Why a monkey suit?

LYNN: She could be mocking him—like he's a monkey. But a tuxedo is also called a "monkey suit."

TEACHER: How could that be seen as relevant?

JANE: Well, a tux is formal, so the dirt seems dirtier on it. It is also sometimes seen as uncomfortable, so it adds to the strangeness and discomfort.

ANDY: Don't forget, we gas jockeys are also called grease monkeys, and those uniforms never quite fit.

TEACHER: Read the next two lines out loud, Jane, and tell me what you hear.

JANE: (Reads). A lot of "s" sounds, a kind of hissing, like snakes.

ANDY: Like tire pumps!

The literary word simile gets introduced in order to describe or reflect on observations.

TEACHER: One of you uses a threatening simile, the other a nonthreatening one. Is the image functioning in both ways?

JANE: Like the sounds and action are unfamiliar, but they could have simple explanations the narrator might not know about.

LYNN: It seems like she's trying to find familiar things in the unfamiliar place. In the next two lines, in the parentheses, she stops and thinks about what she sees. If it's a family filling station, there's something she can relate to.

The language is used to help address an issue raised by readers' experience of the poem.

ANDY: Yeah, she reflects on it, but it's still "quite thoroughly dirty" to her.

TEACHER: The first question in the poem comes next. Why does she ask a question? Whom is she asking?

Conflicts are noted, and sometimes resolved, forming relationships and connections where there used to be confusion.

JANE: Us, but herself too. She's asking herself about the place. She is interested enough to want to know more. I did that at the diner. I wonder what that woman at the counter does? Is that her husband who kissed her after she poured his coffee? What would it be like to work in here, all your life? I thought about the diner like it was a story—until I got my burger.

The readers begin integrating their experience with that of the poem by asking and answering significance questions.

TEACHER: Why would she notice the concrete porch, especially? Why would it be significant to an outsider?

ANDY: Well, she wants to know if they live there. But porches are where people come in—they are where you are invited in. That old greasy furniture is dirty, but it's also crushed, like it's been used a lot. And the dog is dirty, but also comfy.

JANE: I liked that part. Both of her feelings are there—right on the comma! Dirty dog, quite comfy. It's both.

The readers begin to notice that details reveal changes in attitude and that complications make the picture more interesting.

ANDY: I mentioned the comic books before. These guys are not hustling around serving people all the time. Comic books are a little entertainment in a boring day.

TEACHER: Why the line "of certain color." Why "certain"?

ANDY: Well, everything else is dirty. She's not. Certain, I mean. She seems like she still doesn't quite trust the place, quite.

The readers' comments don't always proceed logically from point to point, but all the comments add something to their reading of the poem's overall effect.

LYNN: And "big" and "dim" are not usually words that describe a doily, which is delicate, lacy. That image is contradictory, too. She keeps seeing contradictions and trying to make sense out of them.

JANE: What's a taboret?

TEACHER: A piece of furniture, a bit ambiguous in itself. It's small, cylindrical, without arms or back. It's a stool, and it's a stand. And it's "part of the set." What set?

ANDY: A set of furniture? A stage "set," in a play? She means the things fit together or belong together.

TEACHER: And what about that plant, Andy?

ANDY: What's "hirsute"?

TEACHER: Hairy, I'm afraid. Begonias have thick, fuzzy leaves.

ANDY: A big, hairy, thick plant. Perfect touch of home for a greasy kind of place.

TEACHER: A touch of home? How did this filling station begin to be a home?

JANE: The family, the porch, the dog, the comics, the plant. Things are starting to seem a little more familiar, right?

TEACHER: But she follows, now, with a set of questions. Intense questions. Why? Why? Why oh why?

LYNN: The more she knows, the more connections to her world that she makes, the more she wants an explanation. She does assume there is one. She thinks if she can find how things fit together, she will understand the place better.

JANE: I think that's why I thought of the diner earlier. When I ate there, I was kind of put off by this cigarette burn in the plastic tablecloth. But there was actually a flower vase on the counter with columbine in it. I forgot that.

ANDY: Not a hairy begonia?

LYNN: And that's related to the crochet, maybe. That beneath the heavy gray crochet, there is a pattern. Marguerites are daisies, aren't they?

*The group begins
to connect what
they know into
an idea of the
poem's signifi-
cance by answer-
ing questions the
poem itself invites
them to ask.*

TEACHER: What does the pattern imply? Does the last stanza ask that question? Does it answer it?

ANDY: Well, it doesn't say who is responsible for the touches of home. Is this evidence of a mother? Would a mother water the plant, or "oil" it?

LYNN: It might be evidence of a mother. Maybe that's why I read it from a woman's perspective. You know, the person in the poem tends to look for signs that might suggest a woman's presence. That would make her more comfortable, right?

JANE: Now I feel like the poem was this mystery about who's missing, and we just solved it. But the poem didn't feel that way before. It doesn't really matter who did the embroidery, does it? Or who watered the plant—or oiled it. It just matters that somebody did. Or somebody does.

TEACHER: So the idea of the missing mother may not take the whole poem or the whole experience into account. It's a good question, but as you suggest, Jane, it may not be the issue the whole poem invites us to address. The next image, for example. It has to take us all the way to the final line, which, on first reading of the poem, must have seemed at odds with its content. What are the cans saying to the passing cars? Why do they say it? And why should we listen?

A reader checks the "direction" of the reading against her own response to the poem.

ANDY: Its a soft sound, with the same "s's" that were in stanza two. But now it's more calm, more like a hush.

LYNN: Yes. Hers was one of the high-strung automobiles on the road, and when she came in, she slowed down and looked, and tried to make sense of what she saw. Though she may never have noticed or cared if she didn't need to stop.

TEACHER: Now for the last line. How do you connect it to the rest? What opinion does it offer?

JANE: Somebody loves us all. We know, because when we let ourselves slow down and look at the frightening or the unfamiliar or the different, rather than going on past it, we see that even where things are disturbing, we can find familiar things.

TEACHER: And what does love have to do with it?

LYNN: Well, love is what caused the somebody to make things like home. Maybe love is a kind of connecting. A way to make what is different seem more familiar. Making it a "home." I think the writer wants us to do that.

ANDY: She could have driven on, and with her judgmental attitude, it's surprising that she didn't. But she stayed, and when she left, she felt less put off, more accepting.

The readers speculate about the significance of the poem's experience for them.

TEACHER: And what about your experience as readers?

LYNN: You mean our experience of the place, or of the poem?

TEACHER: Good question! First the place.

JANE: At first, I thought that the diner came to mind because I remembered my anxiety or fear. But it probably also came to me because when I left I was glad I had stayed, and I've been glad since, because I've told the story about the place to others. Telling it made me feel kind of independent.

Now they are encouraged to generalize about the significance of the poem for them as readers, extending the poem beyond its boundaries to another context.

TEACHER: What about the poem? Did anyone's response to the poem change as the discussion went on?

ANDY: Well, I have to say that I didn't like the poem at all, at first. I thought she felt superior, too good for grease monkeys, and having been one, I didn't like her much. I still think the narrator's stiff. But she did change.

TEACHER: Andy, put that together with Lynn's reading of the last stanza. If love in this poem is an expression of connection, of making the unfamiliar more acceptable, then could reading poetry be seen as a kind of caring, of connection, of conversation?

ANDY: Maybe. Yes. Maybe. You have to care enough to understand it, like she had to care enough to look past the dirt and see a home. You can connect with the way the speaker sees things by looking at them the way they do. It's like you're seeing with their eyes. And your own at the same time.

THINKING ABOUT TALKING ABOUT LITERATURE

Your Ideas Matter

Andy's last comment is what persuaded us to include this conversation in this text because it offered one of the best characterizations of interpretation we have heard: seeing with their eyes, and your own at the same time. If you are readers like Jane, Andy, and Lynn, you may be unaware of your own powers of interpretation. You may have thought as you read the conversation, "*I* wouldn't have thought of that." You might not have had those particular responses, but you would have thought of something else that would have enriched the conversation in its own way, changed it, modified it, or extended it. Notice in the conversation that each comment contributed in some way to the overall meaning, to each reader's understanding, even when perceptions differed.

You also may have thought, "This kind of meaning making can happen in a class, but I'd never be able to do that on my own." Look again, however, at the questions posed by the teacher. Did she ask any especially complicated questions? Did she use arcane language or unfamiliar terminology? The key to thinking and talking productively about literature is in knowing what kinds of questions there are, and in discovering what kinds of questions literature asks of you.

The way that Jane, Andy, and Lynn listened to each other, without dismissing or confronting, makes clear that one work will enable many reasonable or probable readings. Although not all readers who talk to each other will arrive at similar interpretations, each reader's reading will be stronger, more informed, and better grounded for having had the conversation.

To make the interpretive process work, you must be willing to change your mind about a work, the way that Andy did, overcoming his initial resistance and finding meaning where he first experienced distance. The reader who insists on an idiosyncratic interpretation based on first impressions and personal biases is not interpreting any more than the reader who simply restates a traditional or teacher-devised interpretation. By using conversation to construct meaning together, we can engage with, inquire about, reflect on, analyze, interpret, and evaluate literary works in ways that make us stronger, more informed, independent readers who can integrate what we know about ourselves and the work with our knowledge of each other and the world.

If you practice the art of interpretation, you will improve your ability to engage with literature, overcome resistances, make connections, and perceive patterns. Reading "art" is different from reading textbooks. When you read textbooks, you read for answers. When you read literature, you read for questions. The questions become problems to work on, problems you can articulate and pursue using methods you can read about in this book and practice in your classes or reading groups. Meaning in literary works is actively created and negotiated, not just found as a static "right answer" hidden in the language or in the teacher's head or in an authoritative work of criticism. Just as Jane, Andy, and Lynn made sense of a poem by engaging, reflecting, analyzing, and evaluating, each contributing uniquely to the interpretive process, so you can participate responsibly and collaboratively in literary interpretation as confidently as you participate in other forms of conversation.

Engaging

The first questions posed by the teacher about "Filling Station" and explored by Jane, Andy, and Lynn concerned their personal engagement with the poem. Most of us connect with works through our personal experiences, and because our backgrounds differ, so will our responses. That's good, not bad. One of the characteristics that separates literature from other kinds of works is in the range and types of questions it asks of readers. Its power is in its ability to show beauty in unity *and* in difference, in diverse human actions and reactions, behaviors and motives. Our conversation about literature must, as much as is possible, reflect the same diversity and attempt the same unity.

After class one day, one student said, "I didn't say anything because I disagreed with what was being said." What if, after Andy had mentioned his gas station experience and his negative response to the narrator, Jane had felt she could not bring up her diner story because it suggested a different response? We may have proceeded to a narrower reading: maybe the narrator was a woman who hated gas stations and who was repulsed by the dirty men at the station. Such a reading seems almost comic against the rich and satisfying discussion the group conducted.

Reflecting and Analyzing

The large group of questions asked and answered by our reading group— why this word, why that comma—were analytical in that they sought answers to how the parts related to the whole. Questions of analysis in any discipline usually draw on knowledge of the assumptions, methods, categories, and conventions of that discipline. In the conversation about "Filling Station," little of the language about literary forms and conventions was incorporated, but this just shows how fruitful and insightful literary discussion can be even without these aids. However, if categories and definitions are seen as tools of perception, ways of making the writer's choices meaningful, then knowledge of literary terminology has a very important function for the responsible, responsive reader. In the same way that knowing a "taboret" is a piece of furniture enlarged the possible meaning of the poem, so knowing that consonance is a kind of sound can offer something of significance to the reader. Literary language about conventions exists to help the reader observe separate elements. It offers an additional set of ways to see how unity and diversity co-exist, constantly reforming each other.

Establishing Significance, Assigning Value

As you noticed in the literary conversation about "Filling Station," reflection and analysis often lead quite naturally to issues of significance because readers are compelled to ask the larger question that motivates all the others: "So what?" Often, as you reflect and analyze, you glimpse the possibility of how you might organize and develop your observations into an interpretive statement you could share with others, a statement that is your specific answer to the question "So what?" This answer will explain what is significant about this work for your self-knowledge or your understanding of language, literature, other ideas, or other people.

As questions get asked and answered, the potential meanings of the literary work may seem to expand beyond your ability to control them. The proliferation of opinions and observations may seem an exercise in frustration, and you may want to retreat into the comfort and isolation of your original responses because everyone seems to have a separate vision. If this happens, attempt to state precisely that difference which makes the conversation worth continuing. In our example, when Andy and Lynn seem to be separately analyzing and expanding the focus, he reflecting on the plant, she on the embroidery, Jane thinks the conversation is losing track of what "matters," and she comments in a way that narrows the focus to shared concerns: "It doesn't really matter who did the embroidery, does it? Or who watered the plant—or oiled it. It just matters that somebody did. Or somebody does." The readers then continue, speculating on what the conflicts, relationships, and changes have to do with each other, with them, or with others in society and in the world.

Other questions of significance that might arise would focus on what this particular literary work has to do with other ideas or works readers have experienced. In any case, establishing significance consists of speculating about meaningful patterns and connections beyond the work itself.

What is beyond the work? Sometimes, our perceptions of pattern and connection will relate the work to our lives as individuals—our prior experiences, our personalities, our goals. Other times, we may understand the significance of the work in terms of a historical moment, that of the work or our own. When we read works that come from a different place or time, we should consider how historical events and forces may have influenced their form of expression and how events and forces within our own time may influence our way of responding to them.

Other works may gain significance when we read as participants in cultural communities—members of families, residents of regions, practitioners of occupations or disciplines, or our affiliations based on gender, ethnic heritage, religion, or economic status. These relationships influence our ways of understanding and expressing meaning and significance, which is why, when reading works that come from cultures different from our own, we can benefit from an awareness of cultural factors that may have influenced the creation, or the perception, of the work. For example, colors often carry **symbolic** significance in literature, but that significance is often related to **culture**. In the European tradition, brides wear white; in the Islamic culture, they wear black; traditional Hawaiian brides wear red. Establishing significance or assigning **value** always happens in a context of assumptions about what is significant and what has value. Seeing symbolic meaning in a color would depend on the set of assumptions about meaning and value you bring to your observations. When you are conscious of the ways individual, historical, and cultural ideas can influence readers and writers, you are more likely to see significance, and less likely to impose your own values on the experience rather than interacting with the work, contributing to it, and being changed by it.

Defined this way, the process of establishing significance or assigning **value** is a process of making connections—between words, across time, among cultures. Sharing a sense of significance about a literary work requires that we converse about what is significant and what has value, and in doing so, form understandings about meanings and values. As human beings, we seem compelled to seek these connections; our desire to connect motivates all conversations, literary and otherwise.

We sometimes wish we had better ways to explain this impulse to look for patterns and connections in experience, but as readers, writers, and teachers, we trust our observations of the phenomenon: human beings want to understand, and the better they are at understanding their experience, the easier it is to live in a complicated world. How else, in matters of human interaction, is it possible to decide what matters?

WRITING ABOUT LITERATURE

Your Contributions

So far in this book we have encouraged you to do a great deal of informal writing about your reading in your reading notebooks. The act of committing thought to paper is a way to clarify your thoughts and beliefs and to communicate with others because part of what encourages you to be clear is an imagined—or real—audience with whom you wish to share your way of seeing your world, the world of the work, or the world of human interaction. In the act of writing, you are accepting the role we have assigned writers of literature. As the writers you read must make choices intended to help you share their significant experiences, emotions, and ideas, so you as a writer, when you shift to public or formal writing, must encourage shared understanding. Your writing is your contribution to public conversations about literature going on within, and beyond, your particular audience.

We present four kinds of writing in the next chapters, each with a different focus and purpose, which can emerge from the kind of literary conversation presented in this chapter. All four kinds of writing—the response essay, the analytical essay, the critical essay, and the literary research paper—require that you engage with works, reflect consciously, analyze carefully, and consider your observations in light of your experience, knowledge of the work, and the readings of others.

We assume, further, that your reflections on any literary work will lead you to at least one question at issue that you care to address with an interpretive statement: one that contributes to an understanding of the work's meaning and significance. In this sense, all of the interpretive statements you will be writing in response to assignments in this book can be considered *arguments*. When you write about literature, you are advancing a particular interpretation you care enough to share with others. You will make choices of content, language, and form designed to help other readers see the literature the way you do, follow and accept your reasoning, and be persuaded to share your ideas.

Response, Analytical, and Critical Essays

The kinds of interpretive statements you choose to make and develop will depend on your decisions about two considerations: What kind of question does my statement answer? What kind of information must I use to arrive at and develop that answer?

A response essay, which you will read about in Chapter 3, focuses on the reader's connection to the literary experience offered by the work. The writer of a response paper uses personal experience to contribute to a reader's understanding both of the world presented by the work and the world experienced by the writer of the essay. The response essay attends to the elements of the work and the responses of others, but it also is enriched by the unique context brought to the piece by the experiences of the writer of the essay. A response paper generally asks "What did I learn from this reading experience that contributes to my self-knowledge or my understanding of the world?" or "What do I know or have experienced that can contribute to an understanding of this work?" or "What did the work make me feel, and how did it make me feel that way?"

Although the origins of an analysis essay, which you will learn more about in Chapter 4, reside within the reader's response to the literature, an analysis essay tends to shift the focus of the writing to the elements of language and form that elicited a particular effect. In the case of "Filling Station," readers might be interested in examining more closely how particular language features—sentence structures, sound patterns, syllabic stresses, line lengths, parenthetical phrases—contributed to their understanding of the last line: what the poem means by "somebody loves us all." That is not because writing about the last line is a typical "teacher-given" assignment; it's because the readers' conversation about the poem led them to ask about it, to deliberate on it, in ways that caused them to consider how elements of language and form lent significance to each other and to the poem as a whole. Writing analytical essays will develop your ability to respond to language and form in a literary work within a community of readers who share understandings about the meaning and significance of the "conventions" of literary discourse. Analytical essays generally answer the questions "What language features created a particular effect I, as a reader, noticed?" or "What is the effect of a pattern of features that I, as a reader, perceived?"

Critical essays, the focus of Chapter 5, require the reader to assign significance or **value** to a work, whether as a literary achievement, a philosophical statement, a social message, a character study, or any other type of contribution to our understanding of literature's significance. This is not the same as asking whether we "appreciated" the work or not, although our opinions about this will inform our inquiry. To write critical essays, we must be clear about what set of assumptions and beliefs about significance we are bringing to bear on our reading, assumptions and beliefs we must share with our readers. These assumptions are the basis for our conclusion and our reasons for believing it. Writing critical essays requires us to ask "What perspective does the writer present?" or "What is the value of the literature in terms of a particular set of shared expectations or criteria?" The answer to these questions will depend on a number of elements: the experiences we bring to the work; our criteria for assessing the kind of work we perceive it to be; our ability to consider historical and cultural assumptions that may influence the work or our reading of it; our observations about language choices and stylistic options and how these influence our reception of the work; our skill at eliciting and responding to questions raised by the work.

Literary Research: Reading with Experienced Readers

Literary works exist within, and can be read within, many layered and multifaceted contexts: the writer's life, a historical moment, a conversation about gender or race, other works by the same or other authors, a cultural community, a mythological system, a regional mode of expression, a set of conventions that describe a **genre**, a similar set of experiences, and so on. Reading material that provides information about these contexts can help us see a particular work or reading experience in new ways. They can inform our reading of a work, offering different, usually additional rather than contradictory, information, and they often make it easier to perceive the patterns and possibilities within and beyond a work.

When you read, you engage in conversation with the work itself, responding and reacting to the experience it offers. You also can engage in conversation with other readers, shaping a richer vision of the possibilities of the literary work. The larger conversation includes the voices of experienced readers—scholars and literary critics—whose reading strategies specify particular sets of assumptions about significance. Chapter 6 will invite you to take part in this critical forum: conducting research, seeing assumptions and perceiving contexts, and identifying and responding to the critical stances of others.

EXERCISE 2.5. KINDS OF INTERPRETIVE ESSAYS

Although each chapter concerns a different type of essay, distinguished by focus and purpose, most writing done in response to literature is likely to include a response, some analysis, and an informing critical argument. Response essays may refer to the work of other readers; research essays are likely to be informed by a question at issue that emerged from a particular reader's response.

Consider the following interpretive statements written about the poem "Filling Station." See if you can determine which kind of essay each statement might generate, and speculate about what kinds of information might be included in the development of that essay.

1. The setting of the poem "Filling Station" seems familiar, in the sense that it could happen anywhere, to anyone. Yet we are led first to imagine it as if it were unfamiliar, and then re-imagine it until it becomes familiar again, but changed, as we learn to see it in a new way. Because of the way Bishop sequences the images, a stop at a filling station becomes a **metaphor** for encountering the unfamiliar and making it familiar.

2. In the poem "Filling Station," Elizabeth Bishop takes us on a journey across a border to a foreign place, from which we return enlightened. As critics have observed, this pattern is common in her poetry; she often addresses the theme of borders perceived, confronted, and crossed.

3. I was fairly intimidated by the poem "Filling Station" when I first read it. I didn't know what to make of most of it. I

felt distanced and disturbed, out of place and out of sorts—not unlike the speaker of the poem when she enters the gas station. As the speaker in the poem comes to understand that the meaning of the place is to be grasped by observing and questioning, so I have come to understand that the meaning of poetry is to be discovered by observing and questioning.

4. In the poem "Filling Station," Elizabeth Bishop's stylistic choices—particularly her syntax and punctuation—reinforce the speaker's evolving attitude toward the station and its inhabitants by marking her sense of distance and connection.

SUMMARY

The purpose of this chapter is to help you understand the *kinds of thinking* that go on as a part of literary interpretation. We have analyzed the process not to complicate it, but to make it more obvious and easier to work with. You might compare the exercises in this chapter to learning to play scales on a piano or bouncing a ball on a tennis racket, in that separating out the skills involved can help you understand your strengths and overcome your frustrations or barriers.

Thinking and talking about interpretation can lead to new knowledge in several ways:

- Paying attention to your own responses can help you identify your assumptions and biases.
- Focusing on details of the work can foster your knowledge of the language and your ability to express your understanding to others.
- Interacting with others can generate knowledge of beliefs, **values**, and expectations held by groups, communities, and **cultures**.
- Developing reasoned, thoughtful statements about literary works encourages you to see yourself as both a discoverer and a creator of ideas as you interpret the world in which you live.

Although literary conversation works conventionally, it is rarely mechanical; it is nearly always surprising and unpredictable; it stays interesting and worthwhile as long as the participants are listening well and responding honestly, but it can also veer off into digressions or confusion when issues are unclear or when we respond to them differently. However, despite the ambiguities of language and the differences among individuals, conversing with others is a way to make meaningful ambiguous events, moments, or observations. You may be attempting to understand something you didn't predict, or make the unfamiliar familiar, but in either case, you think in predictable, nameable ways about your experience.

An Invitation to Write: Discovering Meaning through the Interpretive Process

This chapter has encouraged you to think about reading in ways that will make you more conscious of, and therefore more in control of, your own reading processes. You have been introduced to several strategies for engaging with, reflecting on, and analyzing the composition of a literary work. To test the processes and strategies, read Gwendolyn Brooks's story "Home" and, in your reading notebooks, write your way through the following process toward an interpretive statement about the story.

Engage

1. Summarize the **plot** of the story.
2. React to the story. What emotions does it elicit? What characters or situations do you identify with?
3. Describe the **point of view** or perspective from which the tale is told. Are you invited to share a particular attitude toward events or people in the story? If so, whose? What do you know about the person whose perspective you are asked to share?

Reflect and Analyze

Ask these questions about **characters**, **settings**, **language**, **tone**, **mood**, and **images**, as well as about ideas and attitudes (yours or those of people in the work):

1. What is acting against what? (Conflicts)
2. What relates to what? (Relationships and connections)
3. What changes? (Developments, evolutions, and resolutions)
4. So what? (Significance in relation to each other)

Establish Significance and Assign Value

Using all of the notes you've generated, try to draft possible answers for the following questions:

1. What statement might I make and develop that would contribute to an understanding of the story's meaning and significance?

2. What statement might I make that would connect my experience with the work to my self-awareness and/or my knowledge of the world?

3. What assumptions about **values** underlie my drafted statements? These criteria will emerge from your knowledge and experience and may be concerned with issues as broad as how to be a good human being or as narrow in the disciplinary sense as what makes a good plot or character.

GWENDOLYN BROOKS

Home

What had been wanted was this always, this always to last—the talking softly on this porch, with the snake plant in the jardiniere in the southwest corner, and the obstinate slip from Aunt Eppie's magnificent Michigan fern at the left side of the friendly door. Mama, Maud Martha, and Helen rocked slowly in their rocking chairs, and looked at the late afternoon light on the lawn, and at the emphatic iron of the fence and at the poplar tree. These things might soon be theirs no longer. Those shafts and pools of light, the tree, the graceful iron, might soon be viewed possessively by different eyes.

Papa was to have gone that noon, during his lunch hour, to the office of the Home Owners' Loan. If he had not succeeded in getting another extension, they would be leaving this house in which they had lived for more than fourteen years. There was little hope. The Home Owners' Loan was hard. They sat, making their plans.

"We'll be moving into a nice flat somewhere," said Mama. "Somewhere on South Park, or Michigan, or in Washington Park Court." Those flats, as the girls and Mama knew well, were burdens on wages twice the size of Papa's. This was not mentioned now.

"They're much prettier than this old house," said Helen. "I have friends I'd just as soon not bring here. And I have other friends that wouldn't come down this far for anything unless they were in a taxi."

Yesterday Maud Martha would have attacked her. Tomorrow she might. Today she said nothing. She merely gazed at a little hopping robin in the tree, her tree, and tried to keep the fronts of her eyes dry.

"Well, I do know," said Mama, turning her hands over and over, "that I've been getting tireder and tireder of doing that firing. From October to April there's firing to be done."

"But lately we've been helping, Harry and I," said Maud Martha. "And sometimes in March and April and in October, and even in November, we could build a little fire in the fireplace. Sometimes the weather was just right for that."

She knew from the way they looked at her that this had been a mistake. They did not want to cry.

But she felt that the little line of white, somewhat ridged with smoked purple, and all that cream-shot saffron, would never drift across any western sky except that in back of this house. The rain would drum with as sweet a dullness nowhere but here. The birds on South Park were mechanical birds, no better than the poor caught canaries in those "rich" women's sun parlors.

"It's just going to kill Papa!" burst out Maud Martha. "He loves this house! He *lives* for this house!"

"He lives for us," said Helen. "It's us he loves. He wouldn't want the house, except for us."

"And he'll have us," added Mama, "wherever."

"You know," Helen sighed, "if you want to know the truth, this is a relief. If this hadn't come up, we would have gone on, just dragged on, hanging out here forever."

"It might," allowed Mama, "be an act of God. God may just have reached down and picked up the reins."

"Yes," Maud Martha cracked in, "that's what you always say—that God knows best."

Her mother looked at her quickly, decided the statement was not suspect, looked away.

Helen saw Papa coming. "There's Papa," said Helen.

They could not tell a thing from the way Papa was walking. It was that same dear little staccato walk, one shoulder down, then the other, then repeat, and repeat. They watched his progress. He passed the Kennedys', he passed the vacant lot, he passed Mrs. Blakemore's. They wanted to hurl themselves over the fence, into the street, and shake the truth out of his collar. He opened his gate—the gate—and still his stride and face told them nothing.

"Hello," he said.

Mama got up and followed him through the front door. The girls knew better than to go in too.

Presently Mama's head emerged. Her eyes were lamps turned on.

"It's all right," she exclaimed. "He got it. It's all over. Everything is all right."

The door slammed shut. Mama's footsteps hurried away.

"I think," said Helen, rocking rapidly, "I think I'll give a party. I haven't given a party since I was eleven. I'd like some of my friends to just casually see that we're homeowners."

Writing Group Activity

Compare your interpretive statements with others in your writing group, identifying differences and speculating about them by referring to your notes.

Which questions were most (and least) helpful? Which provoked the most conversation? How would a paper that began with each interpretive thesis statement be developed?

Sample Writing: Reflecting on Your Reading Process

The writing sample at the end of this chapter represents one student's way of reflecting on his interpretive process, noting how his reading evolved from a "gut reaction" to a reasoned interpretive stance, and just as importantly, how his sense of his role in the discussion changed from one of cool detachment to effective involvement. Notice how he engages with, reflects on, analyzes, evaluates, and makes decisions about probable meanings. The assignment was to reflect on the group discussion, reviewing what "changes of mind" occurred in relation to the poem "Filling Station" or poetry in general.

MOVING "INSIDE"

I like poetry. I don't always feel comfortable with it. I'm not always glad I like it, because it somehow makes me responsible for dealing with it, for taking time to think about the questions it raises. But I have always said that if I didn't like a poem right off, I wouldn't bother with it. If I couldn't connect with it right away, it wasn't worth it.

I didn't really like "Filling Station." It seemed sort of narrowly analytical, the kind of over-analysis of the barely significant that makes my friends think I'm crazy when I say I like poetry. "Get your tank filled and get on out of there," they might say to the speaker. What's the problem, anyway? No great issues were being considered in lofty language, the kind of "high" reading which gives you a sense of power and intellectual challenge when you puzzle it out. I didn't really like the speaker, who seemed obsessed by details and sort of nervous and delicate. So I was prepared to sit back and wait it out. Even though I said to myself that my judgment of the poem was "just my opinion," I was also aware, inside, that I was judging the teacher for choosing the poem and maybe even judging my classmates who found something in it to like. (I may be sounding too negative—my attitude was more one of indifference.)

The discussion began, and immediately they were talking, instead of about the language, about places like this and experiences they'd had. Because I had no immediate emotional connection to the speaker, I didn't believe I had any relevant experience or memory. But as one group member started talking about *working* at a gas station, my perspective shifted and I remembered (it should have been obvious to me) trying, and not really succeeding, at the same kind of job. And as I daydreamed, half-listening to him, I realized that maybe my experience gave me something in common with the speaker's. I felt foreign there too. I knew how to put gas in cars and wash windows, but there were a lot of other things about cars I didn't know. I didn't know if I *wanted* to know, either, but I didn't like not knowing.

So I started listening again to the discussion, but with more interest. I thought I heard in the poem the kind of mixed feelings I had about whether to learn the skills and details that would have made me an "insider" at the gas station. At the beginning, the speaker is an outsider, and sees herself as different from (and negative about) everything there. Then she begins to see details which she understands, and she tries to put them together. The group looked at each of these details, asking "Why this, why that," and for each question, I came up with an answer in my head. When we focused on the word "set," I spoke up, adding that a set of something has components that fit together, and that the speaker, at this point in the poem, was beginning to see how things fit together.

After that moment, I started seeing my own observations—and the group's—in a kind of "set" as well. I saw that feeling like an insider is often the result of seeing yourself in the "set," of seeing how the parts make up something complete, of getting a "feel" for how things work together. I also thought how becoming an insider in any situation requires you to make a conscious choice and put out an honest effort. But the poem shows that it can be done, and that doing it, becoming an "insider," is like being loved, belonging, caring enough to "get it."

Now, at home, I've just read my first paragraphs, and I see that my own predispositions and preferences got in the way of my understanding. It's not that I couldn't relate, it's that initially I chose not to, and in choosing not to, I was choosing to stay outside of the experience the poem offers. What made me choose to be an insider, to try to understand the poem, to discuss it with the group? Coincidence, I think. A combination of daydreaming and accidentally remembering my gas station employment gone wrong. But now, when I want or need to, I know I can go about becoming an insider more directly, looking for a connection with the events, the place or the feelings, even if I don't see their relevance right away.

Extra Practice: Additional Writing Invitations

1. In order to help interpretive thinking become more natural and less mechanical, practice with a work you like but which puzzles you. Read it, engage with it. Respond to the experience, the language, the images it offers, and the questions it raises in your mind. Then

write about it. First, record your personal responses, discovering ways in which you identify with the experience. Second, describe what happens in the work: How do the parts seem to relate to the whole? What seems to be in conflict? What changes? Third, suggest connections between the work and others you have read, or other personal or artistic experiences you recall, or other ideas you have encountered.

Discuss the work with others who have read it. Try to identify common ground and points of resistance or difference. What kinds of evidence do your group members bring to bear in support of their observations?

Reconsider your writings. What have you learned? What might you change if you were to use your notes to begin to construct a formal response to the work? What observations might elicit a response paper? What observations might help focus an analysis paper? What criteria emerged that might provide a basis for a critical essay? What questions emerged that cannot be answered by the literary work alone, and how would you go about the process of answering them?

2. If you are taking reading notes from or highlighting statements in this work, take a few moments to review these passages, considering why you marked them. Do they clarify, validate, contradict, or confuse something you had known or assumed about literature and literary interpretation? Write out your observations as statements, questions, or requests for information, and share these with your group and your instructor.

Chapter 3

Interpretation as Experience
Reading and Writing to Respond

WHEN we read, something touches us or strikes a chord. Something reminds us of a similar moment, a glance from another person, the shape of a familiar room, the deafening silence of fear, the smell of a particular warm afternoon, the curve of a dance. This initial response, as uncritical and spontaneous as it may feel, is essential to the process of interpreting. When we cannot find a way to identify with the sensual, emotional, or imaginative sensibility of the work we are reading, we feel as if we are attempting to read a language with which we have no experience. Unless we somehow identify, we may feel that sense of exclusion or separateness that frustrates us enough to close the book, put the poem down, or leave the play at intermission.

Although our initial responses may turn out to be a key to understanding the emotional climate, sequence, conflicts, or resolutions of the work, they also may turn out to have no more to do with the work than a door key does with the room behind it. Sometimes a literary work opens a pleasant memory that is expanded or clarified as we experience it; other times, the work may trigger a memory so powerful that our prior experience colors our reaction and we are unable to hear the writer. If one of the members of the reading community discussing the poem "A Person Is a Person Because of Other People" had a relative who was the victim of a violent crime for which the perpetrator was imprisoned, the memory the work evokes might block that reader's response to the strength of the prisoners' efforts to communicate in the face of such isolation. When our prior experiences control our responses to the emotional impact of the literary experience, we say the work is "charged."

On the other hand, sometimes the familiarity of a work is fleeting, or even deceptive, and behind the inviting, familiar facade waits an experience that challenges, changes, or complicates our former impressions, an experience we may come to embrace or resist as we reflect on it. In any case, the basis of our continued inquiry is our ability to engage with the reading enough to care to contribute to it, transforming it in a way that is at once an individual and a shared experience. This, the readers in Chapter 2 found, was their experience of the poem "Filling Station." The poem, they decided, encouraged them to pause and reflect on their first impressions and resistances, as the **persona** of the poem reflects on hers. Further, they speculated that their interaction with the poem was not unlike her developing, changing response to the place she described. Her initial response to the place is not positive, yet it becomes the key to discovering something about love as a desire to understand and create understandings.

EXERCISE 3.1. REFLECTING ON CLASS DISCUSSIONS

In the previous chapter, you read a reenactment of a group discussion of the poem "Filling Station." The discussion did not end with a summary of one single, carefully argued reading of the poem; rather, each reader had his or her own initial response to the poem—a response enriched by the experiences of others. The discussion of "Filling Station" may not be like one you have experienced before in English classes. History, poetic conventions, and biography were marginal to the initial inquiry; the group focused on the interaction between the readers and the poem. Recall occasions when you discussed a literary work or film in a setting outside the classroom and describe one or more of these occasions in your reading notebook. How did the discussion begin? What information did the participants provide? What roles did they play? How did you feel about your contribution to the discussion? In what way did the discussion differ from the classroom reenactment of the discussion of "Filling Station"?

RESPONDING AS AN INDIVIDUAL AND SHARED EXPERIENCE

In high school or introductory college classes, we all seem to have experienced, at least once, one or two prevalent approaches to discussing literature. The first begins with a description of the characteristics of the work—for example, its **setting, genre, meter, rhyme scheme, imagery**. This analysis may be presented in a lecture by the instructor or conducted by the students while the instructor judges the correctness of their observations. After the analysis, the instructor or class draws one conclusion about what interpretation such analysis compels the reader to draw. Rarely does the class consider competing interpretations. Some students like this approach, but others have described this experience as a frustrating one; it seems as if the instructor has a code book that only one or two other students have read. If students do contribute, they do so tentatively, searching for the right answer. The second approach involves an open class discussion in which students share their reactions to the literary piece and present interpretations of what the work means to them. Every interpretation adds something to the discussion because every reader sees different things in the work. Students who have had this experience in their previous literature classes may feel either a sense of liberation in knowing that such interpretive responses are valid or, in contrast, a sense of frustration that there is no "right answer," or that no answers are better than others, and thus, within the framework of **values** they experience in some of their other courses, the conversation seems to have no point.

We suggest a third model of reading, which we'd like to describe first by comparing it to the way we respond to movies. Most of us go to movies with friends and usually end the evening by talking about the movie. Our conversation begins with our responses: we were puzzled by a particular moment; we thought the director captured the way people act under certain circumstances; we found the film good or boring; we thought it one of the director's best or worst (funniest, most terrifying, most beautiful, best technically); we saw the actors as right or wrong for their roles. Whatever our responses, because we shared the experience with others, we naturally explain and justify our responses to it. Whatever our positions, we tend to defend them enthusiastically without concern for an ultimate right or wrong answer determined by an expert or without assuming that all responses are valid without some justification. We defend them, however, by observing the artistic choices made by the filmmakers, and we assume that such choices are purposeful, designed to help us share and understand the experience the filmmakers envisioned.

When we are engaging in such conversations, we are participating in a shared literary experience with the filmmakers—the writer and director— and other observers, in this case our friends. When we talk with friends about the books we read, we participate in a similar process. Generally, we share our first impressions: a particular moment in the book made us sad or frightened or suddenly aware of some way we often act; we liked the book or we didn't; we found it one of the writer's best or worst; we thought the characters were predictable or engaging; we accepted the writer's presentation of the events as believable. When we talk about such reactions, we usually give reasons that involve how we related to or resisted the way the writer presented the world, what the writer included or excluded, what artistic and stylistic choices made us feel the way we do, and what else we know that seems to offer significance or **value** to the book.

Rather than seeing a literary work as a puzzle with a discoverable solution or as a work that allows all readers to construct whatever interpretations their personal experiences lead them to, we begin our exploration of responses to literary works by acknowledging that when writers write literature, they present emotions or experiences from particular points of view, and that when readers read literature, they hope to share the experience, learning about themselves and others in the process. Often these works are difficult, challenging, or even strange. When we discuss literary works, we look together and challenge each other in an attempt to understand the experience the writer presents. As we share the study, we change our and each others' minds and are changed by the experience.

To illustrate this different way of discussing literature, let's look at a poem together.

WILLIAM DICKEY
The Poet's Farewell to His Teeth

Now you are going, what can I do but wish you
(as my wife used to say) "every success
in your chosen field."

What we have seen together! Doctor X,
having gagged us, hurling his forceps to the floor
and denouncing our adolescent politics,

or the time we had caught trench-mouth in Iowa City
and had to drive west slowing and haltingly,
spitting in all the branches of the Missouri.

Cigar-stained and tired of cavities, you leave.
It is time to go back to the pure world of teeth
and rest, and compose yourselves for the last eruption.

As to those things in a glass by the bathroom sink
they will never communicate with me as you have done,
fragile and paranoid, sensing the world around you

as wild drills and destructive caramel, getting even
for neglect by waking me into the pain of dawn,
that empty and intimate world of our bitter sharing.

Go, under that cool light. I will remember you:
the paper reports that people may still feel pain
in their missing teeth, as with any amputation.

I hope you relax by the shadowy root canals,
and thinking of me with kindness, but not regret,
toast me just once in the local anesthetic.

EXERCISE 3.2. INITIAL RESPONSES

Record your initial responses to Dickey's poem in your reading
notebook. What questions does it raise for you?

- Can you recall similar or different experiences?
- Can you locate the source of your associations or feelings in specific images, words, or phrases?
- Do your responses call attention to conflicts, relationships, or changes?

William Dickey's poem is precisely the kind of poem that might make beginning students of poetry run screaming from literature classes. What does it
mean? What are the symbols? Where do we begin with analysis? What is he
talking about? If we take a deep breath and forget the old scripts, we may be
able to begin the discussion in a new way. Forget beginning with the old questions of "What is literature?" "What are the significant images and
metaphors?" and "What does it mean?" Those were probably never your first
questions anyway. Instead they were questions you thought you ought to
begin by asking. Let's begin, rather, with stories and feelings, the poem's and
our own.

The poem sounds pretty serious, a sad farewell to a good friend and companion, but it is addressed to teeth. That makes it funny in a way, and actually the memories of the relationship between the man and his teeth-buddy
are pretty funny as well, like the doctor gagging them, hurling his forceps, and
railing at their politics, or the two of them spitting in all the branches of the
Missouri. It might even remind you of buddy movies you have seen like *Butch*

Cassidy and the Sundance Kid, in which two men go off on adventures together like a couple of big kids. There's a sense of freedom, youth, and mischief
as the man remembers their early escapades, even though the times he
remembers might be looked at as painful from a different perspective.

Sitting in a dentist's chair or driving west with a bad case of trench mouth
are not inherently funny events, even when recalled a great many years later.
Nonetheless, when we read about them in this poem, they seem funny, particularly when we picture the buddies as a man and his teeth. Yet the poet
seems to express another kind of attitude after he has recounted the early
memories. Somehow everything seems to slow down for a minute and to
focus on the old teeth. When he begins describing the teeth in the present, he
seems sad, even though the way he describes the teeth is amusing in the **personification**: "cigar-stained and tired of cavities," returning to the "pure
world of teeth." The poem might remind you of experiences you have had
that were painful but were strange or ridiculous enough to make funny stories when you told about them later.

These may not be the exact reactions you had when you read the poem
but may include some of your thoughts. They are compiled from responses
we and most of our students began with when first reading the poem together. We agreed on these general observations, but each of us brought unique
personal memories to our reading of the poem. One person may have had
some disease or injury that resulted in the loss of some or all of his teeth.
Another might have lost some precious childhood possession, a bicycle for
example, that was meaningful because it was inextricably linked with the
happiest memories from her youth. The two experiences, although quite different, share an underlying pattern that could become the basis of a conversation about loss, mourning, and the context in which such a loss could be
seen with a certain amount of humor.

Such a conversation might allow its participants to compare the similarities
and differences between their memories and explore the complexity of the overlapping pattern of experience. As the participants discuss the poem in relationship to their own experiences evoked by the poem, they will find themselves not
only coming to a greater understanding of the poem but also beginning to overcome their own limitations as readers of this particular piece. The person who
has had a painful or embarrassing experience with lost teeth might find the
material too close to his own experience to give him the openness he needs to
hear the poet's humor. The person who has a fond memory of something that
represented childhood with all its freedom and foolishness may miss the sad,
reflective resonance of words like "fragile," "empty," and "bitter."

By looking at the poem together, each of these readers may notice more.
Their experiences contribute to the poem's possibilities, and the poem itself

provides a common field of human experience on which they can discover their differences and build an understanding of their similarities. Perhaps each will see elements of bitterness mixed with humor and nostalgia. As they practice the art of interpreting together, they will be strengthening their ability to see beyond their own experiences when reading alone.

EXERCISE 3.3. COMPARING RESPONSES

Read the story "Where Are You Going, Where Have You Been?" by Joyce Carol Oates.

1. Write a set of responses in your reading notebook, commenting on personal associations and emotional effects. Whom do you identify with, if anyone? Why? Where did you find yourself filling in gaps in information or language? How did you do that? When did you find yourself asking questions that made you look back at the story for more information? How would you characterize the overall emotional effect of this story? Why?

2. In your reading group, compare your responses. How do the responses of other readers differ from yours? Speculate about the possible reasons for differences.

JOYCE CAROL OATES

Where Are You Going, Where Have You Been?
(For Bob Dylan)

Her name was Connie. She was fifteen and she had a quick nervous giggling habit of craning her neck to glance into mirrors, or checking other people's faces to make sure her own was all right. Her mother, who noticed everything and knew everything and who hadn't much reason any longer to look at her own face, always scolded Connie about it. "Stop gawking at yourself, who are you? You think you're so pretty?" she would say. Connie would raise her eyebrows at these familiar complaints and look right through her mother, into a shadowy vision of herself as she was right at that moment: she knew she was pretty and that was everything. Her mother had been pretty once too, if you could believe those old snapshots in the album, but now her looks were gone and that was why she was always after Connie.

   "Why don't you keep your room clean like your sister? How've you got your hair fixed—what the hell stinks? Hair spray? You don't see your sister using that junk."

Her sister June was twenty-four and still lived at home. She was a sec-
retary in the high school Connie attended, and if that wasn't bad enough—
with her in the same building—she was so plain and chunky and steady that
Connie had to hear her praised all the time by her mother and her mother's
sisters. June did this, June did that, she saved money and helped clean the
house and cooked and Connie couldn't do a thing, her mind was all filled
with trashy daydreams. Their father was away at work most of the time and
when he came home he wanted supper and he read the newspaper at supper and after supper he went to bed. He didn't bother talking much to them,
but around his bent head Connie's mother kept picking at her until Connie
wished her mother was dead and she herself was dead and it was all over.
"She makes me want to throw up sometimes," she complained to her friends.
She had a high, breathless, amused voice which made everything she said
sound a little forced, whether it was sincere or not.

There was one good thing: June went places with girl friends of hers,
girls who were just as plain and steady as she, and so when Connie wanted
to do that her mother had no objections. The father of Connie's best girl friend
drove the girls the three miles to town and left them off at a shopping plaza,
so that they could walk through the stores or go to a movie, and when he
came to pick them up again at eleven he never bothered to ask what they had
done.

They must have been familiar sights, walking around that shopping
plaza in their shorts and flat ballerina slippers that always scuffed the side-
walk, with charm bracelets jingling on their thin wrists; they would lean
together to whisper and laugh secretly if someone passed by who amused
or interested them. Connie had long dark blond hair that drew anyone's eye
to it, and she wore part of it pulled up on her head and puffed out and the
rest of it she let fall down her back. She wore a pull-over jersey blouse that
looked one way when she was at home and another way when she was away
from home. Everything about her had two sides to it, one for home and one
for anywhere that was not home: her walk that could be childlike and bob-
bing, or languid enough to make anyone think she was hearing music in her
head, her mouth which was pale and smirking most of the time, but bright
and pink on these evenings out, her laugh which was cynical and drawling
at home—"Ha, ha, very funny"—but high-pitched and nervous anywhere
else, like the jingling of the charms on her bracelet.

Sometimes they did go shopping or to a movie, but sometimes they went
across the highway, ducking fast across the busy road, to a drive-in restaurant
where older kids hung out. The restaurant was shaped like a big bottle, though
squatter than a real bottle, and on its cap was a revolving figure of a grinning
boy who held a hamburger aloft. One night in midsummer they ran across,
breathless with daring, and right away someone leaned out a car window and
invited them over, but it was just a boy from high school they didn't like. It
made them feel good to be able to ignore him. They went up through the maze
of parked and cruising cars to the bright-lit, fly-infested restaurant, their faces
pleased and expectant as if they were entering a sacred building that loomed
out of the night to give them what haven and what blessing they yearned for.
They sat at the counter and crossed their legs at the ankles, their thin shoulders rigid with excitement, and listened to the music that made everything so

good: the music was always in the background like music at a church service, it was something to depend upon.

A boy named Eddie came in to talk with them. He sat backwards on his stool, turning himself jerkily around in semi-circles and then stopping and turning again, and after a while he asked Connie if she would like something to eat. She said she did and so she tapped her friend's arm on her way out—her friend pulled her face up into a brave droll look—and Connie said she would meet her at eleven, across the way. "I just hate to leave her like that," Connie said earnestly, but the boy said that she wouldn't be alone for long. So they went out to his car and on the way Connie couldn't help but let her eyes wander over the windshields and faces all around her, her face gleaming with a joy that had nothing to do with Eddie or even this place; it might have been the music. She drew her shoulders up and sucked in her breath with the pure pleasure of being alive, and just at that moment she happened to glance at a face just a few feet from hers. It was a boy with shaggy black hair, in a convertible jalopy painted gold. He stared at her and then his lips widened into a grin. Connie slit her eyes at him and turned away, but she couldn't help glancing back and there he was still watching her. He wagged a finger and laughed and said, "Gonna get you, baby," and Connie turned away again without Eddie noticing anything.

She spent three hours with him, at the restaurant where they ate hamburgers and drank Cokes in wax cups that were always sweating, and then down an alley a mile or so away, and when he left her off at five to eleven only the movie house was still open at the plaza. Her girl friend was there, talking with a boy. When Connie came up the two girls smiled at each other and Connie said, "How was the movie?" and the girl said, "You should know." They rode off with the girl's father, sleepy and pleased, and Connie couldn't help but look at the darkened shopping plaza with its big empty parking lot and its signs that were faded and ghostly now, and over at the drive-in restaurant where cars were still circling tirelessly. She couldn't hear the music at this distance.

Next morning June asked her how the movie was and Connie said, "So-so."

She and that girl and occasionally another girl went out several times a week that way, and the rest of the time Connie spent around the house—it was summer vacation—getting in her mother's way and thinking, dreaming, about the boys she met. But all the boys fell back and dissolved into a single face that was not even a face, but an idea, a feeling, mixed up with the urgent insistent pounding of the music and the humid night air of July. Connie's mother kept dragging her back to the daylight by finding things for her to do or saying, suddenly, "What's this about the Pettinger girl?"

And Connie would say nervously, "Oh, her. That dope." She always drew thick clear lines between herself and such girls, and her mother was simple and kindly enough to believe her. Her mother was so simple, Connie thought, that it was maybe cruel to fool her so much. Her mother went scuffling around the house in old bedroom slippers and complained over the telephone to one sister about the other, then the other called up and the two of them complained about the third one. If June's name was mentioned her mother's tone was approving, and if Connie's name was mentioned it was disapproving. This did not really mean she disliked Connie and actually Connie thought that her mother preferred her to June because she was prettier, but the two of them kept up a pretense of exasperation, a sense that they were tugging and struggling over something of little value to either of them. Sometimes, over coffee, they were almost friends, but something would come up—some vexation that was like a fly buzzing suddenly around their heads—and their faces went hard with contempt.

One Sunday Connie got up at eleven—none of them bothered with church—and washed her hair so that it could dry all day long, in the sun. Her parents and sister were going to a barbecue at an aunt's house and Connie said no, she wasn't interested, rolling her eyes to let her mother know just what she thought of it. "Stay home alone then," her mother said sharply. Connie sat out back in a lawn chair and watched them drive away, her father quiet and bald, hunched around so that he could back the car out, her mother with a look that was still angry and not at all softened through the windshield, and in the back seat poor old June all dressed up as if she didn't know what a barbecue was, with all the running yelling kids and the flies. Connie sat with her eyes closed in the sun, dreaming and dazed with the warmth about her as if this were a kind of love, the caresses of love, and her mind slipped over onto thoughts of the boy she had been with the night before and how nice he had been, how sweet it always was, not the way someone like June would suppose but sweet, gentle, the way it was in movies and promised in songs; and when she opened her eyes she hardly knew where she was, the back yard ran off into weeds and a fence-line of trees and behind it the sky was perfectly blue and still. The asbestos "ranch house" that was now three years old startled her—it looked small. She shook her head as if to get awake.

It was too hot. She went inside the house and turned on the radio to drown out the quiet. She sat on the edge of her bed, barefoot, and listened for an hour and a half to a program called XYZ Sunday Jamboree, record after record of hard, fast, shrieking songs she sang along with, interspersed by exclamations from "Bobby King": "An' look here you girls at Napoleon's—Son and Charley want you to pay real close attention to this song coming up!"

And Connie paid close attention herself, bathed in a glow of slow-pulsed joy that seemed to rise mysteriously out of the music itself and lay languidly about the airless little room, breathed in and breathed out with each gentle rise and fall of her chest.

After a while she heard a car coming up the drive. She sat up at once, startled, because it couldn't be her father so soon. The gravel kept crunching all the way in from the road—the driveway was long—and Connie ran to the window. It was a car she didn't know. It was an open jalopy, painted a bright gold that caught the sunlight opaquely. Her heart began to pound and her fingers snatched at her hair, checking it, and she whispered "Christ. Christ," wondering how bad she looked. The car came to a stop at the side door and the horn sounded four short taps as if this were a signal Connie knew.

She went into the kitchen and approached the door slowly, then hung out the screen door, her bare toes curling down off the step. There were two boys in the car and now she recognized the driver: he had shaggy, shabby black hair that looked crazy as a wig and he was grinning at her.

"I ain't late, am I?" he said.

"Who the hell do you think you are?" Connie said.

"Toldja I'd be out, didn't I?"

"I don't even know who you are."

She spoke sullenly, careful to show no interest or pleasure, and he spoke in a fast bright monotone. Connie looked past him to the other boy, taking her time. He had fair brown hair, with a lock that fell onto his forehead. His sideburns gave him a fierce, embarrassed look, but so far he hadn't even bothered to glance at her. Both boys wore sunglasses. The driver's glasses were metallic and mirrored everything in miniature.

"You wanta come for a ride?" he said.

Connie smirked and let her hair fall loose over one shoulder.

"Don'tcha like my car? New paint job," he said. "Hey."

"What?"

"You're cute."

She pretended to fidget, chasing flies away from the door.

"Don'tcha believe me, or what?" he said.

"Look, I don't even know who you are," Connie said in disgust.

"Hey, Ellie's got a radio, see. Mine's broke down." He lifted his friend's arm and showed her the little transistor the boy was holding, and now Connie began to hear the music. It was the same program that was playing inside the house.

"Bobby King?" she said.

"I listen to him all the time. I think he's great."

"He's kind of great," Connie said reluctantly.

"Listen, that guy's *great*. He knows where the action is."

Connie blushed a little, because the glasses made it impossible for her to see just what this boy was looking at. She couldn't decide if she liked him or if he was just a jerk, and so she dawdled in the doorway and wouldn't come down or go back inside. She said, "What's all that stuff painted on your car?"

"Can'tcha read it?" He opened the door very carefully, as if he was afraid it might fall off. He slid out just as carefully, planting his feet firmly on the ground, the tiny metallic world in his glasses slowing down like gelatine hardening and in the midst of it Connie's bright green blouse. "This here is my name, to begin with," he said. ARNOLD FRIEND was written in tar-like black letters on the side, with a drawing of a round grinning face that reminded Connie of a pumpkin, except it wore sunglasses. "I wanta introduce myself, I'm Arnold Friend and that's my real name and I'm gonna be your friend, honey, and inside the car's Ellie Oscar, he's kinda shy." Ellie brought his transistor radio up to his shoulder and balanced it there. "Now these numbers are a secret code, honey," Arnold Friend explained. He read off the numbers 33, 19, 17 and raised his eyebrows at her to see what she thought of that, but she didn't think much of it. The left rear fender had been smashed and around it was written, on the gleaming gold background: DONE BY CRAZY WOMAN DRIVER. Connie had to laugh at that. Arnold Friend was pleased at her laughter and looked up at her. "Around the other side's a lot more—you wanta come and see them?"

"No."

"Why not?"

"Why should I?"

"Don'tcha wanta see what's on the car? Don'tcha wanta go for a ride?"

"I don't know."

"Why not?"

"I got things to do."

"Like what?"

"Things."

He laughed as if she had said something funny. He slapped his thighs. He was standing in a strange way, leaning back against the car as if he were balancing himself. He wasn't tall, only an inch or so taller than she would be if she came down to him. Connie liked the way he was dressed, which was the way all of them dressed: tight faded jeans stuffed into black, scuffed boots, a belt that pulled his waist in and showed how lean he was, and a white pull-over shirt that was a little soiled and showed the hard small muscles of his arms and shoulders. He looked as if he probably did hard work, lifting and carrying things. Even his neck looked muscular. And his face was a familiar face, somehow: the jaw and chin and cheeks slightly darkened, because he hadn't shaved for a day or two, and the nose long and hawk-like, sniffing as if she were a treat he was going to gobble up and it was all a joke.

"Connie, you ain't telling the truth. This is your day set aside for a ride with me and you know it," he said, still laughing. The way he straightened and recovered from his fit of laughing showed that it had been all fake.

"How do you know what my name is?" she said suspiciously.

"It's Connie."

"Maybe and maybe not."

"I know my Connie," he said, wagging his finger. Now she remembered him even better, back at the restaurant, and her cheeks warmed at the thought of how she sucked in her breath just at the moment she passed him—how she must have looked to him. And he had remembered her. "Ellie and I come out here especially for you," he said. "Ellie can sit in back. How about it?"

"Where?"

"Where what?"

"Where're we going?"

He looked at her. He took off the sunglasses and she saw how pale the skin around his eyes was, like holes that were not in shadow but instead in light. His eyes were chips of broken glass that catch the light in an amiable way. He smiled. It was as if the idea of going for a ride somewhere, to some place, was a new idea to him.

"Just for a ride, Connie sweetheart."

"I never said my name was Connie," she said.

"But I know what it is. I know your name and all about you, lots of things," Arnold Friend said. He had not moved yet but stood still leaning back against the side of his jalopy. "I took a special interest in you, such a pretty girl, and found out all about you like I know your parents and sister are gone somewheres and I know where and how long they're going to be gone, and I know who you were with last night, and your best girl friend's name is Betty. Right?"

He spoke in a simple lilting voice, exactly as if he were reciting the words to a song. His smile assured her that everything was fine. In the car Ellie turned up the volume on his radio and did not bother to look around at them.

"Ellie can sit in the back seat," Arnold Friend said. He indicated his friend with a casual jerk of his chin, as if Ellie did not count and she should not bother with him.

"How'd you find out all that stuff?" Connie said.

"Listen: Betty Schultz and Tony Fitch and Jimmy Pettinger and Nancy Pettinger," he said, in a chant. "Raymond Stanley and Bob Hutter—"

"Do you know all those kids?"

"I know everybody."

"Look, you're kidding. You're not from around here."

"Sure."

"But—how come we never saw you before?"

"Sure you saw me before," he said. He looked down at his boots, as if he were a little offended. "You just don't remember."

"I guess I'd remember you," Connie said.

"Yeah?" He looked up at this, beaming. He was pleased. He began to mark time with the music from Ellie's radio, tapping his fists lightly together. Connie looked away from his smile to the car, which was painted so bright it almost hurt her eyes to look at it. She looked at that name, ARNOLD FRIEND. And up at the front fender was an expression that was familiar—MAN THE FLYING SAUCERS. It was an expression kids had used the year before, but didn't use this year. She looked at it for a while as if the words meant something to her that she did not yet know.

"What're you thinking about? Huh?" Arnold Friend demanded. "Not worried about your hair blowing around in the car, are you?"

"No."

"Think I maybe can't drive good?"

"How do I know?"

"You're a hard girl to handle. How come?" he said. "Don't you know I'm your friend? Didn't you see me put my sign in the air when you walked by?"

"What sign?"

"My sign. And he drew an X in the air, leaning out toward her. They were maybe ten feet apart. After his hand fell back to his side the X was still in the air, almost visible. Connie let the screen door close and stood perfectly still inside it, listening to the music from her radio and the boy's blend together. She stared at Arnold Friend. He stood there so stiffly relaxed, pretending to be relaxed, with one hand idly on the door handle as if he were keeping himself up that way and had no intention of ever moving again. She recognized most things about him, the tight jeans that showed his thighs and buttocks and the greasy leather boots and the tight shirt, and even that slippery friendly smile of his, that sleepy dreamy smile that all the boys used to get across ideas they didn't want to put into words. She recognized all this and also the singsong way he talked, slightly mocking, kidding, but serious and a little melancholy, and she recognized the way he tapped one fist against the other in homage to the perpetual music behind him. But all these things did not come together.

She said suddenly, "Hey, how old are you?"

His smile faded. She could see then that he wasn't a kid, he was much older—thirty, maybe more. At this knowledge her heart began to pound faster.

"That's a crazy thing to ask. Can'tcha see I'm your own age?"

"Like hell you are."

"Or maybe a coupla years older, I'm eighteen."

"Eighteen?" she said doubtfully.

He grinned to reassure her and lines appeared at the corners of his mouth. His teeth were big and white. He grinned so broadly his eyes became slits and she saw how thick the lashes were, thick and black as if painted with a black tarlike material. Then he seemed to become embarrassed, abruptly, and looked over his shoulder at Ellie. "*Him*, he's crazy," he said. "Ain't he a riot, he's a nut, a real character." Ellie was still listening to the music. His sunglasses told nothing about what he was thinking. He wore a bright orange shirt unbuttoned halfway to show his chest, which was a pale, bluish chest and not muscular like Arnold Friend's. His shirt collar was turned up all around and the very tips of the collar pointed out past his chin as if they were protecting him. He was pressing the transistor radio up against his ear and sat there in a kind of daze, right in the sun.

"He's kinda strange," Connie said.

"Hey, she says you're kinda strange! Kinda strange!" Arnold Friend cried. He pounded on the car to get Ellie's attention. Ellie turned for the first time and Connie saw with shock that he wasn't a kid either—he had a fair, hairless face, cheeks reddened slightly as if the veins grew too close to the surface of his skin, the face of a forty-year-old baby. Connie felt a wave of dizziness rise in her at this sight and she stared at him as if waiting for something to change the shock of the moment, make it all right again. Ellie's lips kept shaping words, mumbling along with the words blasting in his ear.

"Maybe you two better go away," Connie said faintly.

"What? How come?" Arnold Friend cried. "We come out here to take you for a ride. It's Sunday." He had the voice of the man on the radio now. It was the same voice, Connie thought. "Don'tcha know it's Sunday all day and honey, no matter who you were with last night today you're with Arnold Friend and don't you forget it!—Maybe you better step out here," he said, and this last was in a different voice. It was a little flatter, as if the heat was finally getting to him.

"No. I got things to do."

"Hey."

"You two better leave."

"We ain't leaving until you come with us."

"Like hell I am—"

"Connie, don't fool around with me. I mean, I mean, don't fool *around*," he said, shaking his head. He laughed incredulously. He placed his sunglasses on top of his head, carefully, as if he were indeed wearing a wig, and brought the stems down behind his ears. Connie stared at him, another wave of dizziness and fear rising in her so that for a moment he wasn't even in focus but was just a blur, standing there against his gold car, and she had the idea that he had driven up the driveway all right but had come from nowhere before that and belonged nowhere and that everything about him and even about the music that was so familiar to her was only half real.

"If my father comes and sees you—"

"He ain't coming. He's at a barbecue."

"How do you know that?"

"Aunt Tillie's. Right now they're—uh—they're drinking. Sitting around," he said vaguely, squinting as if he were staring all the way to town and over to Aunt Tillie's backyard. Then the vision seemed to get clear and he nodded energetically. "Yeah. Sitting around. There's your sister in a blue dress, huh? And high heels, the poor sad bitch—nothing like you sweetheart! And your mother's helping some fat woman with the corn, they're cleaning the corn—husking the corn—"

"What fat woman?" Connie cried.

"How do I know what fat woman. I don't know every goddam fat woman in the world!" Arnold Friend laughed.

"Oh, that's Mrs. Hornby. . . . Who invited her?" Connie said. She felt a little light-headed. Her breath was coming quickly.

"She's too fat. I don't like them fat. I like them the way you are, honey," he said, smiling sleepily at her. They stared at each other for a while, through the screen door. He said softly, "Now what you're going to do is this: you're going to come out that door. You're going to sit up front with me and Ellie's going to sit in the back, the hell with Ellie, right? This isn't Ellie's date. You're my date. I'm your lover, honey."

"What? You're crazy—"

"Yes, I'm your lover. You don't know what that is but you will," he said. "I know that too. I know all about you. But look: it's real nice and you couldn't ask for nobody better than me, or more polite. I always keep my word. I'll tell you how it is, I'm always nice at first, the first time. I'll hold you so tight you won't think you have to try to get away or pretend anything because you'll know you can't. And I'll come inside you where it's all secret and you'll give in to me and you'll love me—"

"Shut up! You're crazy!" Connie said. She backed away from the door. She put her hands against her ears as if she'd heard something terrible, something not meant for her. "People don't talk like that, you're crazy," she muttered. Her heart was almost too big now for her chest and its pumping made sweat break out all over her. She looked out to see Arnold Friend pause and then take a step toward the porch lurching. He almost fell. But, like a clever drunken man, he managed to catch his balance. He wobbled in his high boots and grabbed hold of one of the porch posts.

"Honey?" he said. "You still listening?"

"Get the hell out of here!"

"Be nice, honey. Listen."

"I'm going to call the police—"

He wobbled again and out of the side of his mouth came a fast spat curse, an aside not meant for her to hear. But even this "Christ!" sounded forced. Then he began to smile again. She watched this smile come, awkward as if he were smiling from inside a mask. His whole face was a mask, she thought wildly, tanned down onto his throat but then running out as if he had plastered make-up on his face but had forgotten about his throat.

"Honey—? Listen, here's how it is. I always tell the truth and I promise you this: I ain't coming in that house after you."

"You better not! I'm going to call the police if you—if you don't—"

"Honey," he said, talking right through her voice, "honey, I'm not coming in there but you are coming out here. You know why?"

She was panting. The kitchen looked like a place she had never seen before, some room she had run inside but which wasn't good enough, wasn't going to help her. The kitchen window had never had a curtain, after three years, and there were dishes in the sink for her to do—probably—and if you ran your hand across the table you'd probably feel something sticky there.

"You listening, honey? Hey?"

"—going to call the police—"

"Soon as you touch the phone I don't need to keep my promise and can come inside. You won't want that."

She rushed forward and tried to lock the door. Her fingers were shaking. "But why lock it," Arnold Friend said gently, talking right into her face. "It's just a screen door. It's just nothing." One of his boots was at a strange angle, as if his foot wasn't in it. It pointed out to the left, bent at the ankle. "I mean, anybody can break through a screen door and glass and wood and iron or anything else if he needs to, anybody at all and specially Arnold Friend. If the place got lit up with a fire honey you'd come running out into my arms, right into my arms and safe at home—like you knew I was your lover and stopped fooling around. I don't mind a nice shy girl but I don't like no fooling around." Part of those words were spoken with a slight rhythmic lilt, and Connie somehow recognized them—the echo of a song from last year, about a girl rushing into her boy friend's arms and coming home again—

Connie stood barefoot on the linoleum floor, staring at him. "What do you want?" she whispered.

"I want you," he said.

"What?"

"Seen you that night and thought, that's the one, yes sir. I never needed to look any more."

"But my father's coming back. He's coming to get me. I had to wash my hair first—" She spoke in a dry, rapid voice, hardly raising it for him to hear.

"No, your daddy is not coming and yes, you had to wash your hair and you washed it for me. It's nice and shining and all for me, I thank you, sweetheart," he said, with a mock bow, but again he almost lost his balance. He had to bend and adjust his boots. Evidently his feet did not go all the way down; the boots must have been stuffed with something so that he would seem taller. Connie stared out at him and behind him Ellie in the car, who seemed to be looking off toward Connie's right, into nothing. This Ellie said, pulling the words out of the air one after another as if he were just discovering them, "You want me to pull out the phone?"

"Shut your mouth and keep it shut," Arnold Friend said, his face red from bending over or maybe from embarrassment because Connie had seen his boots. "This ain't none of your business."

"What—what are you doing? What do you want?" Connie said. "If I call the police they'll get you, they'll arrest you—"

"Promise was not to come in unless you touch that phone, and I'll keep that promise," he said. He resumed his erect position and tried to force his shoulders back. He sounded like a hero in a movie, declaring something important. He spoke too loudly and it was as if he were speaking to someone behind Connie. "I ain't made plans for coming in that house where I don't belong but just for you to come out to me, the way you should. Don't you know who I am?"

"You're crazy," she whispered. She backed away from the door but did not want to go into another part of the house, as if this would give him permission to come through the door. "What do you. . . . You're crazy, you . . ."

"Huh? What're you saying, honey?"

Her eyes darted everywhere in the kitchen. She could not remember what it was, this room.

"This is how it is, honey: you come out and we'll drive away, have a nice ride. But if you don't come out we're gonna wait till your people come home and then they're all going to get it."

"You want that telephone pulled out?" Ellie said. He held the radio away from his ear and grimaced, as if without the radio the air was too much for him.

"I toldja shut up, Ellie," Arnold Friend said, "you're deaf, get a hearing aid, right? Fix yourself up. This little girl's no trouble and's gonna be nice to me, so Ellie keep to yourself, this ain't your date—right? Don't hem in on me. Don't hog. Don't crush. Don't bird dog. Don't trail me," he said in a rapid meaningless voice, as if he were running through all the expressions he'd learned but was no longer sure which one of them was in style, then rushing on to new ones, making them up with his eyes closed, "Don't crawl under my fence, don't squeeze in my chipmunk hole, don't sniff my glue, suck my popsicle, keep your own greasy fingers on yourself!" He shaded his eyes and peered in at Connie, who was backed against the kitchen table. "Don't mind him honey he's just a creep. He's a dope. Right? I'm the boy for you and like I said you come out here nice like a lady and give me your hand, and nobody else gets hurt, I mean, your nice old bald-headed daddy and your mummy and your sister in her high heels. Because listen: why bring them in this?"

"Leave me alone," Connie whispered.

"Hey, you know that old woman down the road, the one with the chickens and stuff—you know her?"

"She's dead!"

"Dead? What? You know her?" Arnold Friend said.

"She's dead—"

"Don't you like her?"

"She's dead—she's—she isn't here any more—"

"But don't you like her, I mean, you got something against her? Some grudge or something?" Then his voice dipped as if he were conscious of a rudeness. He touched the sunglasses perched on top of his head as if to make sure they were still there. "Now you be a good girl."

"What are you going to do?"

"Just two things, or maybe three," Arnold Friend said. "But I promise it won't last long and you'll like me that way you get to like people you're close to. You will. It's all over for you here, so come on out. You don't want your people in any trouble, do you?"

She turned and bumped against a chair or something, hurting her leg, but she ran into the back room and picked up the telephone. Something roared in her ear, a tiny roaring, and she was so sick with fear that she could do nothing but listen to it—the telephone was clammy and very heavy and her fingers groped down to the dial but were too weak to touch it. She began to scream into the phone, into the roaring. She cried out, she cried for her mother, she felt her breath start jerking back and forth in her lungs as if it were something Arnold Friend were stabbing her with again and again with no tenderness. A noisy sorrowful wailing rose all about her and she was locked inside it the way she was locked inside the house.

After a while she could hear again. She was sitting on the floor with her wet back against the wall.

Arnold Friend was saying from the door, "That's a good girl. Put the phone back."

She kicked the phone away from her.

"No, honey. Pick it up. Put it back right."

She picked it up and put it back. The dial tone stopped.

"That's a good girl. Now you come outside."

She was hollow with what had been fear, but what was now just an emptiness. All that screaming had blasted it out of her. She sat, one leg cramped under her, and deep inside her brain was something like a pinpoint of light that kept going and would not let her relax. She thought, I'm not going to see my mother again. She thought, I'm not going to sleep in my bed again. Her bright green blouse was all wet.

Arnold Friend said, in a gentle-loud voice that was like a stage voice, "The place where you came from ain't there any more, and where you had in mind to go is canceled out. This place you are now—inside your daddy's house—is nothing but a cardboard box I can knock down any time. You know that and always did know it. You hear me?"

She thought, I have got to think. I have to know what to do.

"We'll go out to a nice field, out in the country here where it smells so nice and it's sunny," Arnold Friend said. "I'll have my arms around you so you won't need to try to get away and I'll show you what love is like, what it does. The hell with this house! It looks solid all right," he said. He ran a fingernail down the screen and the noise did not make Connie shiver, as it would have the day before. "Now put your hand on your heart, honey. Feel that? That feels solid too but we know better, be nice to me, be sweet like you can because what else is there for a girl like you but to be sweet and pretty and give in?—and get away before her people come back?"

She felt her pounding heart. Her hand seemed to enclose it. She thought for the first time in her life that it was nothing that was hers, that belonged to her, but just a pounding, living thing inside this body that wasn't really hers either.

"You don't want them to get hurt," Arnold Friend went on. "Now get up, honey. Get up all by yourself."

She stood.

"Now turn this way. That's right. Come over here to me—Ellie, put that away, didn't I tell you? You dope. You miserable creepy dope," Arnold Friend said. His words were not angry but only part of an incantation. The incantation was kindly. "Now come out through the kitchen to me honey and let's see a smile, try it, you're a brave sweet little girl and now they're eating corn and hotdogs cooked to bursting over an outdoor fire, and they don't know one thing about you and never did and honey you're better than them because not a one of them would have done this for you."

Connie felt the linoleum under her feet; it was cool. She brushed her hair back out of her eyes. Arnold Friend let go of the post tentatively and opened his arms for her, his elbows pointing in toward each other and his wrists limp, to show that this was an embarrassed embrace and a little mocking, he didn't want to make her self-conscious.

She put out her hand against the screen. She watched herself push the door slowly open as if she were safe back somewhere in the other doorway, watching this body and this head of long hair moving out into the sunlight where Arnold Friend waited.

"My sweet little blue-eyed girl," he said, in a half-sung sigh that had nothing to do with her brown eyes but was taken up just the same by the vast sunlit reaches of the land behind him and on all sides of him, so much land that Connie had never seen before and did not recognize except to know that she was going to it.

WHAT SHAPES RESPONSE: OUR EXPERIENCES

Now that you have read the story and noted your responses, you get to listen in on a conversation by other readers responding individually. As you read their comments, watch for places where readers become aware of how their own experiences have influenced their readings. Watch for places where one reader's story or reading experience influences another's. In addition, be aware of how their observations and comments relate to your own: Do they notice similar things? Do they raise similar issues? Do their reactions and stories introduce possibilities you hadn't considered?

TEACHER: What did you think of the story?

AMY: I was confused. I just didn't get the part where Connie was stabbed. What was going on? Wasn't she trying to call the police? But then it seems that she was OK. It just doesn't make sense.

BROOK: She wasn't stabbed, was she? She was on the phone and something happened, but I'm not sure what it was.

TEACHER: Amy, read that paragraph and let's see how Oates narrates the action.

AMY: (reads) . . . Oh, I guess she wasn't stabbed. It says her breath came like Arnold Friend was stabbing her with something. I guess I didn't understand the story.

MARY ELLEN: I find the story haunting. I can't quite say why. I've read it before and I remember that it affected me the same way the first time I read it. I just couldn't stop thinking about it and yet I felt really awful thinking about it. It was so scary and creepy and haunting. And what's all that light imagery about?

TEACHER: What made it so memorable? Is it haunting because it's scary and creepy?

MARY ELLEN: I don't know. I guess I can remember times when I've been alone baby-sitting and watched really frightening movies on television and I've felt really alone and vulnerable. I guess it's the way she discovers that she's vulnerable.

BROOK: When I read it I didn't pick up on the fear. I see it now when I look at the paragraph Amy read but I just read right by it. I guess I was following the plot, but I didn't really hear the fear. It is there though.

TEACHER: Why do you think you didn't see the fear? Do you identify with Connie in any way?

BROOK: Well, I was a pretty normal teenager. I worried about how my hair looked and whether guys noticed me. I don't know. I think it's a story about the devil. I remember discussing the story in another class and we decided that Arnold Friend is the devil. He seems to mark Connie the first time he sees her. He knows everything about her; he knows her name and all about her family and that her family has left for a barbecue. He wobbles in his boots like maybe he has hooves instead of feet, and he makes an X in the air that seems to stay in the air.

STEVE: Yeah, I think he's the devil too. He's so evil and maybe she's being punished, or . . .

ERIN: You think she's being punished? For what? I mean, she's kind of a ditz, but she hardly deserves punishment. I think it's more about power. He has her in a spell, and I think all the music has something to do with that. He's lots older and uses parts of song lyrics to shape his dialogue. It's how he pretends to be younger than he is. And he sounds like the DJ Connie has been listening to. Like a popular singer, he's able to draw women into his power. I think the story is about power and manipulation. Why is it dedicated to Bob Dylan?

KAY: I felt that way too. I remember a time I was getting obscene phone calls and there was something about the way the caller asserted himself that made me feel powerless. I mean, he'd say things sort of explicitly but not completely and with so much power that it kind of pulled me into the phone. I felt kind of weak. I think she feels powerless and terrified. It's like she's being stalked.

MARY ELLEN: Wow, I hadn't thought of it as being like stalking. I guess it kind of is.

ROB: I think she's stronger than people give her credit for. She does pretty well. She does keep her wits about her for a while until she realizes that there's nothing she can do. She's pretty strong. She says things like "Who the hell do you think you are?" and "I don't even know who you are."

BROOK: I don't think so. I think she's just a regular teenager—a kid who is interested in being noticed and is flattered by his attention. I think she stays outside because she's flattered, not because she's strong. She wonders how she looks when he drives up, and while they're talking she lets her hair fall loose over one shoulder. She's kind of playing around and doesn't realize how stupid she's being.

GRETCHEN: I think she kind of enjoys the whole thing.

TEACHER: Laurie, what do you think? I can't read your expression, but you seem to be reacting to something Brook said.

LAURIE: I guess I just don't feel any sympathy. Connie just seems like someone who is concerned about being popular. She's awful to her parents and her sister and she's really shallow. She's making really stupid decisions and she kind of deserves what happens to her. I really hated the story.

TEACHER: That's an interesting reaction. It seems to extend Gretchen's observation that Connie enjoys the attention. What do the rest of you think? Do you identify with her? Do you sympathize?

GRETCHEN: I think she's a product of her family. They're shallow and always ordering her around, telling her not to look in the mirror, for example, or not paying attention to her. So when she meets someone older who orders her around, she is easily manipulated.

BROOK: I guess people would have hated me when I was fifteen. I was like this. She just seems like a typical teenager.

CHANTELLE: Doesn't she have sex with that guy she went out with? She's pretty shallow if she just has sex with a guy she's just met or doesn't really know very well. She was asking for it the way she was acting. I didn't feel sorry for her either.

GRETCHEN: Would you say that if she were a friend of yours? Just because she's promiscuous, if she is, doesn't mean she deserves to be raped.

MARY ELLEN: I agree. There's a difference between the way she responds to the young guys she picks up at the restaurant and this guy. She may have chosen to have sex, or whatever they did, with the other guy, but this isn't sex, this is rape. And rape is about power, not sex.

TIM: I know this sounds kind of stupid, but I thought she was actually raped. She's about to call the police, then she begins to scream into the phone and cry out, and then comes the sentence that describes her breath "as if it were something Arnold Friend were stabbing her with again and again with no tenderness." That sounds like rape to me.

ROB: But he was standing at the door talking to her from the door when he tells her to put the phone back.

TIM: Oh, I guess that's right. Maybe he walked back to the door after he raped her? No, I guess not. Oh well.

TEACHER: The sentence does sound like a rape. What do you make of that?

MARY ELLEN: I think it's the first time that she realized that evil exists. I mean she's what, fifteen? She's just a kid, and maybe she's kind of a rotten kid, but she's really just naive and she flirts the way kids do, without realizing the consequences.

JOHN: When I read the story I thought about Charles Manson, the way he was able to mesmerize his victims. I think the story is about power. The guy doesn't want simply to overpower Connie physically; he wants to make her come to him.

ERIN: What really struck me was the way Connie was paralyzed by her fear. She is so frightened that she has that roaring sound in her ears.

MARY ELLEN: When that happens, she is sort of raped. I mean she realizes that she's powerless. She's completely trapped and then she gives in. She puts the phone down when he tells her to and after that she's changed. She's kind of numb.

TEACHER: I don't know if any of you have ever had a similar experience. It's difficult to talk about. I had an experience that reminds me of this but in many ways was different.

KAY: Will you tell us about it?

TEACHER: It happened when I was seventeen. I guess I was pretty naive at seventeen. I met a guy who was older, college aged, and he was kind of sophisticated and had a neat car. I was flattered when he asked me out and I agreed to go. He said he knew of a great steak place. When we left my house and drove to the other side of town, I had misgivings but I didn't want to sound like a kid so I didn't ask him where we were going but said stupid things like "I didn't know there were any steak places on this side of town." He didn't really reply but just kept driving and pretty soon we were out in the country with no lights left in sight. Still, I was too intimidated to ask where we were going, and I was beginning to feel paralyzed with fear. We turned down a dirt road, drove up a hill, and, much to my relief, came round a corner to a wonderful steak place on the very top of the ridge.

LAURIE: Well, I had an experience like that too. It's pretty hard to talk about, but I was with a friend and we met two guys and I made one decision and she made another, and I guess that affects the way I read this story. This girl was really dumb. She made some bad choices.

TEACHER: The subject matter is charged for some of us. I think if there were anyone who had been raped it would be extremely difficult to discuss this story and not let your own experience overshadow the story. But I think Laurie is noticing something that complicates our reaction to the ending. Connie is not a terribly appealing character, as some of you have noted. How does her character affect our response to the story? How about for next class, you bring a thesis statement that expresses your response to the ending of the story and gives a reason for your reaction?

EXERCISE 3.4. WAYS OF RESPONDING

Reread the conversation about Oates's story, thinking about the various ways of responding to works. With your reading group, categorize these ways of responding using the list below. Where have the readers:

- shared initial responses?
- recalled similar or different experiences?
- located the source of their associations in specific images, words, or phrases?
- identified those responses as perceptions about conflicts, relationships, or changes?
- responded by contributing knowledge that helped identify or resolve an interesting ambiguity?
- modified their responses in the context of new ideas or impressions?
- changed their minds?

WHAT SHAPES RESPONSE: OUR NEEDS

As human beings, we are persuaded when writers or speakers recognize our needs and appeal to them. When we are persuaded to understand and respond to literary works, it is because they have appealed to us emotionally, imaginatively, and logically; that's what makes the works literary. Sometimes the event or situation presented elicits primarily a feeling—of empathy, anger, repose, excitement, longing—as we "feel with" the work. Others strongly engage us with intellectual issues: we find ourselves calling on our logical faculties as we "comprehend" the relationships between the ideas in the work. Still others appeal to us primarily through our senses and imaginations, as we "live through" what the work presents. Although we can locate emotional, imaginative, and logical appeals in all literary works, sometimes one kind of response is complicated by another.

For example, the readers of the story "Where Are You Going, Where Have You Been?" responded in all three ways and looked to the work for reasons for their responses. Mary Ellen connects emotionally, "feeling with" the main character as the story generates emotions she needs to explain to herself ("It was so scary and creepy and haunting"). Erin connects with the story logically, attempting to "comprehend" the way the story's elements relate to each other (the song lyrics, the DJ), using her knowledge of literary language and reasoning inductively that the story is about "power and manipulation." Brook engages imaginatively, "living through" the experience by connecting sense details with her own experience, thus finding Connie credible as a character and the writer knowledgeable about the situation and people she is writing about. If we, as readers, find that a piece of writing offers us less than emotional, intellectual, and imaginative engagement, we are not likely to find it significant. Nonetheless, it is easier to find satisfying and motivating connections with works when we know that there is more than one way to identify with them.

Responsive readers take into account their imaginative, emotional, and logical needs as they respond to the experience the work presents. Writers make choices intended to assist you, as a reader, in identifying with the experience they present. This is a form of persuasion. When writers offer you reasoned statements, they do so to bring you into alignment with their way of thinking by responding to concerns they imagine you have. When writers offer you **images** that engage your senses and emotions, and **metaphors** to help you relate the unfamiliar to the familiar, they want you to see or feel for a moment the way they do. Paying attention to the ways in which writing appeals to your logic, your emotion, or your imagination helps you to listen and respond to the experience of the work. To respond fully as a reader, you have to imagine being in the experience, believe it is possible, accept that the writer knows about what he or she is writing about, and feel that the new knowledge offered is worth something—whether the knowledge is good news or bad, it has significance and value.

IDENTIFYING KEY TERMS AND QUESTIONS AT ISSUE

The participants in the above dialogue ask many interesting questions that could inspire good discussions and papers: Mary Ellen notices a pattern in the light **imagery**; Erin's attention is caught by the way music is used and wonders why the story is dedicated to Bob Dylan; Brook recalls an earlier class that found evidence to support seeing Arnold Friend as a devil; Gretchen wants to explore the influence of the family on Connie's character and choices.

In their conversation these issues are raised but not immediately addressed. Why not? None of these questions will work as papers unless readers first resolve the issues complicating their understanding of Connie's character—her situation, her choices, her degree of victimization or culpability. In other words, *questions at issue must be examined in the context of the experience the literature offers.*

Reflecting on the conversation, you probably noticed that certain words came up repeatedly, words like fear, vulnerable, stupid, manipulation, rape, naive, haunting, and power. These *key terms* emerge naturally in the conversation, lending shape and direction to the give and take as readers share their reading experiences. One of the ways we interpret together is to bring our reactions and our prior knowledge to bear on the key terms, clarifying and agreeing on their meanings in the context of the story and in relation to each other.

Maybe Connie was stupid; if so, why is the story "haunting"? If we are not meant to like her, how else are we invited to identify with her? Is she stupid personally, or stupid in a recognizable, potentially tragic way shared by other girls her age? If you are manipulated, are you stupid? If you are innocent, are you stupid?

Maybe she is vulnerable, but as one reader noted, she also seems strong. What's strong in this story? What's powerful? What kinds of strength may be in conflict?

Maybe she wasn't raped in the sense of physical assault, but if not, why does the descriptive language make it sound like rape? Can there be a non-physical, psychological rape, and if so, what would be its effects? What circumstances would be required?

These inquiries around key terms can help us link the reading experience to our personal experience. When we begin to frame a *question at issue*, we have to take into account several components of response. We have to *identify with a work*, locating a question the work raises that we, too, have found compelling in times or situations outside the reading experience. We have to *listen responsibly to the way the question is complicated and considered* in the work, making sure we don't oversimplify the issue or leave out elements to make the ideas fit our own concerns. We have to *identify ways in which our experience makes a contribution to the meaning* of the work: either the work explains something ambiguous in our lives, or our lives offer some context that helps resolve an ambiguity in the work. Questions at issue emerging from our inquiries about key terms might include:

- Does parent-child conflict make adolescents vulnerable to the manipulations of controlling adults? Do Connie's parents relate to her in a way that makes her more vulnerable to danger?
- Is it tragic when people who behave in predictable, natural ways suffer what appear to be predictable consequences of that behavior?
- What attracts us to explore our darker inclinations? In this story, what persuasions are brought to bear on Connie to make her vulnerable to Arnold Friend's power? How do they work?
- In what ways are we compelled to try to make horrible acts comprehensible? How does the story invite us to find an acceptable, rational explanation for what is finally, horribly, irrational?
- What is power? In what sense is this a story about power, specifically male physical power and female powerlessness?

These questions at issue, and others, emerge from the conversation, and the key terms that offer shape and direction to the conversation typically offer the materials for constructing meaningful thesis statements that can be developed into reasoned interpretations. Although it may seem that the participants have succeeded primarily in articulating their differences, their comments and questions show that they have influenced each other; it's difficult to leave such a discussion with your preconceived notions unchanged.

For example, during this conversation, Amy moves from a confusion about events to an honest response ("She's really shallow. . . . I guess I just don't feel any sympathy") to an awareness of what in her own background might be influencing her response. Brook recognizes the character's vulnerability to flattery and describes her behavior as a kind of "playing around." She calls the character "stupid" but also insists that it's a kind of stupidity she shared as a teenager. Mary Ellen begins with a vague sense of horror and empathy for the victim ("I hadn't thought of it as being like stalking. I guess it kind of is"), but her later statements show she has listened responsibly to Amy and Brook, who have influenced her way of perceiving and presenting her response: "She's just a kid, and maybe she's kind of a rotten kid, but she's really naive and she flirts the way kids do, without realizing the consequences."

As we share our responses, we revise and enlarge them in light of other responses. In the process, we take into account more possibilities, we come to understand and know each other, and we recognize complications that challenge us to clarify our thoughts and beliefs. Clarifying our responses is essential to responsible, responsive interpretation. Mary Ellen can look at light imagery, but it won't have much significance for her unless her analysis allows her to understand the question at issue more fully. Brook may be able to trace the pattern of details that gives Arnold Friend a devilish aspect, but the investigation won't mean much to her unless it helps her articulate her thoughtful, reasoned response to Connie. In Chapter 4, you will learn more about the elements a writer uses to shape and complicate your responses.

EXERCISE 3.5. HOW WRITERS SHAPE OUR RESPONSES

Read "Stalking Muskrats," an excerpt from Annie Dillard's book *Pilgrim at Tinker Creek*. If we can assume that you do not necessarily begin reading with a sense of your need to know more about stalking muskrats, observe what she does to create that need by appealing to your intellect, your imagination, and your emotions.

1. In your reading notebook, reflect on how she is inviting you to identify, to listen responsibly, and to contribute. Where does she include something that makes you think of personal experiences that gave you the same feeling she

describes? Where does she recount an experience using sense **imagery** and **figurative language** that makes you imagine yourself in the story in some way? Where does she give you evidence of her knowledge or credibility and thus a reason to listen to her?

2. In your reading group, respond to the **essay**, keeping a list of key terms that are repeated or seem to give direction to the conversation. What does Dillard seem to want you to do, know, think, or feel? Do you come to identify with her way of seeing muskrats? Do you come to believe that the experience is a significant one? What makes it significant? Out of this discussion, attempt to identify a question at issue that you share with the writer, one that you could explore by referring to your own experience.

ANNIE DILLARD

Stalking Muskrats

Learning to stalk muskrats took me several years.

I've always known there were muskrats in the creek. Sometimes when I drove late at night my headlights' beam on the water would catch the broad lines of ripples made by a swimming muskrat, a bow wave, converging across the water at the raised dark vee of its head. I would stop the car and get out: nothing. They eat corn and tomatoes from my neighbors' gardens, too, by night, so that my neighbors were always telling me that the creek was full of them. Around here, people call them "mushrats"; Thoreau called them "Musquashes." They are not of course rats at all (let alone squashes). They are more like diminutive beavers, and, like beavers, they exude a scented oil from musk glands under the base of the tail—hence the name. I had read in several respectable sources that muskrats are so wary they are almost impossible to observe. One expert who made a full-time study of larger populations, mainly by examining "sign" and performing autopsies on corpses, said he often went for weeks at a time without seeing a single living muskrat.

One hot evening three years ago, I was standing more or less *in* a bush. I was stock-still, looking deep into Tinker Creek from a spot on the bank opposite the house, watching a group of bluegills stare and hang motionless near the bottom of a deep, sunlit pool. I was focused for depth. I had long since lost myself, lost the creek, the day, lost everything but still, amber depth. All at once I couldn't see. And then I could: a young muskrat had appeared on top of the water, floating on its back. Its forelegs were folded languorously across its chest; the sun shone on its upturned belly. Its youthfulness and rodent grin, coupled with its ridiculous method of locomotion, which consisted of a lazy wag of the tail assisted by an occasional dabble of a webbed hind foot, made it an enchanting picture of decadence, dissipation, and summer sloth. I forgot all about the fish.

But in my surprise at having the light come on so suddenly, and at having my consciousness returned to me all at once and bearing an inverted muskrat, I must have moved and betrayed myself. The kit—for I know now it was just a young kit—righted itself so that only its head was visible above water, and swam downstream, away from me. I extricated myself from the bush and foolishly pursued it. It dove sleekly, reemerged, and glided for the opposite bank. I ran along the bankside brush, trying to keep it in sight. It kept casting an alarmed look over its shoulder at me. Once again it dove, under a floating mat of brush lodged in the bank, and disappeared. I never saw it again. (Nor have I ever, despite all the muskrats I have seen, again seen a muskrat floating on its back.) But I did not know muskrats then; I waited panting, and watched the shadowed bank. Now I know that I cannot outwait a muskrat who knows I am there. The most I can do is get "there" quietly, while it is still in its hole, so that it never knows, and wait there until it emerges. But then all I knew was that I wanted to see more muskrats.

I began to look for them day and night. Sometimes I would see ripples suddenly start beating from the creek's side, but as I crouched to watch, the ripples would die. Now I know what this means, and have learned to stand perfectly still to make out the muskrat's small, pointed face hidden under overhanging bank vegetation, watching me. That summer I haunted the bridges, I walked up creeks and down, but no muskrats ever appeared. You must just have to be there, I thought. You must have to spend the rest of your life standing in bushes. It was a once-in-a-lifetime thing and you've had your once.

Then one night I saw another, and my life changed. After that I knew where they were in numbers, and I knew when to look. It was late dusk. I was driving home from a visit with friends. Just on the off chance I parked quietly by the creek, walked out on the narrow bridge over the shallows, and looked upstream. Someday, I had been telling myself for weeks, someday a muskrat is going to swim right through that channel in the cattails, and I am going to see it. That is precisely what happened. I looked up the channel for a muskrat, and there it came, swimming right toward me. Knock; seek; ask. It seemed to swim with a side-to-side, sculling motion of its vertically flattened tail. It looked bigger than the upside down muskrat, and its face more reddish. In its mouth it clasped a twig of a tulip tree. One thing amazed me: it swam right down the middle of the creek. I thought it would hide in the rush along the edge; instead, it plied the waters as obviously as an aquaplane. I could just look and look.

But I was standing on the bridge, not sitting, and it saw me. It changed its course, veered towards the bank, and disappeared behind an indentation in the rushy shoreline. I felt a rush of such pure energy I thought I would not need to breathe for days.

The innocence of mine is mostly gone now, although I felt almost the same pure rush last night. I have seen many muskrats since I learned to look for them in that part of the creek. But still I seek them out in the cool of the evening, and still I hold my breath when rising ripples surge from under the creek's bank. The great hurrah about wild animals is that they exist at all, and the greater hurrah is the actual moment of seeing them. Because they have a nice dignity, and prefer to have nothing to do with me, not even as the simple objects of my vision. They show me by their very wariness what a prize it is simply to open my eyes and behold.

COMPONENTS OF RESPONSE

We have several reasons to understand better this process of responding as a means to understanding and changing. We are individuals, with unique experiences and visions. We also are related to each other, by birth or circumstance, by interest or accident, by love or antagonism. At the same time that we are attempting to make our essential, individual contributions, we also are attempting to help others understand and relate to us. We want to be individuals but not suffer isolation. We want to belong but don't want to disappear into a crowd.

Although Western culture, particularly American culture, has fostered many ways to reward individualism, uniqueness, and independence, the notion of **culture** itself requires that we establish shared ground, common understandings, and the capability to imagine ourselves beyond our present self-knowledge. Managing to engage or identify with an experience unlike one we've had before counteracts the sense of exclusion or separateness that is often a cause of disappointment, even despair, in our most difficult moments. In addition, the ability to confront and accommodate difference is what enables unique individuals to come together as groups with common purposes, whether those groups are based on shared experiences, geography, occupation, ancestors, or Saturday afternoon recreations. Finally, engaging with unfamiliar experiences reinforces our sense of ourselves as individuals by allowing us to both expand and refine our self-knowledge in response to new knowledge.

When we talk about responding to literature, we mean something richer and more complicated than a "gut-reacting" that would reduce the literary experience to something "like" or "unlike" us. Whether we have ever stalked muskrats or even observed animals in the wild should not limit our responses to Dillard's "Stalking Muskrats." We want to encourage an interaction between the reader and writer in which the reader's individuality both affects and is affected by the work and other readers. That is why in this chapter we have explored the ways our responses are shaped by our own experiences, our conversations and interactions with others, our expectations, and our needs.

Three words have been used repeatedly in our discussion of response. The first component of response is *identification*. You respond when you find a way to identify with the unfamiliar. When you read "Stalking Muskrats," you may identify with Dillard's curiosity regarding something she knows little about, her delight in accumulating information and recording details, or her quiet joy in gradually moving toward understanding something so different from herself. Your locus of connection to a literary work may not be the situation, characters, or setting; it may, in fact, be a rather vague sense of having experienced the same emotion before: need, confusion, joy, distance, longing, revenge, reverie. Or your attempt to identify may evoke in you a reaction against the apparent understanding or portrayal of people or events reflected by the work. Response as identification requires that you ask yourself about your reactions and speculate on how they influence and reflect your self-understanding and your understanding of the work.

A second component of response is your *contribution* to the work. If by identifying with a work you find a way to join in an ongoing conversation, then by contributing to that conversation you clarify its meaning and direction. Conversing with written works is not easy; the writer's work is done, and the reader must take up the task of filling in the gaps, of constructing meaning where there is ambiguity, of making connections that are possible and invited but not certain or final. Annie Dillard never tells us why she stalks muskrats, but as we explore our identification with the experience she describes, we consider how the connections between her experience and our own help us come closer to an understanding of her perspective. Literature often raises questions that it insistently refuses to answer, and readers are invited to supply what the narrator or **persona**—who may be limited in consciousness—can't or doesn't supply. As you speculate on what was meant by reflecting on what was read, you are drawn into the experience as a participant. Literature in this sense is a collaborative enterprise, and by the very act of engaging with and attempting to address questions raised by literature, the reader is helping to complete it. Response as contribution requires that you identify and address ambiguity by constructing connection and meaning where there was distance and confusion.

A third component of response is best explained by connecting it to the word *responsibility*. When you respond, you respond "to" something, which requires that you must be aware of it in the first place. You might be intrigued that Annie Dillard begins the explanation of her first sighting with a description of the depths of a pool in the creek. As you explore your reactions to this choice with other readers, you will look carefully at the relationship between the description of the pool and Dillard's response to the sighting, and you will consider various explanations for the relationship. If you are making a statement that does not take into account other interpretive possibilities or other people's ideas or experiences, you are simply asserting a position, but you are not necessarily responding. As we are often reminded in discussions of issues outside of literature, if you come to the question with your mind already made up, there can be no dialogue and therefore no possibility of shared understanding. To converse, you must accept responsibility for hearing the other person. Thus if you come to literature with no desire to hear about or understand views other than those you bring, there can be no response. Responding to works responsibly requires that you take into account other voices inside and outside the work as you make decisions and judgments about probable, reasoned interpretations.

These three components of response are all a part of satisfying readings and interpretations of works. In conversations with literary works, you respond to your own past experiences, to the invitations to contribute contained in the language and substance of the work, and to the possibilities that come to you from your own imaginative extensions or from other readers who confront the work with you. We have identified these components to help you develop your responses in satisfying ways. Readers who don't integrate their literary experience with their own lives may find their efforts to locate meaning in literature sterile and pointless. Readers who refuse the invitations literature offers to make the unfamiliar familiar by contributing their knowledge to the literary conversation isolate themselves from the rich and varied experiences the world has to offer and lose the opportunity to practice clarifying their own thinking and influencing the thinking of others. Readers who fail to pay attention to what the literary conversation offers them beyond their prior knowledge may find in literature nothing but a narrow confirmation of their own unchanging image.

Responsive readers pay attention to their own responses, positive or negative, and inquire about them, asking what features of the work and what factors in their personal lives or values might have caused the responses. Responsive readers observe the form of the work, noting its features and reflecting on its relationship to and significance for the reader's response. Responsive readers listen to the voice or voices of the work, engaging with its perspective, or sometimes varied perspectives. Responsive readers can make up their minds about what a work means, and this includes revising their interpretations when new knowledge or new experiences warrant a change of mind. The process of reading responsively can help us find in literature vital, dynamic human experiences.

READING AND WRITING TO RESPOND

The perspective and organization of your response essay will emerge from your own interaction with the work and with other readers. However, readers have expectations that will help you revise your responses into writing that is more easily read and understood by others. The kinds of interpretive responses you choose and develop will depend on your answers to three questions: What is my response? What kind of question does my response answer? What kind of information must I use to arrive at and develop that answer?

Reading to Respond

In each of the exercises in this chapter, you have practiced habits of reading literature that will help you formulate a response worth sharing. In addition, you know several strategies that could help you read attentively in preparation for sharing your responses. As you read, you can ask yourself questions that will help you *engage* with the work:

- What does this situation, person, or place remind me of?
- Is the feeling created by the work one I've experienced before? When?
- What is similar about the two experiences?
- What is the source or cause of the connection?

If no associations come to mind, you might ask:

- How is it different from what I already know or have experienced?
- What do I like, or not like, about it?
- What in the work makes me uncomfortable, and why?

You also prepare to write a response essay when you ask yourself questions that will help you *reflect on* and *analyze* the work:

- What is acting against what? (Conflicts)
- What relates to what? (Connections)
- What changes?

Discussing your reading of the work with other readers also will help you respond fully. During the discussion, you can ask:

- How are my responses like and unlike theirs?
- How do our differences complicate or clarify my understandings?
- How do some readings reconcile with and complete other readings?
- How do readings in conflict with each other hold up when examined within the context of the work as a whole?

- How has interaction with others validated, changed, or modified my responses and ideas?

Then, in preparation for sharing your responses in writing with others, begin to clarify your purpose and subject:

- Identify significant key terms that emerge from your response and focus your concerns.
- Formulate a question you find intriguing, one to which you can offer an answer that will contribute to the way you and others understand the work.

Kinds of Response Questions

If your response paper asks "What did I learn from this reading experience that contributes to my self-knowledge or my understanding of the world?" you have obligated yourself to these tasks:

- Clearly establishing your prior knowledge or understanding and the basis for it.
- Responsibly representing the reading experience.
- Establishing connections between those two that account for the new knowledge you have discovered.

If your response paper asks "What do I know or have I experienced that can contribute to an understanding of this work?" then you are offering as a writer to answer a question the work raises by filling in the gaps, by constructing meaning where there is ambiguity, by making connections that are possible and invited but not certain or final. In offering your personal experience as a context for the reading experience of others, you must make sure that your contribution works logically and emotionally with the work as a whole and not just a single action or event taken out of context. You promise, in this kind of response paper, to:

- Identify the question raised by the work.
- Explore its implications and complications.
- Place the question in an analogous scene from your own experience.
- Explain how your context resolves the question or clarifies an answer both for you and for others.

If your response paper asks "What did the work make me feel, and how did it make me feel that way?" your paper must do the following:

- Generalize about your primary response.
- Reflect on that response, clarifying what in the work and in yourself produced that response.
- Trace the development and modulation of that response through the experience of the work.
- Modify, accept, or reject that response.

The group discussing "Filling Station" in Chapter 2 engaged in this kind of response without the use of elaborate literary language, and you can too, though Chapter 4 on literary analysis will encourage you to become familiar with the ways of looking and thinking that literary language allows. Your response, however, does not have to be a positive or consistent one. You might begin with an impression of the work which made you resist it, and show how, through the process of reflecting both on your experience and the one the work presents, your response evolved. It might also examine the ways in which a work seems to appeal to some readers and distance others.

SUMMARY

In each of the exercises in this chapter, you have practiced habits of reading literature that will help you formulate a response worth sharing. From earlier chapters, you know several strategies that can help you read attentively in preparation for sharing your responses. In this chapter, we've presented opportunities for you to practice a model of interpretation based on the ways you naturally converse with friends about ideas and opinions. When you share responses, it is natural to explain and justify them without expecting a final or correct answer to the question at issue. When you share responses about literature, you are engaging in a give-and-take that refines and enriches your understanding.

Our responses will be different because our experiences, needs, and questions are different. As we listen responsibly to the way the work is complicated by our diverse observations and ideas, we begin to identify questions at issue raised for us by the work. To answer those questions in terms of our experiences, we need to identify how the work explains some ambiguity in our lives or how our lives offer some context that helps resolve an ambiguity in the work. Thus our interpretations become contributions to the literary conversations as our unique experiences address questions shared with other readers.

Interpretive response requires that we identify with the unfamiliar, share our individual responses and ideas, and contribute responsibly, taking into account other voices and possibilities and making reasoned decisions and judgments. Through interpretive response, we come to understand and value literary works that reflect perspectives like and unlike our own.

An Invitation to Write: The Response Essay

In this chapter, we presented three kinds of questions that can result in response essays. Review these questions, and after reading and responding to a literary piece, try to write at least one question of each type on that piece. Which question do you find most compelling? Which least? Why?

Answer each question with a tentative interpretive statement. What does the statement commit you to including in the essay? Look at each component of your statement. Does it need explaining, defending, defining, illustrating, clarifying?

Choose one statement and refine it so that it emphasizes and promises what you want it to. Develop it into a working draft of an essay you can share with other readers.

Writing Group Activity

After having drafted a response essay, present your draft to your writing group. Give them copies or read it aloud to them, asking them to watch or listen for *your response, the type of response question you have asked*, and *your answer to your question*. Use their responses to your question as guidance to help you clarify your paper. What was clear to your readers? What confused them? Did they ask for more information?

If you have time, ask your readers to describe how you have identified with the work, to indicate how you have contributed to their understanding of its meaning, and to evaluate how responsibly you have represented the work itself.

Sample Writing 1: Response Essay

The following essay was written in response to Annie Dillard's "Stalking Muskrats." In the essay, the reader considers a memory the piece recalls for her. She uses her own experience to try to understand Dillard's, then tries to come to terms with her own memory.

MUSKRATS AND MEMORIES OF MY BROTHER

I spent many hours of my earliest summer days lying on my belly on warm Georgian red clay, watching ants marching relentlessly to and from their mountainous homes or counting the leaves of hundreds of clover stems, greedily anticipating the one elusive four leafed find or breaking the stem off honeysuckle blossoms to suck their tiny drop of sweetness. My brother, in contrast, was always reading, studying, accumulating what seemed to be important information about how the world worked. From an early age, he understood the mysteries of physics. As I ignored the information he loved to share with me, I retreated further into my dream world. I knew he was the family genius while I was only the dreamer. I loved to feel the sun warming the back of my jumpsuit, to smell the onion grass, to see the first lightning bug at dusk, to hear the soft whine of the cicadas.

As I grew into adolescence, I began to look outward to my social world, the splattered canvas of parties and phone calls and slow evenings on beaches where the sounds, sights, and smells of nature provided the landscape for my wakening. As my journey into adolescence accelerated, my brother watched with large pale eyes. Nothing in his studies had prepared him for the dawn of my womanhood. The intensity of my coming of age glittered and rang loudly. While he read Kafka, I held court in my new world. We each resented the other but never made an attempt to know the other better.

We were both fascinated by the world around us. He gathered information; I gathered rosebuds. He knew the way the world worked. I knew how it felt. But neither of us could or would try to look through the other's eyes. Each of us felt ownership of our way of knowing, and yet when I look back, I realize how incomplete each of our ways of knowing was. The encyclopedia of his accumulated facts was as compelling as the march of the ants through my grasses, and the honeysuckle would have tasted as sweet on his tongue as on mine, and yet we each resisted the other's world.

Muskrats fascinate Annie Dillard because they are elusive. She knows a great deal about muskrats from their local reputation and from imaginative and scientific books, and like experts who study them, she has seen signs of them, but before that first chance sighting, she has never seen one. The first muskrat she sees looks strange and moves in a way she has never observed. "Its youthfulness and rodent grin, coupled with its ridiculous method of locomotion . . . made it an enchanting picture of decadence, dissipation, and summer sloth." It was so different from her world, even from the natural world she knows. When it saw her and fled, she chased it. After it disappeared, she was captivated: "all I knew was that I wanted to see more muskrats."

Because she is drawn to them, Annie Dillard begins a study of the behavior of muskrats. Her study proving inadequate, she learns to stalk muskrats by entering their imaginative world. Despite the stories and information she owned when she first saw a muskrat, she says she "did not know muskrats then." She seems to mean that she could only come to know muskrats by observing them and trying to understand the way they think. She is a kind of student of muskrats.

The information from books seems inadequate without the experience but the experience seems to need a reasoning process we use to step back to generalize and synthesize. More important though, our growth depends on looking through another's eyes, someone or some being that is so different, so that having looked we can think about our own lives. It's sad that my brother and I, because we were so different, didn't allow ourselves to grow. We each could have learned so much from each other. We saw our differences as threats to each other. More than wariness, we had inadequacy. Somehow we knew we needed each other, but we shut our eyes.

I think Dillard's story is like the muskrat. It doesn't really see me as an object of its vision and thus in its wariness, it has a nice dignity. Having seen it, having looked through Dillard's eyes, I see something about myself. Maybe I'll call my brother today.

Sample Writing 2: Response Essay

Because we have been using the metaphor of conversation to talk about interpretation, we thought it would be interesting to end this chapter with a story that is almost entirely made up of conversation. In Ernest Hemingway's "A Clean, Well-Lighted Place," two characters converse about another, interpreting his character and behavior and in the process revealing a good deal about themselves—their way of seeing the world and responding to it. After you have read the story, you might reflect on it using the questions in the Reading to Respond section of this chapter.

Following the Hemingway story is a response in which a reader interprets the story in the context of her own experience, allowing each to explain the other. Her paper is an example of the way in which personal knowledge can enrich the reading experience, and vice versa.

Ernest Hemingway
A Clean, Well-Lighted Place

It was late and every one had left the cafe except an old man who sat in the shadow the leaves of the tree made against the electric light. In the day time the street was dusty, but at night the dew settled the dust and the old man liked to sit late because he was deaf and now at night it was quiet and he felt the difference. The two waiters inside the cafe knew that the old man was a little drunk, and while he was a good client they knew that if he became too drunk he would leave without paying, so they kept watch on him.

"Last week he tried to commit suicide," one waiter said.

"Why?"

"He was in despair."

"What about?"

"Nothing."

"How do you know it was nothing?"

"He has plenty of money."

They sat together at a table that was close against the wall near the door of the cafe and looked at the terrace where the tables were all empty except where the old man sat in the shadow of the leaves of the tree that moved slightly in the wind. A girl and a soldier went by in the street. The street light shone on the brass number on his collar. The girl wore no head covering and hurried beside him.

"The guard will pick him up," one waiter said.

"What does it matter if he gets what he's after?"

"He had better get off the street now. The guard will get him. They went by five minutes ago."

The old man sitting in the shadow rapped on his saucer with his glass. The younger waiter went over to him.

"What do you want?"

The old man looked at him. "Another brandy," he said.

"You'll be drunk," the waiter said. The old man looked at him. The waiter went away.

"He'll stay all night," he said to his colleague. "I'm sleepy now. I never get into bed before three o'clock. He should have killed himself last week."

The waiter took the brandy bottle and another saucer from the counter inside the cafe and marched out to the old man's table. He put down the saucer and poured the glass full of brandy.

"You should have killed yourself last week," he said to the deaf man. The old man motioned with his finger. "A little more," he said. The waiter poured on into the glass so that the brandy slopped over and ran down the stem into the top saucer of the pile. "Thank you," the old man said. The waiter took the bottle back inside the cafe. He sat down at the table with his colleague again.

"He's drunk now," he said.

"He's drunk every night."

"What did he want to kill himself for?"

"How should I know."

"How did he do it?"

"He hung himself with a rope."

"Who cut him down?"

"His niece."

"Why did they do it?"

"Fear for his soul."

"How much money has he got?"

"He's got plenty."

"He must be eighty years old."

"Anyway I should say he was eighty."

"I wish he would go home. I never get to bed before three o'clock. What kind of hour is that to go to bed?"

"He stays up because he likes it."

"He's lonely. I'm not lonely. I have a wife waiting in bed for me."

"He had a wife once too."

"A wife would be no good to him now."

"You can't tell. He might be better with a wife."

"His niece looks after him."

"I know. You said she cut him down."

"I wouldn't want to be that old. An old man is a nasty thing."

"Not always. This old man is clean. He drinks without spilling. Even now, drunk. Look at him."

"I don't want to look at him. I wish he would go home. He has no regard for those who must work."

The old man looked from his glass across the square, then over at the waiters.

"Another brandy," he said, pointing to his glass. The waiter who was in a hurry came over.

"Finished," he said, speaking with that omission of syntax stupid people employ when talking to drunken people or foreigners. "No more tonight. Close now."

"Another," said the old man.

"No. Finished." The waiter wiped the edge of the table with a towel and shook his head.

The old man stood up, slowly counted the saucers, took a leather coin purse from his pocket and paid for the drinks, leaving half a peseta tip.

The waiter watched him go down the street, a very old man walking unsteadily but with dignity.

"Why didn't you let him stay and drink?" the unhurried waiter asked. They were putting up the shutters. "It is not half-past two."

"I want to go home to bed."

"What is an hour?"

"More to me than to him."

"An hour is the same."

"You talk like an old man yourself. He can buy a bottle and drink at home."

"It's not the same."

"No, it is not," agreed the waiter with a wife. He did not wish to be unjust. He was only in a hurry.

"And you? You have no fear of going home before your usual hour?"

"Are you trying to insult me?"

"No, hombre, only to make a joke."

"No," the waiter who was in a hurry said, rising from pulling down the metal shutters. "I have confidence. I am all confidence."

"You have youth, confidence, and a job," the older waiter said. "You have everything."

"And what do you lack?"

"Everything but work."

"You have everything I have."

"No. I have never had confidence and I am not young."

"Come on. Stop talking nonsense and lock up."

"I am of those who like to stay late at the cafe," the older waiter said. "With all those who do not want to go to bed. With all those who need a light for the night."

"I want to go home and into bed."

"We are of two different kinds," the older waiter said. He was now dressed to go home. "It is not only a question of youth and confidence although those things are very beautiful. Each night I am reluctant to close up because there may be some one who needs the cafe."

"Hombre, there are bodegas open all night long."

"You do not understand. This is a clean and pleasant cafe. It is well lighted. The light is very good and also, now, there are shadows of the leaves."

"Good night," said the younger waiter.

"Good night," the other said. Turning off the electric light he continued the conversation with himself. It is the light of course but it is necessary that the place be clean and pleasant. You do not want music. Certainly you do not want music. Nor can you stand before a bar with dignity although that is all that is provided for these hours. What did he fear? It was not fear or dread. It was a nothing that he knew too well. It was all a nothing and a man was nothing too. It was only that and light was all it needed and a certain cleanness and order. Some lived in it and never felt it but he knew it all was nada y pues nada y nada y pues nada. Our nada who art in nada, nada be thy name thy kingdom nada thy will be nada in nada as it is in nada. Give us this nada our daily nada and nada us our nada as we nada our nadas and nada us not into nada but deliver us from nada; pues nada. Hail nothing full of nothing, nothing is with thee. He smiled and stood before a bar with a shining steam pressure coffee machine.

"What's yours?" asked the barman.

"Nada."

"Otro loco mas," said the barman and turned away.

"A little cup," said the waiter.

The barman poured it for him.

"The light is very bright and pleasant but the bar is unpolished," the waiter said.

The barman looked at him but did not answer. It was too late at night for conversation.

"You want another copita?" the barman asked.

"No, thank you," said the waiter and went out. He disliked bars and bodegas. A clean, well-lighted cafe was a very different thing. Now, without thinking further, he would go home to his room. He would lie in the bed and finally, with daylight, he would go to sleep. After all, he said to himself, it is probably only insomnia. Many must have it.

OLD MEN

What is it about old age that causes us to retreat? What is it about evidence of human frailty, or weakness, or loneliness that causes us to turn away? He is an old man. He comes into my restau-

rant every evening. Tall and amazingly lanky, he wears clothes
made for someone much heavier and even taller than he is. He hates
everything on the menu. Every evening we go through the same ritu-
al, me reciting dining options, he rejecting all of my suggestions
and finally settling on a bowl of ice cream with chocolate sauce.
"If you hate everything," I think to myself, "why do you bother to
come in here?" I go through the sequence, more and more persuaded
of my right to my irritation. I do not think it is simply that I
am offended when he rejects my suggestions, or the fact that I
have others more needful of my attention waiting as I once again
recite the list. It's not even that I do not like to make ice
cream with chocolate sauce.

The old man in Ernest Hemingway's "A Clean Well-Lighted Place"
sits in the quiet of the evening drinking brandy. He is deaf,
depressed, lonely. I would like to believe that I, that we all, have
some compassion for him. But I also understand as the young waiter
serving him brandy grows increasingly impatient. "I wish he would go
home. I never get to bed before three o'clock." I do not think the
young waiter is impatient simply because he is tired and wants to go
home to his wife. It's not even that he dislikes drunks.

The young waiter has youth, confidence, and a job, all the
things, when we are young, that we believe we will ever need. The
young waiter has a wife, too, who will always, he assumes, be waiting for him. But, as the older waiter reminds us, this is not necessarily the case. The old man once had a wife. I wonder if my
lanky customer has a wife, or had one. I've never asked. I am usually busy working, or visiting with my friends, or closing up so I
can get home to my kids. Occupation, and preoccupation.

The young lovers in Hemingway's story also have youth, confidence, occupation, and a preoccupation with each other. Although the
older waiter worries that the lovers will be picked up by the
guard, the younger waiter does not fear for them, just as long as
the soldier "gets what he's after." The older waiter's concerns—
empathy for the old man, fear for the young lovers—are signs of his
having moved beyond the "getting what he wants," beyond being driven
by his occupation and preoccupations, to a place of contemplation
and reflection, a place which lets him pay attention to the old man.

The older waiter knows the feeling of nothingness that comes with
darkness and night. He can appreciate the need for a clean well-
lighted place and is glad to be able to harbor and attend to others
who do.

Youth takes life, love, and nighttime for granted. The soldier
and his girlfriend, the young waiter, and I all have possibilities: an exciting evening, a warm embrace, accomplishment, hope,
change. The reminder of age casts a haze over this future-gazing,
shortening our vision, defining the limits of our light. The old
men, mine and Hemingway's, look forward as far as a glass of
brandy, or a bowl of ice cream with chocolate sauce.

We avoid the old men. We avoid them until we are forced, by

maturity or the circumstances of our own occasional loneliness, to confront them in nighttime cafes. And when we do, it's obvious that our impatience and irritation with them at other times is the result not only of our rush to leave and love but also of our unwillingness to put a face, much less a name, on our own mortality.

His name is Matt, and next time I will try to face him with more patience. I know I'll still be in a hurry to close the day. My children will still need me at home. But maybe, for my own future, I need to learn from him; maybe I need to understand his way of finding solace with a bowl of ice cream with chocolate sauce.

Extra Practice: Additional Writing Invitations

1. A form of response writing that encourages discovery through exploration involves imaginatively reconstructing a scene in order to understand its significance or motivation. This involves writing creatively in response to a literary work. This kind of writing is successful when it addresses a specific question, such as "Why would she choose to do that?" or "Why did she feel that was important?" Rather than presenting an explanation, the reader attempts to write from within the imagined world of the work, as if he or she were a character, or a friend. Often the stimulus for such writing comes from your own marginal notes, like "Why didn't she just . . . ," or "If I could talk to her, I'd ask her . . ." The intuitive exploration this allows can elicit wonderful literary writing, or it can be a very productive way to focus and clarify your thinking prior to formulating an essay. To write an imaginative response, you should:

   - Locate an ambiguous moment, event, statement, or action in the work that seems significant or puzzling.
   - Gather notes on what you know about that focus.
   - Locate or create a **persona** inside the work—sometimes a main character, sometimes a marginal or missing person—and write a part of a story or poem that would clarify what was ambiguous.

   Then, separately,

   - Explain the ways in which your imagined contribution helps you understand the work as a whole.

2. Our book relies on the metaphor of conversation to explain interpretation, because when we read we converse with works, but also because when we converse, we must interpret in order to under-

stand each other. In classes, we have opportunities to converse directly with others, but as readers in other contexts, we sometimes confront a work alone. However, practicing responsive reading strategies can help you see beyond your own first impressions to observations and reactions that others might have. This ability is called "empathy," feeling like someone else, and is a very important component of the literary experience. To practice this art of "thinking like others," read a literary piece and then imagine a group of other people talking about it with you. (The other people can be real or imaginary, but if you make them up, it helps to write about each one of them first, giving them identities and personalities.) Then write out the dialogue they have about their reading.

When you've finished, reflect on the dialogue. What does it tell you about your own impressions? What did you learn? What interesting questions emerged? Would these make good subjects for response essays?

Chapter 4

Interpretation and Informed Analysis
Making Observations, Perceiving Patterns, Recognizing Conventions

ALTHOUGH our observations are shaped by our unique backgrounds and experiences, we are never actually reading alone. Our observations depend on previous discussions we have had either about poetry or language. In addition, whether we are physically solitary or not, we always read with other voices influencing our responses. Even our definitions of the words in the dictionary are meanings we have agreed to share. For example in the United States, we have agreed as a culture to call the machine that transports us between floors of a building an elevator, whereas in England the same object is a lift. We also determine the way we order the parts of speech in sentences by mutual decision in each culture or language group. In English, we most often use the pattern subject-verb-object, whereas German speakers place verbs at the ends of sentences. Such choices are not ones we make and renegotiate often; rather they are ones we, as a culture, have developed over centuries.

Like our language characteristics, literary conventions are determined by decisions we have made as a culture. We all notice, for example, that conventionally poetry is organized according to a noticeable pattern of lines rather than in paragraphs, that all works of fiction have narrators, or that all plays are divided into scenes and acts. Our initial reactions to a literary work are both personal—that is, influenced by our identities, experiences, and personalities—and communal—influenced by our assumptions about features of literary language.

When we discover patterns and significance in the choices writers make that seem to create particular effects in us as readers, we are engaging in literary analysis. Often readers think they haven't the skills or sensitivity to analyze a piece of literature. Analysis, however, is a natural part of the interpretative process, the process we use as we try to decipher reasons for consequences, such as why an acquaintance seemingly snubbed us. When we examine all possible events that might have led to the acquaintance's actions, we are conducting an analysis of the incident. Likewise, when we have a question of interpretation about a literary work, one part of our search for answers involves examining the details of that work. The range and sophistication of our ability to analyze is a matter of experience and knowledge, which we gain as we practice any activity. There is no mystery to literary analysis. Anyone can observe the number of lines in a poem, the number of syllables in a line, the parts of speech, the kinds of images and descriptions. As we become more proficient, we name these observations, recognize the conventions they represent, and learn the language used to discuss the effects they create. But the entire process begins with careful observation.

Some people may feel that this kind of close observation spoils the enjoyment of a literary work, but arguing that analysis detracts from natural response is not very different from saying that we spoil the joy of looking at the face of someone we find beautiful by observing the color of the person's eyes or shape of the nose. To do so, most would agree, simply intensifies the experience of recognizing and enjoying the beauty. Likewise, to notice that a poet is using a particular technique should not ruin our initial response; doing so should allow us to account for our responses and ideally to enrich them.

EXERCISE 4.1. THE COMPONENTS OF INTERPRETATION

Interpreting art—visual, musical, literary—always involves responding, reflecting, analyzing, and evaluating. Good interpretations weave responses with knowledge to arrive at judgments that take into account the experiences and the expectations of the interpreter.

Read the excerpt from a review by Robert Finn, music critic for the *Cleveland Plain Dealer*.

1. Note in your reading notebooks where the reviewer has incorporated a specialist's knowledge of and language about form and composition; then note where his personal responses have been included, and where he makes a judgment based on his knowledge and guided by his responses.

2. Discuss your notations with others in your reading group, and then define "interpretation" as you think Finn might, illustrating your definition with excerpts from the review.

ROBERT FINN

From the *Cleveland Plain Dealer*, Friday, March 13, 1992

After intermission came the Shostakovich eighth, a work in total contrast to the fairly easygoing concerto.

Ashkenazy molded a mesmerizing account of this massive and very serious piece. He held together the structure of the lengthy first movement, most of which is in slow tempo.

In the two fast middle movements he drew playing of sharp satirical bite from the orchestra, and in the largo movement (something Shostakovich loved to insert in many of his large-scale works) he imparted a sense of brooding calm to the slowly unfolding musical line.

The finale is a little more relaxed in style, at least most of the time. Ashkenazy let it flow with a naturalness and grace that pointed up its big climax and made the soft ending sound like a kind of benediction.

Holding this sprawling symphony together in performance is no mean feat. Ashkenazy and the players brought it off expertly.

The eighth symphony has never been really popular, certainly nowhere near so popular as the pieces that flank it on either side in the list of Shostakovich's symphonies—the bombastic seventh and the pleasant little ninth.

The eighth has the usual Shostakovich mix of high tragic seriousness with vulgar march tunes, bugle calls and percussion patter. It is a little too long, but is nowhere near so overextended as the seventh symphony.

Perhaps the eighth's most remarkable movement is its third, dominated by a chugging motor rhythm that sounds like the clanking of some relentless, evil machine that finally collapses in a kind of orchestral catastrophe.

The performance last night was excellent. There were fine solo bits from many players, notably piccolo and English horn.

Orchestral attacks were sharp; the rhythmic pulse that is so important so much of the time was wonderfully intense.

In the huge noisy climaxes that Shostakovich piles up in three of the movements the orchestra roared out brilliantly with a kind of dissonant fury that was wonderful to hear.

This symphony, predominantly dark in mood, is not for those who seek "easy listening" at symphony concerts. It is unsettling, urgent, serious music, and it is not an easy piece to make work. Last night's performance accomplished this.

Robert Finn's review of the Cleveland Symphony vividly illustrates the way a music critic's analytical observations express and explain his emotional responses and judgments. He presents his personal response and justifies that response with his analysis. His analysis includes such observations as that the first movement is lengthy and in slow tempo, that the largo movement follows a slowly unfolding musical line, and that the work includes march tunes, bugle calls, and percussion patter. Yet despite his emphasis on analysis, Finn discusses the effect of the choices made by the composer and conductor in such comments as that the work is serious, the orchestra plays with satirical bite, the conductor imparts a sense of brooding calm, and the symphony is predominantly dark in mood. Finn also reveals his emotional response as he finds the performance mesmerizing, natural and graceful, held together expertly, and making the piece work. For Finn, the experience included both his response and an awareness of the construction and performance of the piece. In fact, the two seem interdependent. His evaluation of the concert focuses on how effectively the techniques of the composer, conductor, and musicians created his response.

LITERARY ANALYSIS

Observing

When we analyze an artistic work, we are doing more than summarizing a sequence of events. We are observing and examining the details that create the situation or work, the elements that affect the way we respond. If, for example, we were to analyze the reasons for ineffective communication between two people, we might observe a conversation between them. Our analysis would not merely record their words but would also examine the issues they discuss, the kinds of statements they make to each other, the ways they look at each other, how closely they sit, whether they interrupt each other, whether they touch and, if so, how, and so forth. We would try to make connections between and identify the relative importance of these observations. Likewise, when we analyze a painting, a movie, or a poem, we do more than observe its effect on us. We look at the details that constitute it, the way those details are arranged and associations the conventions of arrangement might suggest, and we attempt to connect what we see to form generalizations about meaning. In other words, we examine the choices the artist made in composing the artistic experience, the elements that appeal to our senses and imaginations and bring us into the world of the artistic work.

When we look at a painting, we are concerned with details such as color, texture, shape, and placement of objects in space. When we look at a movie, we are interested in visual details but also are aware of the impact of **language, tone, images, character, setting**, and **plot**. When we examine literature in print, we are concerned with the literary conventions shared with film, and in addition, the role of the narrator and the visual impact of the page, such as in the use of punctuation, **line breaks**, or **stanza** patterns. From these observations, we generalize about the world of the text. Many features of literary language can contribute to the way the writer composes and the reader comprehends the text. In this chapter we invite you to practice looking at and generalizing about some of these features. Others are defined and explained in the Appendix, where literary terms are related to kinds of interpretive questions you might have.

EXERCISE 4.2. ANALYZING A POEM

Read "My Papa's Waltz" and record your reactions and observations in your reading notebook. How did you feel about the experience the poet describes? List everything you notice about the way the poem is constructed:

- Where do the sentences begin and end?
- What is similar about each **stanza**?
- Which lines **rhyme**?
- How many syllables are there in each line?
- Which syllables are stressed, or accented?
- Can you name the **meter** (the pattern of stressed and unstressed syllables)?
- Which words and phrases seem related to each other?

THEODORE ROETHKE
My Papa's Waltz

The whiskey on your breath
Could make a small boy dizzy;
But I hung on like death:
Such waltzing was not easy.

We romped until the pans
Slid from the kitchen shelf;
My mother's countenance
Could not unfrown itself.

The hand that held my wrist
Was battered on one knuckle;
At every step you missed
My right ear scraped a buckle.

You beat time on my head
With a palm caked hard by dirt,
Then waltzed me off to bed
Still clinging to your shirt.

For such a simple poem, "My Papa's Waltz" has many interesting features that express the narrator's attitude and thus affect our response to the poem. Let's put aside for a moment our reactions to the incident the poet describes and talk about our observations regarding the conventions he chooses. You probably noticed that the poem has four **stanzas** of four lines each, that in each stanza the first and third lines **rhyme**, as do the second and fourth, and that the lines seem uniform. You may have counted the number of syllables in each line and discovered that every line has either six or seven syllables. If you are experienced with scanning a poem, you probably recognized the **meter** as iambic—each metrical unit is made up of two syllables, with the first syllable unstressed and the second stressed—and that every line has three units of one unstressed and one stressed syllable: in line one, for example, "The WHIS / key ON / your BREATH." If you were scanning, you also may have noticed that lines two, four, ten, twelve, and fourteen have an extra unstressed syllable: in line two, for example, "Could MAKE / a SMALL / boy DIZZ y."

In addition to seeing the shape of the poem, you probably observed that the kinds of words Roethke chose are relatively simple, and because the words describe an incident rather than comment on its meaning, they are more **concrete** than **abstract.** You also may have noticed that although they are simple and concrete, they give a complicated and ambiguous impression of the narrator's attitude toward the memory. Words such as "whiskey," "death," and "battered" all have negative **connotations**, whereas "papa," "waltz," and "romped" seem to express affection and fun and therefore have positive connotations. All of these observations are examples of close reading.

From these observations, you can begin to form generalizations about some of the techniques the poet has used. The poem is generally balanced and regular in its **meter** and **rhyme scheme**. Although five lines have an extra unstressed syllable, you could argue that even these follow a regular pattern—they occur at the end of the second and fourth lines in the first and third stanzas, and thus create a predictable rhythm. The only other unstressed syllable appears at the beginning of line fourteen, "With a palm," a very small break in an otherwise exceptionally regularly shaped poem. In addition, we can generalize about the words of the poem, which present a combination of negative and positive **images**. These statements are generalizations about the creative process the poet used as he constructed his poem.

Generalizing

The details we included in our discussion above are ones we find important because they are part of our pattern of experience with the poem. Of course, you could make other observations. For example, the poem has 267 letters in it. If you wrote a paper noting that fact, the instructor would probably want to know why you found that observation significant, and you would probably be hard-pressed to discover an answer. (In some poems such an observation could prove interesting, particularly if the poet was playing with the significance of numbers and the number of letters related in some way to the number theory at the heart of the poem.)

Once you've begun to generalize, you have a way to test further observations. For example, what might be interesting to note is that every line has between 19 and 24 letters. This detail probably does not show that Roethke is playing with numerology, but because it does show that the lines are generally uniform in length, it could be seen as contributing to the overall sense of regularity and balance, supporting our first generalization. This process is inductive: you move from observation to generalization, then test your generalization against the entire set of observations, modifying your generalizations when new observations warrant a change of mind.

When you move from analysis to interpretation, you begin to connect your generalizations about the way the poem is created to your response to the experience of the text. As you do so, your observations and responses influence each other. Having seen the regular pattern of Roethke's poem you might argue that the regularity of the poem creates a sense of balance and stability. If you are like most readers, though, such a reading would strain credulity, because the poem is more than its shape. While the poem is regular and balanced, like the waltz of the title, readers respond with a complicated range of emotions. Some recall pleasant interactions with fathers, but are troubled by the seeming dissonance of the negative words. Some recall memories that are ambivalent and oddly unsettling. Others respond with outright anger and have an almost overwhelming sense of the danger of potential or actual abuse. Can our observations about language and form help us mediate and make sense of these responses, related as they are to our own childhood memories?

Interpreting

Let's return to our initial analysis of the poem. If we combine the two generalizations (that the pattern is basically regular and that the language includes a complicated combination of positive and negative images), we may find the starting point for a new generalization that explains why this is such an oddly unsettling poem. We might complicate our generalization then to observe that Roethke combines a regular pattern with unexpected language and **imagery** and by doing so establishes an ambivalent view of a childhood encounter with the narrator's father. At this point, as the generalization establishes a disturbed, or irregular, regularity, we might be able to use our observations about the odd extra syllables, which keep the waltz a little off balance; they function, maybe, as missteps, which make the dance awkward or unpredictable. We might add that all the rhymes in the poem are close rhymes, almost singsong, except one: "dizzy" and "easy." Perhaps the off rhyme accentuates the dizziness and helps us understand just how *un*easy this dance was. Thus generalizations, as we modify them, can offer us new ways to look at the details, just as new details can offer us reasons to modify our generalizations.

We now have the beginning of an interpretation that does more than list details gathered from a close reading. Let's look back at the process we used in reaching this stage as we prepare to write an essay. We began by reading a poem and, as we read, responding to the experience the poet offered. We then looked closely at the details of the poem and generalized two patterns. From our observations we generalized that the poem was regular in pattern, with one potentially significant exception, and also that the language presented a combination of negative and positive images. Each of these observations was in the form of a complete sentence. We then combined the two generalizations so that we could account for our recognition that the poem is less balanced and serene than the first observation suggested. Doing so allowed us to acknowledge that the poem was oddly unsettling. We were then able to see that the two apparently contradictory strategies work together to create an ambivalent view of a childhood encounter with the narrator's father. The process thus reconciled our analysis with our response to the poem.

Observations and responses lead to generalizations; patterns of generalizations give shape to our interpretive statements. These interpretive statements, our ways of representing the world of the poem, relate our reading experience to our old knowledge, validating, challenging, or modifying it. Sometimes we use the word "theme" to talk about the world of the poem. A theme is an implicit generalization the story affirms, a recurrent idea or motif that seems to be the primary idea being explored. However, a work can have more than one theme, and themes will not be expressed identically by all readers. Your initial response will be enlarged and challenged by your close observations; your generalizations will be complicated by their relationships to and conflicts with each other; therefore, although your interpretive statement often will be what is called a "thematic statement," it will integrate your perception of the story's "reason for being" with your sense of its significance for you as a reader.

WHAT DO WE LOOK AT WHEN WE ANALYZE LITERATURE?

If a friend were giving us advice and in the process told us an anecdote that illustrated the value of her proposed solution, we would listen not only to the story she told but also the details she chose and the way she ordered them. We would notice the kinds of words and their connotations, her role in the story and the roles of others, whether she spoke directly to us, and the time and place of the story. We would be concerned with all such details because we would be interested in understanding why it was important for us to hear this story. Literary works sometimes are intended to teach a lesson, but even when they aren't, they nonetheless present an attitude about human existence. This attitude or tone is the voice we respond to when we read, the friend in the text. When we analyze literature, we are examining the details that allow us to know why it's important for us to understand.

Looking at the Language of the Experience

If analyzing literature is looking carefully at its various components and finding patterns that demonstrate the world view it expresses, then in order to analyze, we need to identify and name those components we observe. What makes literary art different from visual art such as a painting, or aural art such as a symphony, is that the literary artist works in the medium of language.

Part of a writer's artistry is evident in word choice. In the previous exercise, we observed that the words Roethke chose were simple and concrete. In addition to looking at whether words are simple or complex, **abstract** or **concrete**, we may look at the way the poet uses parts of speech. We also are interested in what associations the words suggest. In the Roethke poem we noticed that the words seemed to divide fairly evenly into those with negative **connotations** and those with positive connotations. Often writers will do more than just contrast negative and positive **images** in their choice of words and style of phrasing, or **diction**.

Sometimes a writer might choose words that all work together to suggest a particular attitude through the association the reader would share with the general pattern of experience. John Keats, for example, chose harvest images for the first four lines of his **sonnet** "When I Have Fears" to make specific his fear of dying: he doesn't want to "cease to be" before he has written all he wishes, before he has "gleaned" the field of his brain to write "high-piled books" like full "garners," or granaries:

> *When I have fears that I may cease to be*
> > *Before my pen has glean'd my teeming brain,*
> *Before high-piled books, in charact'ry,*
> > *Hold like rich garners the full-ripen'd grain;*

Writers may use **figurative language**, words that suggest levels of meaning beyond their literal level. Central to the mode of figurative thinking is the **metaphor**, a way of exploring the complexity of an idea or image by comparing it to something else different yet somehow similar. For metaphors to be effective, the elements shared between the literal and metaphoric levels of meaning must be accessible to the reader. For example, when William Shakespeare explores feelings of ambiguity and conflict in "Two Loves Have I" by personifying his conflict as being pulled by two spirits, one female, the other male, he is relying on a long tradition of associating the female principle with passion and seduction and the male with reason, an idea familiar to his sixteenth-century audience. Without knowledge of that convention, twentieth-century readers may find his metaphoric comparison somewhat inaccessible.

The **metaphors** and **similes** Joyce Carol Oates uses in "Where Are You Going, Where Have You Been?" to describe Arnold Friend are more contemporary, and thus more easily accessible to twentieth-century readers. Readers who associate Arnold Friend with the devil are responding to strange and frightening images: "the tiny metallic world in his glasses slowing down like gelatine hardening"; the skin around his eyes was "like holes that were not in shadow but instead in light"; his eyelashes were "thick and black as if painted with a black tarlike material." In each case, the comparison is appropriate—it vividly describes the object—but is also unusual and startling. Because the images shock us with their strange threatening quality, the metaphoric level prepares us for Connie's eventual capitulation to his manipulative power. Whether we are reading Shakespeare or Oates, part of the pleasure of reading is being able to recognize and respond to the metaphoric complexity of the expression.

EXERCISE 4.3. ANALYZING DICTION

In the excerpted paragraph from the story "Sonny's Blues," what kind of mood does James Baldwin set? What kind of diction does he use? How does the language contribute to the mood of the paragraph? In your reading notebook, observe and list words, phrases, and figures of speech that seem to set the mood or atmosphere, that tell us how we are to regard the place.

Then, with your reading group, *categorize* the words and *generalize* about them; make some statements about groups of words that go together, that characterize parts of the room or feelings in the room.

Finally, draft some working statements that *interpret* the way mood is conveyed through diction.

JAMES BALDWIN

From "Sonny's Blues"

They were going to play soon and Creole installed me, by myself, at a table in a dark corner. Then I watched them, Creole, and the little black man, and Sonny, and the others, while they horsed around, standing just below the bandstand. The light from the bandstand spilled just a little short of them and, watching them laughing and gesturing and moving about, I had the feeling that they, nevertheless, were being most careful not to step into that circle of light too suddenly: that if they moved into the light too suddenly, without thinking, they would perish in flame. Then, while I watched, one of them, the small, black man, moved into the light and crossed the bandstand and started fooling around with his drums. Then—being funny and being, also, extremely ceremonious—Creole took Sonny by the arm and led him to the piano. A woman's voice called Sonny's name and a few hands started clapping. And Sonny, also being funny and being ceremonious, and so touched, I think, that he could have cried, but neither hiding it nor showing it, riding it like a man, grinned, and put both hands to his heart and bowed from the waist.

Another element we examine when we look at the language of the work is sentence structure, or **syntax**. Analyzing syntax means examining the choices the writer makes in organizing the sentences that constitute the work. Our observations may be as simple as noting that the writer rarely uses complex sentences. Because simple sentences never subordinate one clause to another, a sequence of simple sentences might suggest that we are to assign equal weight to a series of ideas, or they might contribute to a sense of directness, or separateness, or simplicity, depending on the experience offered by the content. We might notice that the writer expands sentences with asides given in parenthetical phrases or clauses, or that one character's speeches are in simple sentences but another's are very complex. By looking closely at **syntax** and **imagery**, we may notice that a poet is playing one against the other or the two together.

In an early fifteenth-century poem, for example, the anonymous writer repeats the same **syntax** and **imagery**, and almost precisely the same words, in the second, third, and fourth **stanzas**. The **repetition** of "He cam also stille" draws attention to the quiet awe and mystery of the conception, while the variation in the description of where the mother was and the natural images as the son moves slowly toward his mother are reminders that conception is natural. The syntax and imagery thus express one of the central Christian paradoxes, that Christ can be both human and God simultaneously.

I Sing of a Maiden

I sing of a maiden	I sing of a maiden
That is makelees;	who is mateless (or matchless);
King of alle kinges	King of all kings
To her sone she chees.	She chose for her son.
He cam also stille	He came as still
Ther his moder was	to where his mother was
As dewe in Aprille	as dew in April
That falleth on the gras.	that falls on the grass.
He cam also stille	He came as still
To his modres bowr,	to his mother's bower
As dewe in Aprille	as dew in April
That falleth on the flowr.	that falls on the flower.
He cam also stille	He came as still
Ther his moder lay,	to where his mother lay
As dew in Aprille	as dew in April
That falleth on the spray.	that falls on the spray.
Moder and maiden	There was never one who was
Was never non but she:	maiden and mother except her:
Well may swich a lady	Well may such a lady
Godes moder be.	God's mother be.

EXERCISE 4.4. ANALYZING SYNTAX

The way a writer chooses to shape sentences affects our perception of meaning. For example, short, single-clause sentences may be used to convey directness, simplicity, or separateness; longer sentences with modifying phrases and clauses may be used to convey complexity, connection, or even deviation.

In your reading group, compare the following passages, the first from "A Clean, Well-Lighted Place" and the second from "Where Are You Going, Where Have You Been?" Observe the number of sentences in each passage, and the sentence types and lengths. Compare the average number of words or clauses per sentence. How are they different? Why might they be different?

You do not want music. Certainly you do not want music. Nor can you stand before a bar with dignity although that is all that is provided for these hours. What did he fear? It was not fear or dread. It was a nothing that he knew too well. It was all a nothing and a man was nothing too.

Connie let the screen door close and stood perfectly still inside it, listening to the music from her radio and the boy's blend together. She stared at Arnold Friend. He stood there so stiffly relaxed, pretending to be relaxed, with one hand idly on the door handle as if he were keeping himself up that way and had no intention of ever moving again. She recognized most things about him, the tight jeans that showed his thighs and buttocks and the greasy leather boots and the tight shirt, and even that slippery friendly smile of his, that sleepy dreamy smile that all the boys used to get across ideas that they didn't want to put into words. She recognized all this and also the singsong way he talked, slightly mocking, kidding, but serious and a little melancholy, and she recognized the way he tapped one fist against the other in homage to the perpetual music behind him.

Looking at the Shape of the Experience

As the previous examples show, it is difficult to talk about the various components of literature separately because the effect of the work depends upon the interaction of all the choices the writer makes. In the poem "I Sing of a Maiden," the writer's syntactic choices work within the structure of the poem. The poem begins with a stanza that expresses the mystery as paradox; it says that a maiden (that is, a young virgin) chose the King of Kings to be her son. The middle three stanzas describe the conception of Christ in three parallel sentences; he came to where his mother was, her bower, where she lay, as still as dew in April that falls on the grass, flower, and spray. Then the final stanza returns to the paradox and restates the mystery but this time with an awareness of the natural explanation from stanzas two through four. Being both maiden (a virgin) and mother, Mary mirrors the paradox of Jesus Christ who is man and God. The poem is, of course, more than a summary of it would indicate. Its form, both in the ordering of the **stanzas** and the **repetition** of syntactic forms and **diction**, helps express the poet's attitude toward the experience and helps shape ours.

From our earliest encounters with language, we learn that the shape of a story or statement offers us information and direction and contributes to our way of responding. For example, when we hear the words "Once upon a time," we know that we are to engage with the story imaginatively, suspending such logical considerations as whether there are or are not such things as evil giants. "As a matter of fact" signals logical support, and "whether you like it or not" calls on us to identify our own stance on an issue. Such forms are like contracts with readers, and when we read, our expectations are influenced by, and therefore our responses are related to, the assumptions we share about them. As readers, you are aware, though you may not have articulated it in words, how reading poetry or drama or fiction requires different "readerly conventions," different kinds of attention.

To paraphrase the twentieth-century literary critic Kenneth Burke, a literary artist begins with an experience so powerful or intriguing that he or she feels compelled to reshape it so that others may experience a similar response. Whether the experience is a visual image such as a bronze leaf against lichen-covered bark or a temporal event such as the death of a parent, its power is realized only if the shape evokes a similar reaction in the reader. The process of shaping involves recognizing what Burke calls the psychology of form. In other words, the writer chooses patterns and images that evoke emotions shared by the writer and most readers.

This is not to say that writers choose predictable patterns that will necessarily trigger the appropriate emotional response. To do so would simply be to use and reuse the same formulas. Some **genres**, such as certain kinds of mysteries or romance novels or westerns, rely on such devices, but typically we admire those works that we say rise above the limitations of their genre. Writers choose patterns and forms that readers will recognize, but also ones that are different enough to make readers notice the difference and ask "why?" When writers make such choices, they are shaping their writing to fit reader expectations or to invite the reader to inquire about the choice. Doing so encourages the reader to participate in the experience of composing—to use a different metaphor, borrowed from another contemporary literary critic, Wayne Booth, writers invite us to dance with them.

The story "Home," in Chapter 2, works both with and against our formal expectations to complicate and intensify our response. It is possible to identify traditional elements of dramatic **plot** structure (exposition, conflict, rising suspense, climax, denouement), but such a structure seems too predictable and solid for a story that achieves such intense feeling with such minimal movement. If we read the story as if it were a poem, we can more intimately follow the modulations in **mood** and **tone** that allow us to identify with and respond emotionally to the prolonged and suspenseful waiting. Reading the story as a poem allows us more easily to accept the odd repetitive syntax of the opening sentence, which asks us to focus attentively on "What had been wanted." We can read the repetitive "l's" in the opening paragraph, "looked at the late afternoon light on the lawn," and find that they intensify the mood as poems, more often than stories, typically do. The selected form here, then, relies not so much on the logical progression of parts as on the way the presence of one state or quality of mind prepares us for another, as on the way an idea gets repeated or comes back again as a variation of what came before. Through the forms we recognize as poetic, we come to understand the sequence, the back-and-forth motion, of the characters' feelings.

Our assumptions about and experience with literary form provides as much preparation for our responses as our personal background and experiences do. These assumptions about detective fiction or folktales or poetry or stories are with us from the time we hear nursery rhymes, and they become part of the culturally acquired mental, emotional, and imaginative equipment with which we go about deciphering our communications with each other. It is easier to find ways to engage with and respond to literature if we are aware of the ways in which literature appeals to us through its shape and conventions. All choices writers make involve anticipating shared conventions, which function like bridges over rivers, or in conversations, like the normal patterns of give and take.

Formal ways of communicating are cultural forces that both permit shared understandings and shape, in significant ways, our responses. Responsive readers are conscious of the ways in which their assumptions about form influence them. The more conscious you are of these cultural influences, the more intelligently you can function within, or challenge, their power and direction.

EXERCISE 4.5. ANALYZING SHAPE (DESIGN)

1. In your reading notebook, define in your own words the
   following **genres**: folktales, poetry, fiction, essays, novels,
   and plays. How do you recognize them? How do you read
   them differently? If it helps, take into account subjects,
   devices, characters, themes and theses, organization and
   relation of parts, style (sounds, words, sentences, figures of
   speech), purposes. Then compare your definitions with
   those of others in your reading group. Where do they
   agree? Where do they disagree? What seems to be the
   cause of the differences: personal experiences, reading
   experiences, or preferences? What common ground do they
   share? Try to revise your definitions collaboratively in a
   way that satisfies all members of your group.

2. Check in your reading notebook for places where your
   assumptions about form have entered into your responses
   to "The Poet's Farewell to His Teeth" and "Home." What
   expectations did you bring to these pieces? What did you
   see that fulfilled or frustrated those expectations? Did these
   concerns influence your positive or negative impressions of
   the story? Did they make it easier or harder to identify with
   the situations presented?

Sometimes the shape of a short poem is easier to talk about than that
of a longer fictional work because in a longer fictional work the shape man-
ifests itself in the chronology of the **plot**. Often when we think about plots
we simply think about the story rather than the order in which it is told,
but the way a story is shaped or ordered contributes to our understanding of the world it expresses. When we tell each other stories, we carefully choose an order that will elicit the response we desire from our listeners. When we tell jokes, we give each clue at just the right moment so that
the listener will be both surprised and delighted by the appropriateness of
the punch line. We want them to think, "I should have seen that coming."
At the same time they are amused that they didn't, so that they might feel
the pleasure of the surprise. Mysteries work in ways not unlike jokes. The
gradual revealing of clues shape the reader's response so that the solution
is satisfying.

EXERCISE 4.6. ANALYZING SHAPE (DEVELOPMENT)

After reading "The Story of an Hour," record your reaction in your reading notebook. How do you react to the ending?

With your reading group:

Observe: List the separate actions of the story.

Generalize: Speculate about how each is chosen to influence your reaction.

Interpret: How does the order of the actions prepare you to respond in a particular way to the ending?

KATE CHOPIN

The Story of an Hour

Knowing that Mrs. Mallard was afflicted with a heart trouble, great care was taken to break to her as gently as possible the news of her husband's death.

It was her sister Josephine who told her, in broken sentences; veiled hints that revealed in half concealing. Her husband's friend Richards was there, too, near her. It was he who had been in the newspaper office when intelligence of the railroad disaster was received, with Brently Mallard's name leading the list of "killed." He had only taken the time to assure himself of its truth by a second telegram, and hastened to forestall any less careful, less tender friend in bearing the sad message.

She did not hear the story as many women have heard the same, with a paralyzed inability to accept its significance. She wept at once, with sudden, wild abandonment, in her sister's arms. When the storm of grief had spent itself she went away to her room alone. She would have no one follow her.

There stood, facing the open window, a comfortable, roomy armchair. Into this she sank, pressed down by a physical exhaustion that haunted her body and seemed to reach into her soul.

She could see in the open square before her house the tops of trees that were all aquiver with the new spring life. The delicious breath of rain was in the air. In the street below a peddler was crying his wares. The notes of a distant song which someone was singing reached her faintly, and countless sparrows were twittering in the eaves.

There were patches of blue sky showing here and there through the clouds that had met and piled above the other in the west facing her window.

She sat with her head thrown back upon the cushion of the chair quite motionless, except when a sob came up into her throat and shook her, as a child who has cried itself to sleep continues to sob in its dreams.

She was young, with a fair, calm face, whose lines bespoke repression and even a certain strength. But now there was a dull stare in her eyes, whose gaze was fixed away off yonder on one of those patches of blue sky. It was not a glance of reflection, but rather indicated a suspension of intelligent thought.

There was something coming to her and she was waiting for it, fearfully. What was it? She did not know; it was too subtle and elusive to name. But she felt it, creeping out of the sky, reaching toward her through the sounds, the scents, the color that filled the air.

Now her bosom rose and fell tumultuously. She was beginning to recognize this thing that was approaching to possess her, and she was striving to beat it back with her will—as powerless as her two white slender hands would have been.

When she abandoned herself a little whispered word escaped her slightly parted lips. She said it over and over under her breath: "Free, free, free!" The vacant stare and the look of terror that had followed it went from her eyes. They stayed keen and bright. Her pulses beat fast, and the coursing blood warmed and relaxed every inch of her body.

She did not stop to ask if it were not a monstrous joy that held her. A clear and exalted perception enabled her to dismiss the suggestion as trivial.

She knew that she would weep again when she saw the kind, tender hands folded in death; the face that had never looked save with love upon her, fixed and gray and dead. But she saw beyond that bitter moment a long procession of years to come that would belong to her absolutely. And she opened and spread her arms out to them in welcome.

There would be no one to live for during those coming years; she would live for herself. There would be no powerful will bending her in that blind persistence with which men and women believe they have a right to impose a private will upon a fellow creature. A kind intention or a cruel intention made the act seem no less a crime as she looked upon it in that brief moment of illumination.

And yet she loved him—sometimes. Often she had not. What did it matter! What could love, the unsolved mystery, count for in the face of this possession of self-assertion which she suddenly recognized as the strongest impulse of her being.

"Free! Body and soul free!" she kept whispering.

Josephine was kneeling before the closed door with her lips to the keyhole, imploring for admission. "Louise, open the door! I beg; open the door—you will make yourself ill. What are you doing, Louise? For heaven's sake open the door."

"Go away. I am not making myself ill." No; she was drinking in the very elixir of life through that open window.

Her fancy was running riot along those days ahead of her. Spring days, and summer days, and all sorts of days that would be her own. She breathed in a quick prayer that life might be long. It was only yesterday she had thought with a shudder that life might be long.

She arose at length and opened the door to her sister's importunities. There was a feverish triumph in her eyes, and she carried herself unwittingly like a goddess of Victory. She clasped her sister's waist, and together they descended the stairs. Richards stood waiting for them at the bottom.

Some one was opening the front door with a latchkey. It was Brently Mallard who entered, a little travel-stained, composedly carrying his grip-sack and umbrella. He had been far from the scene of accident, and did not even know there had been one. He stood amazed at Josephine's piercing cry; at Richards' quick motion to screen him from the view of his wife.

But Richards was too late.

When the doctors came they said she had died of heart disease—of joy that kills.

Looking at the Participants in the Experience

Beyond the choices we have already discussed, there are other ways the author expresses his or her attitude. One of these ways is in the choice of speakers. When we read the language of literature, we hear voices: the voice of the writer, of course, expressed by all the choices of detail and form; the voices of the narrators or speakers in a poem; and in novels, short stories, drama, and narrative poetry, voices of the characters who participate in the action. These voices influence our interpretive response because how we regard what they tell us will depend on what it is we know about them.

Who tells the story? The voices of the narrators or the speakers (there may be one or several) may be in first person as they recount their experiences, or they may be in third person, describing what happened to others. In either case, narrators can know everything, not just events and details but also the thoughts and feelings of all the characters; or they can have limited understanding, observing and recounting but not necessarily comprehending fully or clearly the events and details around them. When narrators seem to be all-knowing, we need to inquire about their way of looking: Can they be trusted? Do they project an attitude toward characters or events and, if so, is it based on assumptions we can identify? When narrators have limited perspective, what are those limitations? How do they influence the action, or our perception of characters or events? Sometimes a writer may chose to give the narrator an ironic voice. Writers use irony when they present the opposite view from the one they hold so that readers have enough distance from the events being recounted to judge them. We need to ask: Does the writer expect us to take the narrator's words at face value, or are we to share the writer's delight or outrage in seeing the absurdity of the narrator's words or the characters' beliefs or actions?

Who speaks within the story? In addition to the voice of the narrator, we also hear the voices of those who participate in the action. Our evaluation of each character depends on what the character says and how he or she says it, images associated with the character, what others say to the character, what is said about the character by the narrator or other characters and in what ways, what the character does, and the consequences of those actions.

EXERCISE 4.7. ANALYZING CHARACTER

In your reading group, compare the voices of the passages by Ralph Ellison and Terry McMillan. In the first, from *The Invisible Man*, a narrator begins to tell his own story; in the second, from *Disappearing Acts*, a narrator who is a participant in the story introduces a second character.

How do the two voices differ? *Observe* details about each character. Based upon the little information you have, *generalize* the character of the individuals you have just met: the man who introduces himself, the woman who introduces her future lover, and the lover. What details contribute to the impression you have of each character?

RALPH ELLISON

From *Invisible Man*

I am invisible man. No, I am not a spook like those who haunted Edgar Allan Poe; nor am I one of your Hollywood-movie ectoplasms. I am a man of substance, of flesh and bone, fiber and liquids—and I might even be said to possess a mind. I am invisible, understand, simply because people refuse to see me. Like the bodiless heads you see sometimes in circus sideshows, it is as though I have been surrounded by mirrors of hard, distorting glass. When they approach me they see only my surroundings, themselves, or figments of their imagination—indeed, everything and anything except me.

Nor is my invisibility exactly a matter of a bio-chemical accident to my epidermis. That invisibility to which I refer occurs because of a peculiar disposition of the eyes of those with whom I come in contact. A matter of the construction of their inner eyes, those eyes with which they look through their physical eyes upon reality. I am not complaining, nor am I protesting either. It is sometimes advantageous to be unseen, although it is most often rather wearing on the nerves. Then too, you're constantly being bumped against by those of poor vision. Or again, you often doubt if you really exist. You wonder whether you aren't simply a phantom in other people's minds. Say, a figure in a nightmare which the sleeper tries with all his strength to destroy. It's when you feel like this that, out of resentment, you begin to bump people back. And, let me confess, you feel that way most of the time. You ache with the need to convince yourself that you do exist in the real world, that you're a part of all the sound and anguish, and you strike out with your fists, you curse and you swear to make them recognize you. And alas, it's seldom successful.

TERRY MCMILLAN
From *Disappearing Acts*

I heard the sound of hammering from the top of the stairs, so I took my chances and ran up. Sawdust was flying around the white room like gold snow. I looked down, saw a curved red back, then a long arm flying up, thick black fingers grasping a hammer, and when it swung back down, the sound of the impact scared me. I jumped.

He looked up, then stood. "What can I do for you?" he asked.

"Lord have mercy," was all I heard inside my head. I couldn't move, let alone speak. I really couldn't believe what I was seeing. This man had to be six foot something, because he was towering over me. His eyes looked like black marbles set in almonds. He wore a Yankees baseball cap, backward, and when he lifted it from his head to shake off the dust, his hair was jet black and wavy. That nose was strong and regal, and beneath it was a thick mustache. His cheeks looked chiseled; his lips succulent. And those shoulders. They were as wide as any linebacker's. His thighs were tight, and his legs went on forever. He was covered with dust, but when he pushed the sleeves of his red sweatshirt up to his elbows, his arms were the color of black grapes.

Looking at Other Literary Elements

Diction, syntax, form, point of view, and character are not the only elements writers choose and shape when they write literature. You will find others in the Appendix. As you become more proficient in reading, writing, and talking about literature, the questions you ask about a literary work will probably lead you to examine these elements as well. For now, as we talk about writing an analysis paper, we will concentrate on the elements we have looked at in this chapter.

READING AND WRITING TO ANALYZE

The response essays included in Chapter 3 all answered questions readers raised in response to a text. Analysis essays, too, answer questions:

- What language choices created an effect I, as a reader, perceived?
- What is the effect or significance of a particular pattern of details I noticed?

In both cases, you are linking your analysis of the work or one component of the work with your response to the experience of reading it. We rarely write analysis papers simply to show our ability to see the way a text works. Rather, we do so because we are interested in exploring how the choices a writer makes shape our response. As you begin to prepare your essay, you will be considering not only what your response is but how your close reading justifies, explains, or complicates your response. The paper you write will be your explanation. The thesis of this paper will have two parts: the *conclusion* you have drawn combined with a *justification* for believing the conclusion to be valid. Your response to the work is your conclusion, and your analysis is your justification for drawing your conclusion.

Keep in mind that the thesis is rarely your first writing act. Nor is it a simple task to shape one effectively. Much exploration and refinement of ideas—engaging, reflecting, analyzing, observing, and generalizing—have first occurred. If you are fortunate enough to have a reading group, formulating a thesis will follow a discussion with other readers in which all participants have expressed responses to the piece and pointed to details in the text that have explained their responses. After you have observed, generalized, and linked your generalizations in ways this chapter and previous chapters have described, you are prepared to plan and test a thesis statement.

Drafting a Thesis Statement

Drafting and refining a thesis statement is a good exercise because the thesis helps you see what you are committing yourself to writing as you compose the paper. Drafting and testing will allow you to clarify your purpose and make changes when it's still easy. The thesis statement helps us focus on a particular subject, suggests a purpose, and provides a sense of direction for the essay. Because it does so, it helps us find effective ways of developing and organizing our essay.

Let's return to the paper we began on "My Papa's Waltz." You will recall that we ended with a sentence that combined our generalizations with our response: "Roethke combines a regular pattern with unexpected language and imagery and by doing so establishes an ambivalent view of a childhood encounter with the narrator's father." The statement asserts two actions: the poet combines a regular pattern with unexpected language, and he expresses an ambivalent view of a childhood encounter. The two observations are not separate; the second is the effect of the first. When we read the poem we responded to the ambiguity in the narrator's description of waltzing with his father. When we examined the rhythmic patterns and language of the poem, we found reasons for our reaction. To turn this into a thesis statement, we need to state clearly what part of the statement is our conclusion and what our justification. The conclusion is the effect we identified. The justification is our analysis. Simply stated, they read:

Justification: Roethke combines a regular pattern with unexpected language and imagery.

Conclusion: Roethke expresses an ambivalent view of a childhood encounter with the narrator's father.

Testing a Thesis

Ask questions about this thesis to decide whether or not you want to do what it suggests, and whether you can do what it promises.

- Does it make an assertion you believe is accurate?
- Does it answer a question at issue that came from your reading and responding experience?
- Does it say exactly what you want it to?
- Have you considered other possibilities?
- Can it be developed using your observations?
- Does it leave out any significant observations?

Using the Thesis Statement to Plan a Paper

You could plan and write a very clear analysis paper using the thesis statement on "My Papa's Waltz" as your organizing principle. Your essay will follow the reasoning implied by your thesis statement:

Introduction	Presents the question your essay will answer: Why did I respond the way I did?
Development	Your justification and evidence: What choices did the writer make that relate to my response?
Conclusion	Answers your question by linking your justification to your conclusion: Why did these choices affect me the way they did?

This possibly unfamiliar but simple strategy for focusing and organizing an analysis paper requires some practice. You will be able to compose a thesis statement like this, a thesis that links response and analysis and provides a guide for structuring your writing, only after you have read responsively, reflected honestly, and observed and generalized carefully. When it works well, the thesis becomes a simple statement of the significance you find in the text. Thesis statements are not as easy to derive as our sequence might imply;

however, writing them insures that your analysis will never become discon-
nected from the human experience the text offers and the personal experience
you contributed to it.

SUMMARY

Language is a powerful, vital force in our lives, and the forms and functions
of the language we use—the language of the **cultures** we are born in or come
to know—influence how we see and understand our world. Through the
process of naming, we become conscious of things we may not have seen
before. Thus the study of literary language not only helps us talk about what
we see and hear, but changes and enriches the way we look and listen. When
we read about consonance, for example, we may become more aware of a particular pattern of sounds in the same way that the big 194-color box of crayons
changes the way we think about "red."

As a reading community, we share assumptions about the ways words get
put on the page, and about how those shapes and sounds lend meaning and
direction to our communication. Literary conventions help us perceive and
use those shapes and sounds to our advantage as participants in conversations about meaning. Our responses to texts—and events, conflicts, relationships, and changes—are always mediated and influenced by our powers of
language.

Making sense of your observations about literary language requires that
you connect your response to your observations. The thesis writing strategy
presented at the end of this chapter is a way to think responsibly about the
power and potential of language forms both to influence and help us articulate our interpretations. In the next chapter, you will learn more about organizing your thoughts by refining and focusing your subject and identifying
the assumptions and premises underlying your justifications and conclusions.

An Invitation to Write: The Analysis Essay

Read the following poem, and then use your reading notebook to record your
responses to the experience the poet expresses. Does the work engage you?
Did anything puzzle you? Then list your observations about the composing
choices Silko has made: look at **imagery** and **syntax**, shape, and participants.
From your list of observations, state a generalization about a characteristic of
the poem. After writing this generalization, write a conclusion in which you
relate your response to the poem to your generalization about the characteristic you have observed. Write an essay that expands and explains the connection between your response and analysis.

LESLIE MARMON SILKO
In Cold Storm Light

In cold storm light
I watch the sandrock
*   canyon rim*
*   The wind is wet*
*   with the smell of pinon.*
*   The wind is cold*
*   with the sound of juniper.*
*   And then*
*   out of the thick ice sky*
*   running swiftly*
*   pounding*
*   swirling above the treetops*
*   The snow elk come,*
*   Moving, moving*
*   white song*
*   storm wind in the branches.*

And when the elk have passed
*   behind them*
*   a crystal train of snowflakes*
*   strands of mist*
*   tangled in rocks*
*   and leaves.*

Writing Group Activity

Bring your analysis essay drafts to your writing group for their responses. As you present your work, ask your group members to read for the question at issue. Ask them to explain the way each paragraph contributes to your answer to your question. Then ask them to express your conclusion as your question linked to your justification. Use their comments and questions to guide your revision process. What was clear to them? What was confusing? Did they ask for more information? For extra practice, identify and define the literary terms each writer includes. Is the writer focusing on language? On shape? On the participants?

Sample Writing: Analysis Essay 1

At the end of Chapter 2 you were invited to read and respond to "Home," by Gwendolyn Brooks, a story that is quiet, lyrical, and full of rich language. The piece comes from what has been described as a "poetic novel" called *Maud Martha*, a collection of moments in the growing up of an African-American girl. "Home" can be puzzling because of its difficulty to categorize, because it manipulates conventions to complicate our expectations. One reader was puzzled because in the absence of full character development or events or actions, he couldn't see the significance of or the impulse for the story, and yet the piece evoked a powerful response he was unable to account for. The story made him recall his own childhood and the fear he felt as a child that he might lose all that was familiar and special despite its ostensibly ordinary appearance. After a discussion of the flexibility of conventions, he tried to see the way a blending of poetic and narrative conventions might create new reader expectations and consequently account for his reaction to the story. When he returned to the work to analyze it on its own terms, he found reasons for his response. He discovered that Gwendolyn Brooks's use of an omniscient narrator, poetic language, and syntactic form focused his attention on the logic of feeling and allowed him to see the ordinary as extraordinary. As you read the essay, consider how different it might have been had the writer omitted the response he explores in the first four paragraphs before he begins his analysis of the story.

SEEING THE ORDINARY AS EXTRAORDINARY

My father was a pharmaceuticals salesman. And a car salesman. And a security guard. He lost the bottom half of his right arm in Viet Nam, and I came to think of that truncated limb as his temper. He lost it too, so often I imagined it simply gone forever, and what we experienced as calm and relaxed moments were the equivalent of the imagined feeling he sometimes had past the point where the arm ended.

My mother worked, and we lived in a comfortable, easy-to-keep home with plenty of annuals around to brighten up the place. We had chores to do, schedules to keep, rules to obey. In all, our routines were predictable and manageable. My experience of my father's temper was like a metal plate in my head, a dull, flat place for the yelling to bounce off when it began. I went about my days cheerfully, plate and all, hiding in the holly bushes, making bows and arrows from tree branches, and cutting down alleys where I felt special for recognizing the houses from the back.

When he didn't have a job, he was angry because the world was unfair. When he had a job, he was angry because he hated it. When he had a bad day either way, he and my mother would, kindly enough, get us out of the house so they could fight. My sisters and I would sit and listen and make plans and even joke; it had happened before, and it would happen again. And despite the fact that my mother frequently declared she "had enough," we survived it all.

When my sisters and I get together now, we laugh about it, all of us good at avoiding conflict and sharing confidences. But after I read Gwendolyn Brooks's story "Home," I sent it to them. We all had the same reaction. None of us had remembered until the story brought it to mind the amount of time we had spent as the fights went on speculating about what would happen if we had to move. Our home was our concrete steps in the warmth of summer. It was our habit of sticking wooden tulips into the flower beds before the sun grew hot enough in spring to bring up the real ones. It was the hill, too small for us now but perfect when we were little, for rolling and sledding and king on the mountain. And though I don't ever remember a specific threat of divorce or separation issuing up from the fray, our understanding of the worst possible consequence of these arguments was that we might have to move. We simplified the family problems into an equation we could understand and which avoided assigning blame: if they can't come to terms, we'll have to pack our bags.

What enabled us to reconstruct and make sense of our own memories? The significance of this short, simple story is in the way characterization, form, and language all heighten our sensitivity to the significance of a threatened loss of "home," whatever that comes to mean to a particular, everyday person.

The characters in this story are particular, everyday people, and that is their significance. The point of view in the story is represented by an omniscient narrator who sees through Maud Martha's eyes, and it is her way of responding, her revelations, her complicated reactions that unify the story. We know little about her; Brooks replaces usual characterization with careful descriptions of everyday interactions and observations. But because we notice what Maud Martha notices, we come to identify with her way of seeing as extraordinary the ordinary things around her, and begin to comprehend how, though her external life is ordinary, her internal life is rich and complicated: "[S]he felt that the little line of white, somewhat ridged with smoked purple, would never drift across any western sky except that in back of this house. The rain would drum with as sweet a dullness nowhere but here." Though the family members share the fear of losing their home, it is Maud Martha's thoughts we hear, and her resistance to the possibility of the loss is expressed in images that attach us to her home with the power of our senses. We see the ordinary as extraordinary, as she does.

The heightened sensitivity Maud Martha brings to her surroundings is also intensified by the form of the story. The plot does not proceed along the usual dramatic structural points but moves from one state or feeling to another through a sequence of moods or attitudes evoked by words and phrases, each one preparing us for the next. In the beginning, words and phrases like "emphatic" and "little hope" and "hard" let us know the seriousness of the situation. We then listen to Mama test the believability of the alternative to hope, the "silver-lining hunting" that fearful people must engage in: "We'll be moving into a nice flat somewhere," she imagines. Maud Martha, aware of the ordinary pattern being played out but individual enough to counter it with the alternative *of* hope, argues against Mama's rationalizing, refusing to see its purpose. Then in the release that could be seen as the emotional climax, Maud Martha cries out "It's just going to kill Papa! . . . He *lives* for this house!" And Helen follows with the response to the fear, the quiet, necessary resolution: "He lives for us. . . . It's us he loves. He wouldn't want the house, except for us." "And he'll have us," Mama adds, "wherever."

What follows is a sigh, and a sense of relief, and a little clue that Maud Martha, too, has come to terms with the possibility of leaving. In the beginning, she gazes at a little bird in "the tree, her tree," an order that emphasizes her possession of her surroundings. In the end, she witnesses her father coming in "his gate—the gate," the order now illustrating a letting go not of hope, but of fear. And the denouement, the bank's answer, while it reinstates their possession and brings a light to Mama's eyes, reinstates the status quo as well—the mortgage is still delinquent, the reprieve is temporary.

The poetic language, too, heightens our sensitivity to the ordinary. While sound and rhythm are more typically characteristics of poetry than prose, Brooks uses alliteration and pacing to intensify and compress the feelings as well. For example, in the lines "Mama, Maud Martha, and Helen rocked slowly in their rocking chairs, and looked at the late afternoon light on the lawn," the rhythm of the rockers is reinforced by the patterns of accented syllables; in addition, the alliterative "l's" emphasize the length and longing of their wait.

Brooks uses syntax both to wrench ordinary word order and to press our emotions out past the ends of sentences. "What had been wanted was this always, this always to last—" begins the story, reversing normal word order and forcing us to wait until the end for the subject phrase, a phrase that ends with the words "to last," which is what they are all hoping will happen. "These things might soon be theirs no longer" creates the same effect, ending this time on the word "longer," which again stretches our hope out past the sentence and connotes "longing," offering us a way to identify emotionally with their situation. To focus our attention on the particular, immediate, present, and quiet moment with which this story is concerned, Brooks uses three short, simple sentences to isolate it from the past and future: "Yesterday

Maud Martha would have attacked her. Tomorrow she might. Today she said nothing." Poetic syntax thus concentrates and telescopes our attention to combine a heightened awareness of the present with a longing for its suspension.

A longing for its suspension. Don't take away the familiar. Don't take away my home. Reading "Home" and discovering my identification with Maud Martha allowed me to rediscover my memories of a time when I, too, perceived the wonders of the everyday world with heightened awareness. Whatever else was going on in the world, however ordinary my life or my existence, my own child's view was of a world resonant with small but significant dreams. The significance of Brooks's story is that it allows us to re-experience through the power of language the knowledge that everyone's life is fearful, joyous, and extraordinary.

Sample Writing: Analysis Essay 2

In this paper, a student objected to ways in which the class's discussion of Shakespeare's **sonnet**, in Chapter 1, set aside the gender issues she felt the poem was inviting us to ask. Though she accepted intellectually the ways the poem could be seen as a division between abstract oppositions, especially as a working out of the Renaissance opposition between reason and passion, she still felt hostility being expressed toward women as representative of passion, and she looked for sources of her response in features of the poem.

GOOD, EVIL, AND GENDER IN SONNET 144

Two LOVES / I HAVE / of COM / fort AND / des PAIR,
Which LIKE / two SPI / rits DO / sug GEST / me STILL:
The BET / ter AN / gel IS / a MAN / right FAIR,
The WOR / ser SPI /rit a WO / man, COL / or'd ILL.
To WIN / me SOON / to HELL, / my FE / male E vil
TEMPT eth / my BET / ter AN / gel FROM / my SIDE,
And WOULD / cor RUPT / my SAINT / to BE / a DEV il
WOO ing / his PUR / i TY / with HER / FOUL PRIDE.
And WHE / ther THAT / my AN / gel BE / turned FIEND
Sus PECT / I MAY, / but NOT / di RECT / ly TELL
But BE / ing BOTH / from ME, / BOTH to / EACH FRIEND,
I GUESS / one AN / gel IN / an OTH / er's HELL:
Yet THIS / shall I / ne'er KNOW, / but LIVE / in DOUBT,
Till MY / bad AN / gel FIRE / my GOOD / one OUT.

The sonnet is perceived by some as the ultimate form for roman-
tic expression. Yet in Shakespeare's "Two Loves I Have of Comfort
and Despair," the sonnet is used more for combat than affection.
In this poem, the duality of good and evil is personified by the
sexes, a strategy which does more to set men and women apart than
to resolve gender disputes in some ideal abstraction.

Because the language of the poem seems blatantly misogynistic,
we naturally want to recast the conflict in other terms. Our reading group found evidence of an internal dispute, a crisis of conscience, even a division between the masculine and feminine
"sides" of the narrator's personality. Those who responded to the
anger present in the poem assumed a failed relationship, and recognized the tendency to dismiss the woman as the result of love
gone wrong. Others excused the writer for the way he matched the
male with purity and the female with evil, acknowledging that if
the writer were a woman, the tables might be turned, or speculating that the parallels had something to do with cultural ideas of
the time. All of these explanations, it seemed to me, were
attempts to find a way to talk around our resistance to the language about women as conniving whores.

The first two lines of the poem introduce the conflict between
comfort, a freedom from worry, pain, and trouble; and despair, a
loss of hope. Line two specifically compares these two conditions
to spirits which pull us in opposite directions. Lines three and
four assign sexual identity to the conditions: "The better angel
is a man right fair, / The worser spirit a woman color'd ill."

The choice of the words angel and spirit is significant and sets
the tone for the rest of the sonnet. While angel conjures up a
picture of holiness, spirit also relates to less religious supernatural beings, ghosts, devils, and other demonic presences. The
word "ill," too, carries a range of connotations: Webster's The-
saurus lists bad, evil, hostile, and damaging as synonyms. Ill, as
in ill repute, carries a moral judgment when paralleled with fair,
which suggests one who is unblemished and honest.

The fifth line firmly casts the female in the role of devil. The
female evil has set out to drag the narrator to Hell by tempting
the man/angel away in line six. The word "tempteth" carries a powerful association to the Adam and Eve myth, lending cultural
authority to the narrator's judgment of women. The word "TEMPTeth"
also represents a variation on the usual meter, emphasizing even
more the perverseness of the power of "female evil." To tempt is
to induce or entice, especially to that which is immoral or sensu-
ally pleasurable. The narrator is in effect saying that women
wield sensuality as a tool to destroy men.

In line seven, man and woman are again cast in the roles of
"saint" and "devil," but the key word in this line is "corrupt."
To corrupt is to sway one to that which is morally unsound, per-
verse, debased, evil, and depraved. The appearance of the woman
spirit in the poem again corrupts the meter, warping the expected

rhythms: the phrases "female evil" and "be a devil" each add an extra, irregular syllable to the line endings. Her presence, we understand, tempts, corrupts, and "woos" the male/angel away from the correct path.

Line eight both begins and ends with the kind of metrical perversion which underscores the female evil. The first foot, "WOO-ing," replaces an iamb with a trochee, reversing the accent and thus calling attention to the conniving intent. The last words, "FOUL PRIDE," seem to require an equal, and therefore doubly emphatic, stress. "Wooing" reinforces the stereotypical picture of women as manipulators. The male association with purity, freedom from sin and evil, is repeated, lest we forget. "Foul" serves as an exclamation of disgust and calls to mind that which is extremely dirty, impure, or rotten, which makes the paired word "pride" all the more disturbing.

Lines nine through twelve contemplate the probable success of the devil/woman in pursuit of the angel/man. The word "fiend" again links the woman to Satan, a fiend being an evil spirit, devil, or the effect of an addiction to some activity; here, the implied addictive activity is sex. To suggest that the devil/woman will inevitably corrupt the angel/man is to suggest that sexuality is a matter of women exercising sexual power to demonic ends. Lines nine and eleven also incorporate the use of slant rhyme with "fiend" and "friend." Since the rest of the poem is consistent in maintaining true rhyme, this suggests a weak link in the implied friendship; it may even suggest that the friendship is fraudulent. The perversion here is, once again, reinforced by an interruption in the iambic meter; read naturally, "BOTH to EACH FRIEND," the variation makes the friendship seem unnatural, strained.

Lines ten through twelve show the author in a state of suspicion, wondering if the two spirits are cavorting without his knowledge and if the man/angel is falling in the path of wickedness. In the couplet, he admits he will never know unless the female extinguishes the male, leaving him in a constant state of hopelessness, or despair. It is the manner in which he conveys this thought that suggests a final insult. The author will not know if the two "angels" are friends until the "bad angel fires" the "good one out." Fire, according to the *Oxford English Dictionary*, is Elizabethan slang for venereal disease. Thus with this knowledge we can understand the metaphor to imply that through connivance and manipulation of sexual wiles, the devil/woman will destroy the angel/man through a sexually transmitted disease.

It can be argued that Shakespeare was uncommonly fair to women in the majority of his works. In this work, too, he carefully characterizes both conditions, comfort and despair, as "angels" whom he "loves." However, the evidence in the language of the poem accounts for the problem that I, as a reader, encountered. Other readings, those which resolved the polar tendencies neatly into an abstract statement about human frailty, conscience and temptation,

or the "sides" of personality, did not lessen the powerful and
challenging effect of the way evil and good were paired with the
female and male genders. In his personification of the battle of
right and wrong in Sonnet 144, Shakespeare has done a disservice
to both genders, portraying women as evil aggressors and men as
unwilling or unable to resist the stereotypical dark side of femi-
ninity, an alignment for which few excuses can be offered. For
those who would buy into the farce represented in this sonnet, I
offer the words of Oliver Goldsmith: "Don't let us make imaginary
evils, when you know we have so many real ones to encounter."

Extra Practice: Additional Writing Invitations

1. Look back through your reading notebook and find a place where
   you have noticed the way a writer's choice of word or phrase
   sparked your interest. Write a paragraph in which you explore why
   the particular choice elicited your reaction. Speculate about
   whether other readers might have had similar reactions. Share your
   writing with others in your reading group. What assumptions do
   you find that you share about literary conventions? Do you have
   different assumptions? Explore the similarities and differences in
   your group's definitions of literary conventions.

2. Both the questions "What language choices created an effect I, as a
   reader, perceived?" and "What is the effect or significance of a particular pattern of details I noticed?" can be answered with thesis
   statements that combine a conclusion (your response) with a justification (your observation of a particular pattern of details). Practice
   writing statements like these based on your observations of and
   readings about literary pieces in this chapter. Then write three-part
   outlines of what the essays based on each thesis statement would
   contain. Pick one thesis statement and draft a short essay stating
   your question and presenting your justification in a way that leads
   to your conclusion.

3. Select a term from Part B of the Appendix with which you are unfamiliar. Find a detail or a pattern of details that illustrates the term
   in a literary piece where it calls attention to itself. How do you
   respond to the piece? How is the detail or pattern of details related
   to that response?

Chapter 5

Interpretation and Responsible Reasoning
Developing the Literary Argument

WE have been arguing and interpreting for the last four chapters, but in this chapter, we will introduce some strategies for more successfully integrating your responses, reflections, observations, and analyses into interpretations through critical reasoning. Our students have often complained that the more they learn about literature, the more difficult it is to write papers. That may be because the more you know, the less likely it is that you'll be satisfied with simple answers. Literature, like human beings, is not simple. Unlike soap operas that give you a vacation from the complexities of life by being predictable, literature can help you learn to cope with the complications of life by giving you an opportunity to face and respond to them, coming to know yourself and your world a little better in the process of making critical decisions.

A critical decision is the end of a critical essay. Being critical is not the same as criticizing, in the sense of "finding fault." Being critical is not simply "arguing against," although some people seem satisfied with the role of devil's advocate. To think critically, you must be willing and able to:

1. Identify questions at issue.

2. State your responses and reactions to those questions honestly and clearly.

3. Use those responses and reactions to identify and reflect on your prior knowledge and assumptions.

4. Challenge your prior knowledge and test your assumptions through observing details and listening to the opinions of others.

5. Clarify your responses and reactions in light of new knowledge, taking into account your experience, your reading, your observations, and your interactions with others.

6. Formulate an answer to your question at issue that you have good reasons to believe and no good reason to doubt.

In this chapter, you will learn strategies that encourage two kinds of conversation. The first is the one you have with yourself as you acknowledge your assumptions, allow the work to challenge them, and combine your new knowledge with your prior understandings. The second is the one you must have with *your* reader when you are ready to make a reasoned, provisional commitment on paper: as you and your reader name your common ground and your differences, as you critically examine reasons for accepting one stance or another, you both discover and create an interpretation that goes beyond preconceived ideas to an examined, supportable statement.

Although you have been practicing these habits of mind in earlier chapters, the task is not easy, and things can suddenly fall apart as you try to write about your process of discovery and change. For example, when some students listen to other readers or conduct close literary analysis, they feel they lose track of their own experience. If this happens, they may either revert to their original "gut reaction" and ignore the complications they have found through their study of their work, or they may mimic the ideas of others. In other words, when they learn much more than they feel equipped to handle, they may resort to something that looks and sounds like a solid argument but doesn't take into account their experience or the complicating elements of the work. Other students may find it difficult, even in the face of their new knowledge, to change their minds; they may argue fiercely for their right to their initial opinions. However, when everything comes together, when your personal knowledge is integrated with your reading experience and you come to understand more about the work, yourself, and your world, the process of inquiry and discovery can be one of the most exciting learning opportunities of your education.

Rather than focusing on arguing against others, this chapter demonstrates how critical argument helps you to make up your mind on questions at issue through critical reasoning, and to express your discoveries in a way that takes your new knowledge and your audience into account.

ARGUMENT AND LITERATURE

As you read this chapter, consider that literature can be seen as a form of argument. Raising questions at issue, literature presents relevant evidence through sense details, complications, situations, and plots that appeal to our intellect, emotions, and imagination. Some works seem to argue more obviously than others, but even the poet who shares an experience with us wants us to see the world, for that moment, the way she does.

Writers of literature don't insist that their arguments are "right" finally and forever, but they do believe their arguments contribute to a fuller understanding of a work's meaning and significance. A single poem, story, or play may not move you from one opinion to its opposite, but it will contribute to the complex array of experiences and evidence you use to make up your mind. As we identify questions raised by a literary work, we find our shared concerns and our differences; as we consider the positions or perspectives offered by the work, we must first identify with the experience, then distinguish ourselves from it, engaging, reflecting, and responding. In that process, the work changes us (in that we've experienced something new) and we change the work (in that we contribute our own experiences and knowledge, which add meaning and significance to the reading experience). In this text, both the literary works and the sample papers can be examined in light of the arguments they are making.

EXERCISE 5.1. READING FOR ARGUMENTS

Review Annie Dillard's essay "Stalking Muskrats," Gwendolyn Brooks's story "Home," and the sample paper called "Seeing the Ordinary as Extraordinary." In your reading notebooks, write statements in response to the following: What might be Dillard's argument about seeing wild animals? What does Gwendolyn Brooks seem to argue about the meaning of "home"? What argument does the student writer make about how we judge things as ordinary or extraordinary?

Now examine your statements with other readers in your reading group to determine how the writers present and develop the arguments you identified. What evidence has the author presented that supports the argument as you have stated it? As you examine your statements, feel free to modify and clarify them.

When you identify the arguments writers seem to be making and then transform these statements into questions, you are discovering writers' questions at issue. When you identify puzzling places in a literary work or problems of interpretation, you discover your own questions at issue. Exploring *your* questions at issue requires that you reason critically, keeping your response, your assumptions, your observations, your analyses, and your audience in mind.

ASKING AND ANSWERING INTERPRETIVE QUESTIONS

You may have heard instructors say that the first stage in reading literature well is asking the right questions. When they say so, they seem to imply that a set of correct questions exists for each literary work. We doubt that they meant you to draw such a conclusion. When we say that reading well involves asking the right questions, we usually mean questions that respond to the problems and concerns raised by the work through choices the author made. If we are listening well to the writer, our responses come from a connection with the writer's issues and concerns. It also means we are responding to the way the shape and details of the writer's experience engage our own similar and different experiences.

Reading literature changes us by making us think about our lives, and it does so by presenting a perspective on particular kinds of experiences that we share in some way. As we read and respond, we begin by exploring and attempting to understand the perspective presented in the work. That perspective is expressed in the shape and features of the work. Our discussions of literature are attempts to see the connections between our lives, the shape of the work, and the perspective the work assumes toward a complex set of feelings or observations. To interpret is to be concerned with the *significance* of these connections.

In the discussion of "Filling Station" recounted in Chapter 2, Jane noticed that although the narrator seemed to feel just a bit frightened by the place, she didn't leave, and Jane wondered why. When she did so, she was responding to a moment of tension in the poem. The narrator seems disturbed by the scene, yet she remains in the place long enough to make very detailed observations about the scene before her and the inhabitants who must have constructed it. Because she does so when we might expect her not to, we are puzzled. Our interest is aroused and we want to find out why she stayed and what difference it made that she did so.

After posing the question, Jane suggests a possible answer: "She's kind of interested." If Jane begins exploring the connections between the observation and the hypothesis, she will be engaging in the conversation with the writer by responding to a question raised by an event in the poem. She will do so through analysis—by examining how the details and conventions of the poem make the question seem important. Our interest in the significance of the moment is in some way affected by our own memories, but the choices the poet made establish a particular **atmosphere** that raises the question.

Proposing and explaining an answer involves interpreting the significance of the connections between our experience, the perspective of the work, and the writer's choices of shape and language. A question of interpretation is one with at least two possible answers. When we ask why we responded the way we did or what effect a pattern has, we are looking for an answer that is an interpretation. Our answers, although circumscribed by limits set by the author's choices, will propose different readings. The possibility of different and competing readings raises the problem that often comes up in literature classes. If there are different ways to read components of a work, does that mean that all meanings are simply a matter of opinion and therefore equally valid, and if so, why argue about them?

What we have been asserting throughout this book is that we operate in a community of readers, a community that shares assumptions about what literature does and the way literature works; consequently, we share certain responses to and understandings about literary works. When we read, we identify and respond to the way in which the writer has discussed ideas and experiences with readers by presenting a view of some aspect of the world. When we discuss or write about literature, we respond, analyze, and attempt to understand that view of the world. Part of what we do is identify the shared experience and understanding of the work; as we do so, we explore the complexity or ambiguity in the work. In our shared examination of a work's complexity or ambiguity—the tensions in the literary piece, if you will—we achieve a fuller understanding of the world view of the poem, story, or play. Each new viewpoint offers a potential modification, clarification, or enrichment of the understanding.

THREE KINDS OF INTERPRETIVE QUESTIONS

In Chapter 2, we discussed the different but overlapping actions of responding, analyzing, and criticizing and evaluating a literary work. Although these three activities are interdependent, when we write about literature we generally emphasize one of the three. The emphasis depends on what question we focus on. When we explore our own responses to a work, we are interested in our own experience with the piece we have read, our **identifications** with the conflicts, relationships, and changes presented in the work, and how our identification changes us. When we analyze, we are interested in how the writer shaped these responses; our focus then is on the writer and his or her choices of literary conventions. When we interpret or judge a work, we do so because we are interested in understanding why the writer chose to write about a particular experience in a particular way, what attitude the writing expressed, and what difference it makes. When we write papers, the different questions will determine the way we shape our explorations and discussions of the work.

The following poem by William Stafford elicits a powerful response from most readers. Though apparently effortless in its structure and **diction** and conversational in **tone**, "Traveling through the Dark" is a very carefully constructed poem. After reading the poem, take a moment to consider what questions of response, analysis, and interpretation or judgment occurred to you while reading it.

WILLIAM STAFFORD
Traveling through the Dark

Traveling through the dark I found a deer
dead on the edge of the Wilson River road.
It is usually best to roll them into the canyon:
that road is narrow; to swerve might make more dead.

By glow of the tail-light I stumbled back of the car
and stood by the heap, a doe, a recent killing;
she had stiffened already, almost cold.
I dragged her off; she was large in the belly.

My fingers touching her side brought me the reason—
her side was warm; her fawn lay there waiting,
alive, still, never to be born.
Beside that mountain road I hesitated.

The car aimed ahead its lowered parking lights;
under the hood purred the steady engine,
I stood in the glare of the warm exhaust turning red;
around our group I could hear the wilderness listen.

I thought hard for us all—my only swerving—,
then pushed her over the edge into the river.

QUESTIONS OF RESPONSE: ENTERING THE DISCUSSION BY REASONING ABOUT OUR IDENTIFICATION WITH THE POEM

Our individual response to this poem might be one of sadness, and our question would probably concern what personal experience causes us to feel sadness when we read such a poem, or why the poem makes us remember it, or how reading the poem affects our reaction to the sort of experience the poem describes. In a discussion of responses to Stafford's poem, one student identified with the poem in the following way:

> *This poem makes me remember a time when I was driving down a road and saw a squirrel that had been hit by a car. I couldn't tell whether it was dead or alive, but it was lying face up and I remember the face. I couldn't decide whether or not I should stop. I realized that I probably wouldn't know what to do if I did stop but I felt somehow responsible. I remember feeling sick and sad and guilty. I didn't stop but I still remember the face. I haven't thought of the incident for a long time, but reading this poem brought it back.*

As this student discussed the experience with the other members of her discussion group, she realized that her reaction was more than sadness. By comparing her own experience and other readers' to that of the poem, she realized that what she was responding to in Stafford's poem was a sense of hopelessness, loss, guilt, and regret. The participants in the conversation raised multiple answers to such questions as "What happened?" "How did the events create the complex set of feelings?" "What details in the poem reminded you of this experience?" "In what ways did your experience differ from that of the narrator?" "What difference might it have made had the poet chosen to write about a squirrel instead of a deer?" "Are there other experiences you have had that are quite different from the experience detailed in this poem but that elicited the kinds of emotions you felt in reading about this particular experience?" In the discussion, individuals related stories, speculated about the differences and similarities of various responses, and discussed how various experiences, although quite different, may share an underlying pattern that is at issue for the poet. The interaction then was an **identification** with the work and with other readers of the work to come to an understanding of the emotional pattern of a shared experience.

Because this discussion of the poem involved identifying individual and shared responses to the experience the poet describes, the focus of the discussion was on the common experience. The questions focused on what was shared or different. In Chapter 2, we presented three questions that lead to response papers: What did I learn from this reading experience that contributes to my self knowledge or my understanding of the world? What do I know or have I experienced that can contribute to an understanding of the poem, play, novel, or short story? What did the work make me feel, and how did it make me feel that way? In each case, we are concerned with the relationship between our own experiences and the one the writer explores.

The reader who recalled her inability to help the squirrel was responding to the work by realizing that her sadness, guilt, and shame at not being able to save the life of a suffering creature shows the condition of humans as merely human, incapable of playing God. She developed this idea in a paper by exploring the similarities and differences of the experiences, all the while demonstrating that, despite the differences, the two situations showed humans' regret at their inability to make happy endings.

When we write response papers, we take positions about how the work affected us or changed us, and we justify those responses by considering the connections between our own experiences and those of the writer. Thus response essays, which take positions and support them with justifications, are also arguments.

QUESTIONS OF ANALYSIS: ENTERING THE DISCUSSION BY REASONING ABOUT THE PATTERNS THAT ELICIT RESPONSES

When we turn to analyzing the way a poem works, we generally ask how the poet constructed a work that elicited the responses we feel when we read it. Both the questions "What language choices created an effect I, as a reader, perceived?" and "What is the effect or significance of a particular pattern of details I noticed?" focus our attention on the choices the writer made in shaping the work. We examine details such as where the sentences begin and end, what is similar about each **stanza**, what order the details of the experience follow, what kind of words or **images** we find. Our study leads us to form generalizations about the poet's choices.

When you analyzed the William Stafford poem, you probably noticed many interesting patterns of details and reflected on what effects these patterns created. If you looked at the narrator, you might have noticed that in the first stanza the narrator is alone traveling through the dark when he sees the deer and identifies it as an object obstructing a narrow road. In the second stanza, he is still alone but joins the deer behind the car. He stands next to the deer then drags it off the road and, in the process, notices its gender, a doe "large in the belly." His observation makes the deer seem more alive, less an object. In stanza three, when the narrator touches the doe's belly and feels the warmth of the live fawn, he is clearly no longer alone. In the fourth stanza, the narrator is part of a group, "our group" he calls it, that includes the dead doe, live fawn, and his car. The scene seems full of life, as around them the wilderness listens. In the final stanza the relationship between the narrator and others seems to be central, but while the narrator thinks for "us all," his final act is an individual one. He pushes the deer "over the edge into the river"—but with a heightened awareness of his relationship to the "group."

If we generalize about these observations, we might conclude that this pattern initially emphasizes the isolation of the individual, then presents the individual as a member of a community that includes the natural world, yet ends with a solitary individual who must finally make his own decision but is painfully aware that the choice is not an easy one. We can see this change in the contrast between his initial statement of certain belief "To swerve might make more dead" and his final "I thought hard for us all."

The focus of this discussion is then on the patterns found in the poem because the question of analysis is both what patterns exist in the literary work and what are the effects of the particular patterns observed. The conclusion to the analysis of the Stafford poem provides an answer to the question "What patterns exist" and takes a position on the question "What difference does it make that Stafford's narrator is isolated until he confronts his decision?" or, more specifically, "Does the pattern indicate that the narrator acted as an isolated individual who had no real choice as to what action he had to take, or did he do so with an awareness of the implications his decisions had on the community, both natural and social?"

When we write analysis papers, we are concerned with the writer's choices. The process of study generally begins with observing patterns of analysis, then moves to generalizations regarding the effects of the patterns. We have an opinion about what effect the writer's choices made, and our essay explains how those choices create the effect. We might argue that Stafford constructs a poem that shows an individual ready to choose an action that he considers to be a simple, clear-cut decision until he is faced with the complicated nature of such a choice. We would base such a reading on our analysis of a pattern we find in the poem: when the narrator comes upon the carcass of a dead animal, he knows action must be taken; when he allows himself to reflect on the natural world he encounters—first the doe and then the wilderness "listening"—he realizes that decisions are not so simple; having taken the surroundings and implications into account, he decides, but his action, though seemingly inevitable, is now resonant with human complexity.

Our analysis essay then would use our observations about language and form to show the movement in the poem—from isolation to community and back to isolation—reflected in the words, phrases, **syntax**, **tone**, design, and development of the poem. Analysis essays, too, are arguments which take positions on questions at issue and offer justifications based on the writer's choices.

QUESTIONS OF INTERPRETATION AND EVALUATION: ENTERING THE DISCUSSION BY REASONING ABOUT SIGNIFICANCE AND JUDGMENT

Although we are involved in interpretive argument when we respond to or analyze a literary work, we often begin our study of the work by explicitly focusing on a question about the meaning and implications of the perspective on life the work offers. Most people who read Stafford's poem wonder why the narrator pushes the deer over the cliff or argue about whether the decision was justified. In one class discussion, a student who had read the poem for the first time exclaimed, "I'm furious with Stafford. I loved the poem, but I hated the ending. Why did he have to end it that way? How could he make the narrator push the doe into the river?" This is a poem that elicits strong responses because it raises questions of significance and judgment. These are questions of interpretation and evaluation. The focus of the discussion of such a question is on the problem to be solved, in this case the act of the narrator pushing the deer into the river.

When we write critical essays we begin with an interpretative or evaluative question, one that asks us to understand or assign **value** to options or choices or alternatives. We take positions that give our opinion regarding the probable implications of the work, then give a justification for believing our answer to be more probable than other possible answers. If the question asked about Stafford's poem is how does the poet expect us to respond to or value the narrator's decision to push the doe over the cliff, our answer will include both our response to a careful reading of the poem and our analysis of the way the poet has shaped the experience. If we believe that the poet is presenting the decision as a kind of inevitable one, or one that most people would make though perhaps with regret or even a sense of guilt, we base that conclusion on our response to the emotional pattern of the poem, a pattern that forces us to relate and balance our notions of the **value** of the human and animal worlds, or of isolation and connection, or of pragmatism and the sacredness of life.

We see this pattern of arguing in the various readings of the ending. The student who recalled her own similar experience argued that the poem makes the reader identify and therefore sympathize with the narrator's sense of hopelessness, loss, guilt, and regret. She based this line of reasoning on her observation of the poem's movement from isolation to identification and back, following the narrator as he chooses to make his own decision after considering his position as a member of a larger community that includes the natural world. She generalized that the pattern makes the reader identify and therefore sympathize with the narrator's emotional state.

Another reader saw the ending illustrating the coldness and selfishness of the human world because the ending's use of pronouns from the plural "us" of the second to the last stanza to the singular "I" acting in the final stanza shows the narrator choosing to turn from the community that included the natural world as he single-handedly pushes the deer over the canyon. This reader's reasoning is based on the assumption that the emphasis placed on the shift from the community of the natural world back to the isolation of the human condition, as illustrated by the pattern of pronouns, demonstrates the coldness and selfishness of the human world.

A third reader connected the pronoun pattern with the **repetition** of the word "swerving," demonstrating the narrator's sad recognition that he must decide to act as he does because the shift back to "I" joined with the repetition of the word "swerve" reminds the reader of his responsibility, that "to swerve might make more dead." This reader assumed that the intertwined pattern of pronouns and repeated word focuses the reader's attention on the inevitability of responsible action despite our and the narrator's sadness. In each case, the reasoning process begins with a shared assumption about the way literary conventions work. The answer to the question in the critical essay is the reader's conclusion, and the justification, a generalization based on analysis, is the reason for believing it to be the answer.

EXERCISE 5.2. KINDS OF CRITICAL QUESTIONS

Read or reread a work of literature selected by your group or your instructor. For that work, write at least two questions of response, two of analysis, and two of interpretation or judgment that could be answered in at least two ways. Then generate possible answers, or trial thesis statements, that might answer the questions. Share your questions and statements with your reading group.

READING AND WRITING TO CONSTRUCT ARGUMENTS

Identifying the Question at Issue

For a question to be at issue, it must be a real question, that is, a question for which we do not already know the answer and recognize that more than one possible answer exists. In the discussion of "Where Are You Going, Where

Have You Been?" the students explore issues by considering possible answers. Erin, Kay, and Ron took different positions on the question of who had power. There were competing readings of Arnold Friend, Steve and Brook seeing him as the devil, John as a Charles Manson figure, Erin and Kay as a man obsessed with power. Brook, Gretchen, and Chantelle disagreed about their judgment of Connie. While they presented their positions, they also shared their responses to the story (for example, Mary Ellen identified with the fear of being alone and vulnerable), and examined details from the work (as when Brook argued that Friend must be the devil because he marks Connie, knows everything about her, wobbles in his boots, and makes an "X" in the air). Mary Ellen wondered why the story is filled with light imagery; Erin wondered why Oates dedicated the story to Bob Dylan. Throughout the discussion, the students struggle to find the questions they share. At the end of the discussion, they focus on the ending as a place to begin exploring their different readings of the significance of the story.

In the discussion of "Traveling through the Dark," one issue was more clearly delineated—the three readers all found the poem sad but differed on how the poet wished the reader to respond to the ending. Was the ending sad because the narrator turned his back on a lesson he should have learned through an encounter with the forces of nature, or because he had no other choice given the danger to other lives, or because human beings have lost their sense of community? The discussion proceeded as the students began constructing arguments that stated their positions and gave reasons for someone who held a different conclusion to consider the validity of their positions.

EXERCISE 5.3. FINDING QUESTIONS AT ISSUE

Review the poem "A Poet's Farewell to His Teeth" and the story "A Clean, Well-Lighted Place." In your reading notebooks, write at least three questions at issue for each piece. Share these questions with your reading group. What kinds of questions are they? How are they alike and different? What are some possible answers? What reasons could be given for accepting each answer? Find a general question that seems at issue for all members of your reading group.

Seeing the Components of a Thesis Statement

All the interpretive questions we ask about a literary work lead us into a process of inquiry to find answers to our questions. As we attempt to answer the questions we have, we look at the way the writer has shaped the work and the context in which it was written. When we disagree about the answers to those questions, we enter discussions that involve taking positions and giving reasons for our answers. Doing so involves presenting arguments. Simply stated, an argument is a position on a question at issue for which there are other competing answers and a justification for the position.

We begin constructing arguments by stating an opinion on a question at issue, and then we justify our position by giving our reasons for believing as we do. We do this formally by writing thesis statements that guide our reasoning process. A thesis statement includes the answer to a question at issue and a reason for believing that answer to be a good one. Recognizing the thesis statement that answers your question can help you determine whether your reasoning is effective, because identifying the terms and their relationships makes the line of reasoning explicit. In addition, making yourself aware of your own line of reasoning can help you discover what you must explain and justify and how you must support your claims in order to persuade your audience that your answer is plausible.

When Brooke said, for example, that Arnold Friend must be the devil because he marks Connie, knows everything about her, wobbles in his boots, and makes an "X" in the air, she was addressing a question about how Joyce Carol Oates expects readers to respond to Arnold Friend. Brooke's answer was that Arnold Friend must be the devil, and her justification was that he acted in ways only a devil would act. Her line of reasoning began with the generalization that anyone who does all of these things is the devil. When we look at her reasoning formally, we see the following line of reasoning:

> *Generalization*: Anyone who marks another person, knows everything about that person, wobbles in his boots, and makes strange marks in the air must be the devil.
>
> *Justification based on the generalization*: Arnold Friend marks Connie, knows everything about her, wobbles in his boots, and makes an "X" in the air.
>
> *Conclusion*: Therefore, Arnold Friend must be the devil.

Is this good reasoning? Once we look at Brook's argument in this form, we find a number of problems. In the first place, although what she has observed about Arnold Friend's description and behavior are correct, they do not present a full picture. Arnold Friend has other traits as well. In addition, her conclusion is based on an assumption very few of us would accept. When we care about demonstrating that our answers to significant questions are plausible and compelling, we construct lines of argument that begin with generalizations our readers or listeners will accept. Identifying the line of reasoning allows us to see the problems with arguments as we plan them.

Recognizing the Thesis Statement behind an Argument

In order to see how identifying and clarifying our thesis statements can also help us answer the logical problems doing so may reveal, first let's examine the parts of a thesis statement. Before examining our own potential thesis statements, we'll look at a thesis statement we might find in a literary piece. At the end of "Stalking Muskrats," Annie Dillard writes:

> *The great hurrah about wild animals is that they exist at all, and the greater hurrah is the actual moment of seeing them. Because they have a nice dignity, and prefer to have nothing to do with me, not even as the simple objects of my vision. They show me by their very wariness what a prize it is simply to open my eyes and behold.*

Dillard's essay raises a question at issue for any reader who has not previously considered that stalking muskrats could be worthwhile: Why should I learn to stalk muskrats? Dillard's job as a writer is to make choices that result in your answering the question as she does, because you have identified with her experience and found it valuable. Dillard is drawing a conclusion based on her experience, a conclusion she expects you to share because you accept her reasons and her assumptions. Her conclusion might be stated like this:

> Learning to stalk muskrats is good because it can lead us to
> find pleasure and significance in seeing beyond the obvious.

This statement is a thesis statement. In literature, arguments are usually implied rather than stated, but the process of constructing them, in response to our reading, forces us to examine the connection between our old knowledge and the new information the author has provided. A thesis statement demonstrates this connection by combining a conclusion with a justification for believing it. Underlying the conclusion and reason is an assumption the writer believes she shares with her audience.

> *Conclusion*: Learning to stalk muskrats is good.
>
> *Justification*: Because it can lead us to find pleasure and significance in seeing beyond the obvious.
>
> *Underlying assumption*: Anything that leads us to find pleasure and significance in seeing beyond the obvious is good.

If Dillard has argued effectively, she will have based her argument on an assumption we share, or she will have brought us to share the assumption in the process of her argument, making language choices that resulted in our experiencing pleasure and significance as we identified with the work. If the underlying assumption can be called our "old knowledge" and the details of the work our "new information," then the conclusion should relate our old knowledge to our new information in a way that results in the "new knowledge" represented by the conclusion.

Generalization/old knowledge

An assumption shared by the writer and the audience.

Anything that leads us to find pleasure and significance in seeing beyond the obvious is good.

Justification/new information

A particular case or application of the major premise; the justification.

Because learning to stalk muskrats can lead us to find pleasure and significance in seeing beyond the obvious.

Conclusion/new knowledge

A conclusion that is the logical consequence of reasoning deductively from the shared assumption to the specific case.

Learning to stalk muskrats is good.

What characterizes such a thesis statement is the relationship it implies between the person who presents it and the person to whom it is directed. Whether or not we accept the reasoning of an argument depends on whether or not we accept the assumption underlying the statement or assertion. Recognizing the thesis statement behind an argument on a question at issue can help you discover whether to believe the author's line of reasoning because the thesis statement can expose what the author assumes you will believe without proof.

EXERCISE 5.4. RECOGNIZING THESIS STATEMENTS BEHIND ARGUMENTS

Recognizing the thesis statement behind an argument on a question at issue can help you discover whether to believe the author's line of reasoning because the thesis statement can expose what the author assumes you will believe without proof.

1. The preceding sentence is a thesis statement. Can you identify its parts? What assumption have we made? Do you agree with the statement?

2. In your reading notebooks, use the process below to practice constructing thesis statements behind arguments you
   have read:

   a. Identify the question at issue.

   b. State what you see as the author's answer as a com
      plete clause (this is the conclusion).

   c. Summarize the bulk of the author's arguments in a
      "because" clause (this is the reason).

   d. Put the clauses together as a complete statement.

   e. Identify the assumptions implied by the statement.

   f. Examine the assumptions, the reason, and the conclu
      sion for validity.

3. In your reading groups, review the discussion of "Filling
   Station." Using the process above, construct a thesis statement that could be used to begin a paper. What seems to be
   the argument Bishop is making about the **value** of her stop
   for fuel or the implications of the high-strung automobiles?

*Constructing the Thesis Statement behind Your
Argument*

You may have recognized the formal pattern we are using to discuss the thesis statement as a syllogism. We find the syllogistic form a convenient tool
for examining our lines of reasoning, but it is only a tool because syllogisms
are typically associated with certainty, truth, and proof, whereas responding
to, analyzing, and interpreting literature involve uncertainty, belief, and
probability. We could use the syllogism to show, as Aristotle does, that
Socrates is mortal because he is a man, and in doing so, we would be concerned with establishing certainty through the logic of proof. What makes
most human argument different is that we rarely argue about issues that are
either right or wrong. Rather, we tend to enter discussions on issues without simple answers, and thus we examine what is probable rather than what
is provable. Even more significantly, we argue based on a premise held in
common with someone who holds an opposing position. We call this premise
a shared assumption. Despite this distinction, we may borrow the form of the
syllogism in order to reveal the structure of our argument, the reasoning it
implies, and the justification we must explain and support. We begin the
process by stating our argument as a position and justification for our posi-

tion and identifying the assumption implied by the relationship between the two statements.

In our everyday conversations, whenever we say "I believe" something, we follow the statement of belief with a justification for why we believe it, and we try to justify it in a way that our listener will find convincing. If we do not do so, our listener often will ask for justification. If our justifications are based on assumptions the listener does not share, we either try a different line of reasoning or reconsider and modify our positions. If in a group discussion about William Stafford's "Traveling through the Dark," one participant in the discussion says, "Stafford makes the narrator's decision inevitable," the rest of the group will want to know why this person finds the decision inevitable. The person who took the position might argue that he thinks so because the narrator is cut off from the world of societal rules. The implied line of reasoning can easily be stated in syllogistic form:

> *Conclusion*: Stafford makes the narrator's decision inevitable.
>
> *Justification*: He isolates the narrator from the world of societal rules.
>
> *Assumption*: Cutting the narrator off from the world of societal rules makes the narrator's decision inevitable.

Obviously, this line of reasoning does not rely on a statement of truth but rather is based on an assumption that the writer thinks the listeners will accept, and yet a discussion of this thesis statement will probably reveal that readers who do not accept the conclusion may not share the assumption. If the person who constructed the thesis statement discovers that the assumption is not shared by the other participants, the discussion will lead him to explore another line of reasoning, perhaps something along the lines of "Isolating the narrator from society makes the narrator's choice to push the doe over the edge of the road inevitable because removing the narrator from the rules of his society and placing him in the wilderness compels him to follow the rules of the wilderness." This new assertion can be stated as a syllogism as well:

> *Conclusion*: Isolating the narrator from society makes the narrator's choice to push the doe over the edge of the road inevitable.
>
> *Justification*: Removing the narrator from a setting controlled by the rules of his society and placing him in the wilderness compels him to follow the rules of the wilderness.

Assumption: Compelling an individual to follow the rules of
the wilderness makes any choice that is in accordance with the
laws of nature inevitable.

As this example illustrates, our discussions with each other suggest lines
of reasoning and do so by implying connections between ideas. Further, it
shows the way we dig deeper into our reasoning process when we discover
that the assumptions at the heart of our arguments are not necessarily shared
by the people with whom we are conversing. These discussions naturally rely
on assertions that could be stated in syllogistic form. The syllogism simply
allows us to see the position taken, the justification for accepting it as plausible, and the assumption implied by the relationship between the two statements, an assertion that must be shared by the listeners or readers involved
in discussing the question. If we have considered our positions and the ways
they relate to the positions held by others, the result of this thought process
will be a thesis statement worth arguing, a defensible answer to an interpretive question.

Clarifying the Terms of Your Argument

Good reasoning depends on the logical relationship of the terms of the argument and the clarity of those terms. Every thesis statement contains three
terms. To talk about the reasoning in the thesis statement, we identify the components or terms of the assertions and the relationship among the components. Every thesis statement includes two assertions, each being a complete
idea or clause and therefore having a subject and a predicate. The subject is
the focus of our attention, and the predicate is what we wish to say about it.
The subjects and predicates are the terms of our thesis statement. Technically, we thus have four terms, but what makes a thesis statement a statement
of reasoning is that two of the terms are shared, which means simply that they
are either the same term or one is a synonym or paraphrase of the other term.
We may say, for example:

Subject	Predicate
Stafford	makes the narrator's decision inevitable
because	
he	isolates the narrator from societal rules.

In this thesis statement, Stafford, the shared term, is the subject of both
clauses. The predicates of the two clauses are our second and third components or terms. Because we can easily see the shared term, we can identify the

relationship between the unshared terms, the two predicates. The student assumes we agree that "isolating the narrator from societal rules makes the narrator's decision inevitable." When we identify the connection between the two unshared terms, we discover the assumption behind the line of reasoning. If a writer has not constructed a thesis statement with one shared term, readers may not be able to identify the argument's underlying assumption and, as a result, will have difficulty understanding the argument. This lack of coherence in the thesis statement was evident in the first statement the student made when he asserted "Stafford makes the narrator's decision inevitable because the narrator is cut off from society's rules." The lack of a shared term makes the line of reasoning less explicit and consequently more difficult to analyze.

The choice of subject indicates the focus of the argument. If we make Stafford the subject of both assertions, we suggest that we are addressing the question "What does Stafford intend us to conclude about the decision the narrator makes?" In the thesis statement that explores the premise this line of reasoning implies, we addressed a different question and thus shifted to a new subject. With that thesis we wondered why Stafford has chosen to isolate the narrator on a dark road away from the conventions and expectations of his society. Our answer was:

Subject	*Predicate*
Isolating the narrator from society	makes his choice inevitable

because

removing him from a setting controlled by society's rules and placing him in the wilderness	compels him to follow the rules of the wilderness

Because we are now interested in the choice Stafford has made to isolate the narrator from society, the subject of the conclusion is no longer the poet but rather a decision he has made in constructing his poem. The shared term may be somewhat more difficult to see. The subject of the justification, "removing him from a setting controlled by the rules of his society and placing him in the wilderness," paraphrases and explains the subject of the conclusion, "isolating the narrator from society." As we construct thesis statements, we decide what the focus of our attention ought to be and make that the subject, then we decide what we are asserting about the subject, and that becomes our predicate. Which thesis statement we choose to argue will depend on which question we wish to explore.

When we argue, we construct lines of reasoning based on an assumption we are pretty sure our readers or listeners will accept. If you were disputing the grade you had received in a class, you probably would not say, "I should have received an A because I completed all the assignments." You would never assume that the professor would agree with the premise this line of reasoning implies, that students who complete all the assignments deserve A's in the class. The argument you would use in such a case would need to imply a premise the professor would accept, that all or most of your grades on assignments were A's, for example.

The assumption implied by any line of reasoning shows the connection between the two unrelated terms of the thesis statement. In the example of the student speaking to a professor, the shared term is the subject of the two statements, "I," and the unshared terms are the predicates of the two statements, "should have received and A" and "completed all the assignments." In the first thesis statement above, the shared term is the subject, "Stafford," and the unshared terms are the predicates, "isolates the narrator from the world of societal rules" and "makes the narrator's decision inevitable." The logical connection implied by the line of reasoning of the argument is "Isolating the narrator makes his decision inevitable." In the second thesis statement, the logical connection implied by the line of reasoning is "Compelling the narrator to follow the rules of the wilderness makes his choice to push the doe over the edge of the road inevitable."

Recognizing the thesis statement can help you discover what commitment you have made to your readers, what they will expect you to address, and how they expect you to reason in order to convince them that your position is plausible, because the thesis statement exposes the terms of your argument and the logical relationship among your terms. When we argue effectively, we always begin by deciding whether our readers or listeners will accept our assumptions.

EXERCISE 5.5. CONSTRUCTING THESIS STATEMENTS

1. In order to construct and analyze the thesis statement
    behind your argument:

    a. Identify the question at issue, and state your answer
        as a complete clause.

    b. Ask yourself why you believe the answer, and state
        your reason as a clause beginning with "because."

    c. Check your reason to see if you can support it with
        information that is new to your reader—your experi-

ences, your reading, your new perspective on your subject.

    d.   Create a thesis statement from your two clauses. Using the first clause as the conclusion and the "because" clause as one of the premises, make a syllogism, supplying the missing premise or assumption.

        Check your thesis statement to see if the subject of both clauses is the same, a shared term.

    e.   Check your syllogism to see if your audience is likely to agree with your assumption and accept your reason.

2. Select a paper you have written in this class, or one of the student papers in this text. In your reading notebook, construct and analyze the thesis statement behind the argument. Then discuss the paper with your writing group. Examine each paragraph of the paper to see how it relates to the components of the thesis statement. Is each component of the thesis statement addressed in the paper? Are all key terms defined?

CRITICAL REASONING ILLUSTRATED: THE EVOLUTION OF A THESIS STATEMENT

To illustrate the process of constructing and analyzing a thesis statement using a literary work, let's return to our discussion, begun in Chapter 4, of Theodore Roethke's poem, "My Papa's Waltz." Our analysis of the interaction of the shape and language of the poem verified our response to the complexity of the situation described in the poem. You recall our conclusion that the poem expresses an ambivalent view of the narrator's childhood encounter with his father. The question we raised was one of analysis: what is the effect of the combination of regular **meter** and unexpected, threatening language and **imagery**?

Let's look back at the process we used in reaching this stage in our preparation for the essay. We began by reading a poem, and as we read, responding to the experience. We then looked closely at the details of the poem and generalized two patterns. From our observations we generalized that the poem was regular in its metrical pattern and also that the language combined negative and threatening images with more positive images. The thesis statement we constructed drew a conclusion based on our analysis:

Roethke expresses an ambivalent view of a childhood encounter by com-
bining a regular metrical pattern with unexpected, threatening language
and imagery.

Now let's examine this statement using critical reasoning. As written, this thesis statement suggests that the subject of the paper we intend to write will be Roethke because he is the subject of both the conclusion and the justification (he did the combining). It indicates that we believe this conclusion to be the case because Roethke combines a regular pattern with unexpected and threatening language and imagery. Our assumption is that when a poet combines a regular metrical pattern with unexpected and threatening language and imagery in a description of a childhood experience he expresses an ambivalent view of such an experience.

If we are interested in Roethke, the thesis statement is fine as written. However, if we are interested in his choice of conventions, we ought to revise the thesis statement to reflect the subject we intend to examine in our essay. The findings of our analysis, Roethke's combining a regular metrical pattern with the unexpected and threatening language and imagery, become the subject we wish to discuss, and what we wish to conclude is what effect such a choice creates. If we rewrite the thesis statement to reflect this shift in focus, the new argument may read:

Roethke's choices of conventions express an ambivalent view of a child-
hood encounter with the narrator's father
because
the combination of a regular metrical pattern with unexpected and threat-
ening language and imagery creates responses of stability and predictabili-
ty complicated by uncertainty and threat.

Our thesis then includes a subject, the focus of our discussion, which represents our analysis; a predicate, which asserts that this subject contributes to the effect we feel when we read the poem; and a justification for drawing this conclusion, or what it is about this combination that creates the ambivalence we feel. Now look at the components of this thesis statement. Does it offer you the information you need to begin structuring a sound, unified, responsible paper? It obligates you to several things: you must examine your assumptions; you must support your reasons; you must identify and define key terms that may have ambiguous meanings for your readers. Although this thesis statement as written may never appear in the essay you write, the reasoning you conduct will provide you with a guide to the critical thinking responsibilities implicit in your thesis statement.

When we move from analysis to conclusion, we are constructing an argument that explains the connection between our examination of the poem and the question we share with other readers. We take our findings from an examination of the details of the work and align them with our response to the poem. The process may begin instead with a different kind of question at issue—if we begin by determining different and competing responses to the experience Roethke describes in the poem, our question is how Roethke might expect readers to respond. In fact, when we teach this poem in literature classes, we find that some readers view the attitude expressed in the poem as quite dark; they argue that the father is a menacing figure and the waltz frightening. Others find it far lighter, contending that the father is playful if somewhat forbidding, as fathers often are to young children, and the waltz a shared game. Clearly, the question is at issue for a typical group of readers. As these readers explore their response, they will be using their analysis of the poem to help them find answers.

PLANNING YOUR PAPER

The following discussion suggests a procedure to follow as you plan and write your paper. We are not implying by this suggestion that writing a paper follows a simple linear pattern. Often you will find yourself changing your mind, changing your question, looking at new information, picking up the process at different stages, or rethinking or starting over. What we offer is a very general roadmap to consider.

The preparation for a critical essay begins with your considering your response to the literary work and determining the question that is at issue for you. If you are in a classroom setting or a reading group, this initial stage can take place in a discussion with others. As you share responses as a group, you will identify differences of opinion on ambiguous moments in the work, and by doing so will determine the question at issue. If you are writing about a work you are reading alone or for a class that includes very little discussion, it may help to imagine a hypothetical, internalized discussion with other readers you know and whose intelligence you respect. When you read alone, you must manufacture the dissenting voices, but if you reflect sincerely and thoughtfully, your own interpretive responses are usually far more complex and ambivalent than your initial impressions might suggest.

We have often had students acknowledge that they chose to write certain papers because they seemed "easy," and to make their arguments work, they ignored the complexities of the literary experience. This suggests to us that dissenting voices were at work, that each of us converses with potential others when we read and try to interpret the meaning of literary works. The beginning of a study of a work, then, is the recognition of our responses and the exploration of questions about the meaning of the work.

Exploring responses and questions involves trying out potential answers to the questions you raise. As you think about hypothetical answers, test them against your knowledge and experience, the literary conventions the writer has chosen, and your assumptions about the effects and significance of these observations. As you test the persuasiveness of your ideas, begin to shape possible thesis statements, and then focus on the most promising combination of conclusions and justifications. An important part of this process is deciding on a method of inquiry, in other words, determining what you need to examine to answer your question. With your question in mind, revisit the work, allowing it to challenge and modify your hypothetical conclusion.

When you have reexamined the work in light of the question you are exploring, you may be ready to refine your thesis statement in light of your analysis. Examine the subject of each of your assertions to be sure it is the focus of your interest and that the terms you use are precise and clearly state your position and justification. An important part of this stage of refining your thesis statement is determining your assumption and honestly assessing whether it would be acceptable to a dissenting audience. If you are working through this stage in a group setting, this assessment is fairly easy. You can simply ask those who disagree with you whether they would accept your assumption. If you are working alone, you will have to imagine your opposition. If you determine that the assumption is not shared by your audience, you will have to reshape your thesis statement so that it depends on an assumption your audience will accept, or determine how you will address and support the assumption in the context of your argument.

Allow the components of your thesis statement to suggest a structure for your essay. A well-reasoned thesis statement will indicate both the key ideas and the connections between them, which will help keep your paper on track and unified. If you have worked with your thesis statement extensively and think that the logic of your argument is strong, you should find this stage far easier than you have as you wrote papers in the past.

As you begin your paper, you will need first to let your reader know what question you will be answering and why you think it is important. You may explain what method of analysis you will be using to answer the question and what assumption your line of reasoning depends on. After this introduction, you will begin explaining and supporting your justification. This stage of an argument is often called the burden of proof. In other words, for a dissenting reader to find your argument plausible, that reader must see the evidence you have found and the generalizations based on that evidence that led you to draw your conclusion. An important part of this section of your argument is an explanation of the terms of your minor premise or justification. Finally, you will show how your justification earns your conclusion. What you are arguing now is that if a reader accepts the shared premise and is convinced by your justification, the conclusion follows. This structure of argument is seen in the following sketch:

Introduction

The question at issue

The significance of the question

The assumption your reasoning will follow

The method of your analysis

Body of the essay

Definition of the terms of your justification

Evidence explaining and supporting your justification

Conclusion

How your justification allows you to draw your conclusion given the assumption you originally proposed

You might think of this structure as recreating your own process of inquiry. You began with a question that seemed important to you and others, a question with more than one possible answer. You used a particular kind of analysis to explore possible answers. As you looked at the possible answers, you discovered what assumptions the divergent answers shared. All this information begins the discussion your paper will present. It is helpful information to present in your introduction. Having given the preliminary introductory remarks, you then turn to the discussion of the generalization your analysis has led to and any clarification of the terms you use in those generalizations. This discussion includes your reasons for drawing the conclusions and how the information you have gathered from your study supports the generalizations you have drawn. Finally you conclude by pulling your argument together, explaining how these generalizations and their supporting information add up to the position you have taken as the result of your study. When we plan a paper in this way, we typically sketch out the line of the argument with a sentence outline. If we did so in planning the critical essay on "My Papa's Waltz," the sentence outline might look like this:

What is the narrator's attitude toward his father?

The language and rhythm seem to indicate a fond memory.

Yet much of the language seems violent, and thus the experience seems somewhat frightening.

Further, while the rhythm is predictable, the language is puzzling; maybe his reaction is more complex than it appears on a first reading.

If we examine the rhythm and diction of the poem we may see whether the patterns indicate a more positive, more negative, or mixed response.

The rhythmic pattern is regular in its three metrical feet per line (trimeter), each foot being iambic (unstressed, stressed).

Part of the reader's response is to the regular rhythm of an experience we may have all had when dancing.

The physical reaction to such rhythm is one of balance and satisfaction in the predictability of the three-beat waltz step.

Yet this balance and satisfaction seem undercut by the unexpected and threatening language.

The diction is often surprising in associating the memory of the narrator's father with the whiskey on his breath and even threatening in the battered wrist and the buckle that scrapes the child's ear.

Associating the memory of a father with whiskey, a battered wrist, a buckle that scrapes the child's ear, and a palm caked hard by dirt makes the reader feel somewhat off balance, not knowing what to expect next and fearing that there may be violence.

The combination of a regular metrical pattern with unexpected and threatening language and imagery creates responses of stability and predictability complicated by uncertainty and threat.

When readers feel both satisfaction and balance and instability and potential threat their response is complicated.

Therefore the poet's choices of such conventions express an ambivalent view of the childhood encounter.

EXERCISE 5.6. DEVELOPING ARGUMENTS

1. Reread the story "Where are You Going, Where Have You Been?" and the dialogue about the story in Chapter 3. Choose one question that you share with the students in that dialogue. In your reading notebook, compose a thesis statement that one of the students might have written about this question. What evidence might the student have chosen to

support the justification? Use a sentence outline to indicate the structure of an argument the student might follow.

2. Compose a thesis statement of your own that answers the question at issue. Does it begin with an assumption a student who disagrees with your answer would accept? What evidence would you use to support your justification? Outline the structure of the argument your thesis statement suggests and present your outline to your writing group. How do they respond? What do they suggest?

SUMMARY

Successful academic writing uses knowledge of the audience to develop and justify a thesis in response to a question at issue. Recognizing the thesis statement within your argument can help you discover what you must address and how you must reason in order to persuade your audience. In addition, as you will learn in Chapter 6, recognizing the thesis statement behind an answer to a question at issue in critical research essays can help you decide whether to accept the author's reasoning, because the thesis statement can expose the terms of the argument.

In this chapter, we've argued that incorporating explicit reasoning into your process of constructing literary arguments can help you as you plan your critical essays. We do not want to give the impression that the thesis statement is a mechanical device for generating arguments. If you have spent any time with the practices suggested in this chapter, you already know that critical reasoning does not simplify ideas, but it is a way to help you relate, examine, and align complex combinations of ideas. Focusing your questions at issue and constructing thesis statements based on good reasoning can clarify your arguments by encouraging you to acknowledge and examine your assumptions and reasons, and to meet the responsibilities you have accepted by making assertions about meaning.

An Invitation to Write: The Critical Essay

In Chapter 4, we used the first quatrain of the following **sonnet** to illustrate how patterns in word choice can suggest a particular attitude toward the subject matter. Now we'd like to invite you to share the whole sonnet with your reading group. In your discussion of the poem, begin with your response, then determine at least one question at issue for your group. State each person's position in a thesis statement and find the argument's implied assumption. Revise the thesis statements so that the assumption is a shared one and the terms are clearly stated. Decide together what method of analysis would help you clarify your positions and test your thesis statements against the details of the work. Then, independently, write a sentence outline and a draft of your critical essay, linking your responses to your conclusions, and your observations to your justifications.

JOHN KEATS
When I Have Fears

When I have fears that I may cease to be
*   Before my pen has glean'd my teeming brain,*
Before high-piled books, in charact'ry,
*   Hold like rich garners the full-ripen'd grain;*
When I behold, upon the night's starr'd face,
*   Huge cloudy symbols of a high romance,*
And think that I may never live to trace
*   Their shadows, with the magic hand of chance;*
And when I feel, fair creature of an hour,
*   That I shall never look upon thee more,*
Never have relish in the faery power
*   Of unreflecting love!—then on the shore*
Of the wide world I stand alone, and think
*   Till Love and Fame to nothingness do sink.*

Writing Group Activity

Share your drafts with your group members. How are they alike? How are they different? What does each emphasize? Ask the group to compose a sentence outline that illustrates the progression of your points, and then compare it to the original. What is clear? What is confusing? Use their questions and comments to guide your revision process.

Sample Writing: From Response to Analysis to Thesis Statement to Critical Essay

In the dialogue about Joyce Carol Oates's "Where Are You Going, Where Have You Been?" the students whose discussion you read in Chapter 3 all had strong but differing emotional responses to the ending of the story. Some felt sympathy for Connie; some saw her as weak, naive, and vulnerable; some thought her actions were brave given her situation; others believed she deserved punishment. With such different and opposing positions, the class had found a question at issue: "How does Oates expect her readers to respond to Connie's predicament at the end of the story?" When Steve suggested that Connie was being punished, he narrowed the focus of the question. Erin responded so strongly that she interrupted him:

> *You think she's being punished? For what? I mean, she's kind of a ditz,*
> *but she hardly deserves punishment. I think it's more about power. He has*
> *her in a spell, and I think all the music has something to do with that.*
> *He's lots older and uses part of song lyrics to shape his dialogue. It's how*
> *he pretends to be younger than he is. And he sounds like the DJ Connie*
> *has been listening to. Like a popular singer, he's able to draw women into*
> *his power. I think the story is about power and manipulation. Why is it*
> *dedicated to Bob Dylan?*

Because she responded so strongly, Erin decided to pursue this question. The question as she began her study was "Is a girl of fifteen, however superficial she might be, responsible for the manipulations of an older man?" As a method of analysis, she decided to look at what contributed to Connie's self-concept and how that profile of her personality affected her responses to Arnold Friend. Her first tentative thesis statement was:

Oates allows the reader to feel sympathy for her by making Connie helpless.

Or stated as a two-part thesis statement with a conclusion and justification:

Oates allows the reader to feel sympathy for her because Oates makes Connie helpless.

The assumption implied by this thesis statement is: "Making a character helpless allows readers to feel sympathy for the character."

This is a good beginning thesis statement. It has a shared term, "Oates," and two terms that when linked in the assumption become a premise most of her readers would accept. A problem with the thesis is that it is rather general and, as a result, may lead to a rather superficial development of the argument. It also suggests that the focus of the paper is the writer. Looking back at her controlling question, Erin realized her real interest was what made her feel that Connie was not responsible for her predicament. As she returned to her analysis of the story, she discovered that what she wanted to examine was what made Connie seem vulnerable, and therefore sympathetic.

She reread the story and found that Connie's relationship with her family was either a distant or verbally abusive one. Erin thought most people would agree that this pattern would make a teenager who needs attention and affirmation open to the advances of a man who wanted power over young girls and knew how to speak to them. She then revised her thesis statement to reflect the findings of her analysis and the assumption she believed dissenting readers would accept. Her new thesis statement was:

Connie's upbringing makes readers see her as blameless at the end because her relationship with her family left her totally unprepared to deal with a man who understood the teenage culture and was controlling and destructive.

Her underlying assumption now is that being raised in a way that leaves one unprepared for the advances of a power-hungry man who knows the teen **culture** well enough to manipulate young women makes the victim of such a seduction blameless. With this new focus, Erin is ready to begin planning her essay, which she does by constructing a sentence outline of the ideas of her argument.

1. Many people hold victims who are less than upstanding citizens responsible for the crimes committed against them.
2. Connie is one of these victims, but as a fifteen-year-old girl should she be held responsible?
3. Connie lives in a household that is either distant or verbally abusive.
4. Rejection and verbal abuse weaken a person's self-esteem.
5. A lack of self-esteem often makes a person seek approval elsewhere.
6. Arnold Friend was an older man who knew the teen culture.
7. He knew their insecurities and what teens valued.
8. Arnold was able to use his knowledge to get close enough to manipulate Connie, and because she was unprepared and vulnerable, she is not held accountable for her predicament at the end of the story.

After constructing her sentence outline she wrote the following paper.

CONNIE, WHERE ARE YOU GOING, WHERE HAVE YOU BEEN?

Society only wants to hear about the injustices done to people who are upstanding, productive, and promising citizens. The news will flash photographs of college students who are killed in a car accident on the six o'clock broadcast while ignoring the routine deaths of young kids who live in the projects. When undesirable members of society are victimized, it may be viewed by others as a reflection of their questionable lifestyle. Or perhaps the death of these shunned individuals is a blessing to an already imperfect society. Since Connie isn't perfect, it might be easy for the reader to blame her for the situation involving Arnold Friend. Is a girl of fifteen responsible for the manipulations of an older man?

One aspect of Connie's life that influenced her negatively was her relationship with her family. Connie's father remained distant from the family. Her "father was away at work most of the time and when he came home he wanted supper and he read the newspaper at supper and after supper he went to bed" (1055). By avoiding the family, Connie's father was unable to give her the attention she might have needed. Her mother also distanced herself from Connie, but she did it through verbal abuse. The mother scolded her about her appearance and her laziness. Often the verbal abuse contained references to her sister, June: "Hair spray? You don't see your sister using that junk" (1055). Connie even said to a friend one time that she wished her mother was dead so it was all over (1055). The constant attack may have caused Connie to stop trusting and confiding in her parents. Perhaps she could have reached out to her sister for support, but June "saved money and helped clean the house and cooked" (1055), and this perfect image may have intimidated Connie too much for her to trust her sister. Alienated from all members of her family, Connie may have developed a vulnerable state of mind.

Verbal abuse can weaken a person's self-esteem. In our society, parents are told by child-rearing specialists that reinforcing the child's positive self-concept is essential. Connie, however, had no such support from either her absentee father or her abusive mother. Perhaps Connie sensed their rejection and stayed away from home to avoid feeling like an outsider.

While speaking on the phone, "If June's name was mentioned her mother's tone was approving, and if Connie's was mentioned it was disapproving" (1057). The favoritism might have forced Connie to seek escape in a world still too mature for her. "Everything about her had two sides to it, one for home and one for anywhere that was not home," and trying to fit into the older crowd may have been an attempt to find herself. Statements such as "Stop gawking at yourself, who are you? You think you are so pretty" (1055) may have led Connie to secretly search for someone who would accept her for herself. Ironically, her search for love and acceptance led her to someone who cared too much.

Arnold Friend may have sensed Connie's loneliness and need for attention. He could then use her weakness to manipulate her into leaving with him. Arnold's appearance also was used to make her feel a false sense of security. Oates explains,

Connie liked the way he was dressed . . . : tight
faded jeans stuffed into black, scuffed boots, a belt
that pulled his waist in and showed how lean he was,
and a white pull-over shirt that was a little soiled
and showed the hard small muscles of his arms and
shoulders (1060).

Dressing like one of the boys she went to school with enabled
Arnold to lull Connie into believing that he was as innocent as a
high school boy.

Music also helped Arnold gain control over Connie. When Arnold
drove up to the house he was playing the same radio station Connie
had been listening to.

"Bobby King?" she said.

"I listen to him all the time. I think he's great."

"He's kind of great," Connie said reluctantly.

Appearing like someone she'd be interested in and having similar
music taste were both ways to capture Connie's trust. After Connie
realized the seriousness of the situation, she had the idea "that
everything about him and even about the music that was so familiar
to her was only half real" (1063). Throughout the story music was
present. For example, Arnold "spoke in a simple lilting voice,
exactly as if he were reciting the words to a song" (1061). Perhaps Arnold sensed how important music was to teenagers and
shrewdly used it to his advantage.

Another way Arnold used Connie's vulnerabilities to his advantage was by verbally claiming her as his own. From the moment he
uttered "Gonna get you, baby," Connie's fate was sealed. Even
though he implied rather obscene things, he offered Connie more
attention than her family ever gave her. Arnold said, "Seen you
that night and thought, that's the one, yes sir. I never needed to
look anymore" (1065). He went to the extreme and learned everything about her family and even knew when they'd be away at a barbecue. When he was trying to convince Connie to take a ride with
him, he stated, "You're my date. I'm your lover, honey," as if it
were her fate rather than a choice. From the moment they met,
Arnold played on her strongest insecurity—her fear of not being
accepted.

Arnold suggested a life of all-encompassing devotion. Although
the reader was aware of the unhealthy dimensions of his suggestion
to go for a ride, Connie may have been unable to resist such an
offer. Due to the parents' lack of interest and involvement in
Connie's life, she was emotionally vulnerable to someone who
thrives on control. Arnold's manipulations were far too complex
for Connie to deal with successfully. The constant belittling by
her mother could have created a confidence problem in Connie that
left her unable to deal with someone as demanding as Arnold. After
Arnold successfully gained control over Connie, she felt numb when
she felt her heart and "thought for the first time in her life that

it was nothing that was hers, that belonged to her, but just a pounding, living thing inside this body that wasn't really hers either" (1067). The way Connie's family treated her made her vulnerable to a person as controlling and destructive as Arnold.

Therefore, the way the family treated Connie makes us empathize with her and makes her seem less responsible for the situation's outcome. The reader can't blame someone for the choices she makes if that person lacks emotional stability. Connie's upbringing would have left her totally unprepared to deal with a character like Arnold. Maybe if Connie's family had given her a better sense of who she was, then Arnold wouldn't have had such an easy time convincing her to leave with him. Connie never had control over her own destiny. Even though some may say that Connie brought about her own demise, the reader must remember that Connie's parents had considerable influence over the kind of person she became, so they must also be held accountable for the situation.

Extra Practice: Additional Writing Invitations

1. Write a response to Erin's essay. Would you argue that it is a convincing argument? Why or why not? What might she do to strengthen her position? Compose a thesis sentence that states your position on the effectiveness of her essay and your justification for your assessment. Write a sentence outline of the reasoning of your argument, then write the essay that critiques Erin's paper.

2. Reread a paper you wrote before you read this chapter. Find and articulate the question at issue and your answer to that question— it may be a directly stated thesis, or it may be implied. Examine the thesis statement for a conclusion, a justification, and an underlying assumption. Are the terms clear? Are they clearly related? Are any underlying assumptions likely to be shared by your audience? Are all the parts of the paper clearly related to the thesis statement, and does the thesis statement guide the progression of points? Let the answers to your questions guide a revision of the paper with the purpose of translating it into a critical essay.

Chapter 6

Interpretation within a Literary Community:
Reading with Experienced Readers

IN previous chapters, you were introduced to several ways to think about reading literature as conversation. You have participated in literary conversations with the friend in the work and with your reading companions in classroom conversations. You have studied the vocabulary of literary conventions in order to improve both the content and quality of those conversations. You have learned to converse with yourself as you acknowledge your assumptions, allow the work to challenge them, and combine your new knowledge with your prior understandings. You have learned to converse with your reader when you are ready to make a reasoned, provisional commitment on paper.

In this chapter, we will expand the voices in the conversation to include literary scholars practiced in the art of interpretation. As is evident to those of you who have discovered the treasure of interpretive works in the library, many readers take pleasure in this art—*so* many that the reader who wants to listen in on a literary conversation recorded in books and articles may get intimidated by the range and quality of arguments that have already taken place. As one of our students said, "I wanted to write about Frost's poem 'The Death of the Hired Man,' but when I saw how many people had already written about it, I decided there was nothing left for me to say."

It's easy to feel that way, unless you have a way to think about these other readers as companions in conversation, and unless you remember that *your* experience of the work will be necessarily different from that of any other reader. It's important to remember that the ways we see significance in patterns of sound, image, event, and emotional reaction are in part personal, the result of our own backgrounds—age, class, ethnicity, and life experiences—and in part training and experience, resulting from an ongoing conversation about interpretation and meaning making that was going on long before we entered it and will go on long after we are no longer participants. Do you remember Kenneth Burke's description of the parlor gathering in Chapter 1? He envisioned the way we participate in literary studies as being in a room of people conversing, all contributing to and each changed by the interaction. We'd like you to recreate that scene in your imagination, adding to the room literary scholars, whom we will call "experienced" readers.

HOW EXPERIENCED READERS CAN ENRICH OUR READING EXPERIENCE

In a literary conversation, as in any other, not everyone has the same questions. However, the more you read the writing of experienced readers, the more obvious it will be that similar questions come up over and over again. In any list of questions you or your reading group might compose after having read a literary work, there are likely to be questions about text features, the author's life, the period and **culture** out of which the work emerged, the implications for gender, racial, class, or inter-generational relationships in the work, the way the structures of the work represent or fail to represent a significant pattern, or what patterns work their way from unconscious recesses to conscious images and behaviors in the work.

These questions can be categorized, and the categories can be identified with particular schools of literary criticism. Each school evolved as a method of looking for interpretive patterns and meanings in response to real reader questions and concerns. These methods are so rich and various that some scholars spend their careers testing the possibilities of a single interpretive method. Although literary theories, as methods of inquiring, are interesting in their own right, we are concerned here not so much with developing a thorough working knowledge of the various theories, but with helping you understand how reading the writing of experienced readers can enrich your experience of literature.

Reading publications of experienced readers can help us:

- Explore the range of possibilities and variety of questions asked by expert readers.
- Consider ways in which critical dialogues precipitate interesting and complicated answers to questions at issue.

- Discover new critical questions that emerge as works and readings are generated in reaction or resistance to each other.
- Develop options for integrating other critical voices into our own interpretive writing.

When we write our own essays, reading the work of experienced readers can help us:

- Investigate an observation that seems significant but for which we have no explanation.
- Provide a context for an observation that, alone, seems inconsequential.
- Cite an experienced reader to lend support to our interpretive statement.
- Cite an interpretive statement made by another reader in order to distance ourselves from it or refute it.
- Make use of a statement made by an experienced reader because it is a better expression of an idea than we could craft ourselves, one that offers clarity to our own observations.
- Trace the development of a pattern of thinking into which our interpretation seems to have a place.
- Explore an observed dilemma or paradox in terms of one or several critical paradigms that seem to explain it.

These are just some of the ways research can help us. The similarity among all of them is that the research *serves* our purpose, it does not *dictate* it. Writing a critical research essay, like writing all the essays described in this book, requires you to respond, reflect, analyze, and reason your way to a tentative answer to a question at issue.

EXERCISE 6.1. ENGAGING WITH A POEM

Read the poem that follows and note your responses in your reading notebook, reflecting, when it's helpful, on the questions you have practiced in earlier chapters:

What does this situation, person, or place remind me of?

Is the feeling created by the work one I've experienced before? If so, when?

What is the source or cause of the connection?

What is similar about the two experiences?

If no associations come to mind, you might ask:

How is it different from what I already know or have experienced?

What do I like, or not like, about it?

What in the work makes me uncomfortable, and why?

MATTHEW ARNOLD

Dover Beach

The sea is calm tonight.
The tide is full, the moon lies fair
Upon the straights; on the French coast the light
Gleams and is gone; the cliffs of England stand,
Glimmering and vast, out in the tranquil bay.
Come to the window, sweet is the night-air!
Only, from the long line of spray
Where the sea meets the moon-blanched land,
Listen! you hear the grating roar
Of pebbles which the waves draw back, and fling,
At their return, up the high strand,
Begin, and cease, and then again begin,
With tremulous cadence slow, and bring
The eternal note of sadness in.

Sophocles, long ago
Heard it on the Aegean, and it brought
Into his mind the turbid ebb and flow
Of human misery; we
Find also in the sound a thought,
Hearing it by this distant northern sea.

The Sea of Faith
Was once, too, at the full, and round earth's shore
Lay like the folds of a bright girdle furled.
But now I only hear

Its melancholy, long, withdrawing roar,
Retreating, to the breath
Of the night-wind, down the vast edges drear
And naked shingles of the world.

Ah, love, let us be true
To one another! for the world, which seems
To lie before us like a land of dreams,
So various, so beautiful, so new,
Hath really neither joy, nor love, nor light,
Nor certitude, nor peace, nor help for pain;
And we are here as on a darkling plain
Swept with confused alarms of struggle and flight,
Where ignorant armies clash by night.

EXERCISE 6.2. REFLECTING AND ANALYZING

1. Read the poem again, reflecting on the writer's choices, using the four main questions described in the section on "Reflecting" in Chapter 2 to guide your inquiry. Divide your reading notebook pages into two columns. On one side, write down all the questions that occur to you. Ask of particular images, how do they *relate* to or *conflict* with each other? Ask about words and phrases and punctuation, what is the *relationship* of these choices to the development of the poem? Ask about the **persona** of the poem, does the way he sees the sea *change* as the poem progresses? Think of as many questions as you can.

   On the other half of your paper, note possible answers to your questions. Jot down details or ideas that seem significant. Phrase these answers as questions if it helps, considering how the answers support or challenge your personal response and how they connect with or are supported by other features of the poem. If general statements about the poem's purpose or significance occur to you, write them down for later consideration.

2. Share the questions and answers with your reading group. What questions occurred to more than one reader? What

new answers emerged from the combination of responses offered by group members? What differences of opinion were expressed? What readings or ways of answering particular questions modified your own observations? Why?

3. Using all the notes you've generated, try to draft possible answers to the following questions:

   a. What statement might I make and develop that would contribute to an understanding of the poem's meaning and significance?
   b. What statement might I make that would connect my experience with the work to my self-awareness and/or my knowledge of the world?
   c. What assumptions underlie my drafted statements?

   These criteria will emerge from your knowledge and experience and may be concerned with issues as broad as how to be a good human being or as narrow in the disciplinary sense as what image or sound or structural choice works well in the poem as a whole. Talk to others in your reading group to try to identify the criteria implied by your interpretive statements and judgments of the work.

CRITICAL POSSIBILITIES EMERGE FROM OUR RESPONSES

The preceding exercise asks you to practice, once again, the arts of engagement, reflection, analysis, and argument that were introduced in chapters 2, 3, 4, and 5. As you ask yourselves about your experience of the poem, you will be reflecting on the possible sources of or explanations for your responses in your personal knowledge, the work's features, or the time and **culture** of the poem. In comparing your questions and responses to those of others, you will undoubtedly identify differences. One outcome of this comparison is that we understand better how our lives influence our readings. Another is typically that we enrich and complicate our own readings as we struggle to take into account and make sense of the observations and analyses of others. Another is that we become aware of challenges, either to our usual way of reading a work or to the way in which it has typically been read by others. These challenges become the critical questions that motivate the conversations of literary study, conversations that have at their center the issue of literary merit. Is it worth reading? If so, how? If so, why?

In one recent course, as students responded to "Dover Beach," they argued about whether the central **symbol**, the sea, was "compelling" or not. Some thought it irrelevant, a cliché, general enough to front many greeting cards for lovers or mourners. One saw it nostalgically, thinking about old war movies in which military men gaze at the sea over the ship-rails. Others were moved by the poem but seemed somewhat embarrassed by their reactions. The next day, the instructor began the discussion by asking that a student read the poem aloud. A woman who had been absent the prior day volunteered. She stood and began to read, but before she reached the last stanza, her eyes misted over and her voice trembled. She struggled to explain her reaction. "The way he sees the sea," she said, "is so overwhelming. My father was in World War II, and once in a while, when he talked about his experience, it sounded like this poem. He was a proud veteran, but he also remembered fear and darkness and confusion, and he wanted to come home." What accounts for these different responses? What do we bring to our reading that governs our emotional engagement and influences our reflection and analysis? How does our personal reading relate to our critical questions and methods?

Experienced readers bring previous experience and assumptions to their studies of literature. Often these prior experiences and assumptions become as much a part of the critical conversation as the competing interpretations of the work itself. What these readers bring to the work may directly affect the questions these critics may ask or the methodology they employ to answer the questions. By publishing their responses and the studies that their responses initiate, they may raise questions or offer perspectives that differ from those of other readers and thereby may enlarge or enrich the experience of reading the literary work.

The critical conversation about "Dover Beach" has been going on for a long time. This chapter includes two essays about the poem. The first, by Theodore Morrison, tells a tale that illustrates the way several imaginary critics come to evaluate the significance of "Dover Beach." In the second, Gerald Graff finds the conversation still going on and the issues still being defined as modern readers struggle to assign **value** and significance to literary works in a diverse and changing world. All readers of literature, it seems, continue to respond, reflect, and analyze as they attempt to explain for now, if not for always, what is worth reading, and how, and why.

EXERCISE 6.3. ASSIGNING VALUE AND SIGNIFICANCE

1. As you read the following article by Theodore Morrison, record your reactions and responses in your reading notebook. What is Morrison's concern? What does he want us

to do, think, feel, and know about the relationship between literature and criticism? About how we assign value to works? About the relationship between ourselves as readers and our ways of seeing?

2. (This part of the exercise might be divided among several groups, each taking responsibility for one professor.) For each of Morrison's professors, note the following: What is the purpose of literature? What are the criteria that identify literary significance? What kinds of evidence does each professor see as important to making his judgment? What judgment does each offer about the value of "Dover Beach" as literature?

Then look at the stories that Morrison constructs which describe these professors, their lives and experiences. Why has he chosen to include the information about each professor? What is the connection of each story to each critical judgment?

Finally, describe each professor's position on the poem's value and try to construct a thesis statement for an evaluative argument that would reveal both the criteria for the judgment and the judgment itself.

3. With volunteers acting as moderator and panel members, present a panel discussion among Morrison's professors. Whoever plays the moderator, Peter Prampton, should begin with an assertion he might make about the poem, using where appropriate the observations made by other professors, synthesizing them into a statement about the poem's significance. To get into character as a panel member, ask yourself what is relevant? What is irrelevant? What will you accept? What will you refute?

THEODORE MORRISON

Dover Beach Revisited
A New Fable for Critics

Early in the year 1939 a certain Professor of Educational Psychology, occupying a well-paid chair at a large endowed university, conceived a plot. From his desk in the imposing Hall of the Social Sciences where the Research Institute in Education was housed he had long burned with resentment against teachers of literature, especially against English departments. It seemed to him that the professors of English stood square across the path of his major professional ambition. His great desire in life was to introduce into the study, the teaching, the critical evaluation of literature some of the systematic method, some of the "objective procedure" as he liked to call it, some of the certainty of result which he believed to be characteristic of the physical sciences. "You make such a fetish of science," a colleague once said to him, "why aren't you a chemist?"—a question that annoyed him deeply.

If such a poem as Milton's "Lycidas" has a value—and most English teachers, even to-day, would start with that as a cardinal fact—then that value must be measurable and expressible in terms that do not shift and change from moment to moment and person to person with every subjective whim. They would agree, these teachers of literature, these professors of English, that the value of the poem is in some sense objective; they would never agree to undertake any objective procedure to determine what that value is. They would not clearly define what they meant by achievement in the study of literature, and they bridled and snorted when anyone else attempted to define it. He remembered what had happened when he had once been incautious enough to suggest to a professor of English in his own college that it might be possible to establish norms for the appreciation of Milton. The fellow had simply exploded into a peal of histrionic laughter and then had tried to wither him with an equally histrionic look of incredulity and disgust.

He would like to see what would happen if the teachers of English were forced or lured, by some scheme or other, into a public exposure of their position. It would put them in the light of intellectual charlatanism, nothing less . . . and suddenly Professor Chartly (for so he was nicknamed) began to see his way.

It was a simple plan that popped into his head, simple yet bold and practical. It was a challenge that could not be refused. A strategically placed friend in one of the large educational foundations could be counted on: there would be money for clerical expenses, for travel if need be. He took his pipe from his pocket, filled it, and began to puff exultantly. To-morrow he must broach the scheme to one or two colleagues; to-night, over cheese and beer, would not be too soon. He reached for the telephone.

The plan that he unfolded to his associates that evening aroused considerable skepticism at first, but gradually they succumbed to his enthusiasm. A number of well-known professors of literature at representative colleges up and down the land would be asked to write a critical evaluation of a poem prominent enough to form part of the standard reading in all large English courses. They would be asked to state the criteria on which they based their judgment. When all the answers had been received the whole dossier would be sent to a moderator, a trusted elder statesman of education, known everywhere for his dignity, liberality of intelligence, and long experience. He would be asked to make a preliminary examination of all the documents and to determine from the point of view of a teacher of literature whether they provided any basis for a common understanding. The moderator would then forward all the documents to Professor Chartly, who would make what in his own mind he was frank to call a more scientific analysis. Then the jaws of the trap would be ready to spring.

Once the conspirators had agreed on their plot their first difficulty came in the choice of a poem. Suffice it to say that someone eventually hit on Arnold's "Dover Beach," and the suggestion withstood all attack. "Dover Beach" was universally known, almost universally praised; it was remote enough so that contemporary jealousies and cults were not seriously involved, yet near enough not to call for any special expertness, historical or linguistic, as a prerequisite for judgment; it was generally given credit for skill as a work of art, yet it contained also, in its author's own phrase, a "criticism of life."

Rapidly in the days following the first meeting the representative teachers were chosen and invited to participate in the plan. Professional courtesy seemed to require the inclusion of an Arnold expert. But the one selected excused himself from producing a value judgment of "Dover Beach" on the ground that he was busy investigating a fresh clue to the identity of "Marguerite." He had evidence that the woman in question, after the episode hinted at in the famous poems, had married her deceased sister's husband, thus perhaps affecting Arnold's views on a social question about which he had said a good deal in his prose writings. The expert pointed out that he had been given a half-year's leave of absence and a research grant to pursue the shadow of Marguerite through Europe, wherever it might lead him. If only war did not break out he hoped to complete this research and solve one of the vexing problems that had always confronted Arnold's biographers. His energies would be too much engaged in this special investigation to deal justly with the more general questions raised by Professor Chartly's invitation. But he asked to be kept informed, since the results of the experiment could not fail to be of interest to him.

After a few hitches and delays from other quarters, the scheme was ripe. The requests were mailed out, and the Professor of Educational Psychology sat back in grim confidence to await the outcome.

II

It chanced that the first of the representative teachers who received and answered Professor Chartly's letter was thought of on his own campus as giving off a distinct though not unpleasant odor of the ivory tower. He would have resented the imputation himself. At forty-five Bradley Dewing was handsome in a somewhat speciously virile style, graying at the temples, but still well-knit and active. He prided himself on being able to beat most of his students at tennis; once a year he would play the third or fourth man on the varsity and go down to creditable defeat with some elegiac phrases on the ravages of time. He thought of himself as a man of the world; it was well for his contentment, which was seldom visibly ruffled, that he never heard the class mimic reproducing at a fraternity house or beer parlor his manner of saying: "After all, gentlemen, it is pure poetry that lasts. We must never forget the staying power of pure art." The class mimic never represents the whole of class opinion but he can usually make everyone within earshot laugh.

Professor Dewing could remember clearly what his own teachers had said about "Dover Beach" in the days when he was a freshman in college himself, phrases rounded with distant professional unction: faith and doubt in the Victorian era; disturbing influence of Darwin on religious belief; Browning the optimist; Tennyson coming up with firm faith after a long struggle in the waters of doubt; Matthew Arnold, prophet of skepticism. How would "Dover Beach" stack up now as a poem? Pull Arnold down from the shelf and find out.

Ah, yes, how the familiar phrases came back. The sea is calm, the tide is full, the cliffs of England stand. . . . And then the lines he particularly liked:

> Come to the window, sweet is the night air!
> Only, from the long line of spray
> Where the ebb meets the moon-blanch'd sand,
> Listen! you hear the grating roar
> Of pebbles which the waves draw back, and fling,
> At their return, up the high strand,
> Begin, and cease, and then again begin,
> With tremulous cadence slow . . .

Good poetry, that! No one could mistake it. Onomatopoeia was a relatively cheap effect most of the time. Poe, for instance: "And the silken sad uncertain rustling of each purple curtain." Anyone could put a string of s's together and make them rustle. But these lines in "Dover Beach" were different. The onomatopoeia was involved in the whole scene, and it in turn involved the whole rhythmical movement of the verse, not the mere noise made by the consonants or vowels as such. The pauses—only, listen, draw back, fling, begin, cease—how they infused a subdued melancholy into the moonlit panorama at the same time that they gave it the utmost physical reality by suggesting the endless iteration of the waves! And then the phrase "With tremulous cadence slow" coming as yet one more touch, one "fine excess," when it seemed that every phrase and pause the scene could bear had already been lavished on it: that was Miltonic, Virgilian.

But the rest of the poem?

> The Sea of Faith
> Was once, too, at the full, and round earth's shore
> Lay like the folds of a bright girdle furl'd . . .

Of course Arnold had evoked the whole scene only to bring before us this metaphor of faith in its ebb-tide. But that did not save the figure from triteness and from an even more fatal vagueness. Everything in second-rate poetry is compared to the sea: love is as deep, grief as salty, passion as turbulent. The sea may look like a bright girdle sometimes, though Professor Dewing did not think it particularly impressive to say so. And in what sense is *faith* a bright girdle? Is it the function of faith to embrace, to bind, to hold up a petticoat, or what? And what is the faith that Arnold has in mind? The poet evokes no precise concept of it. He throws us the simple, undifferentiated word, unites its loose emotional connotations with those of the sea, and leaves the whole matter there. And the concluding figure of "Dover Beach":

we are here as on a darkling plain
Swept with confused alarms of struggle and flight,
Where ignorant armies clash by night.

Splendid in itself, this memorable image. But the sea had been forgotten now; the darkling plain had displaced the figure from which the whole poem tacitly promised to evolve. It would not have been so if John Donne had been the craftsman. A single bold yet accurate analogy, with constantly developing implications, would have served him for the whole poem.

Thus mused Professor Dewing, the lines of his verdict taking shape in his head. A critic of poetry of course was not at liberty to pass judgment on a poet's thought; he could only judge whether, in treating of the thought or sensibility he had received from his age, the poet had produced a satisfactory work of art. Arnold, Professor Dewing felt, had not been able to escape from the didactic tone or from a certain commonness and vagueness of expression. With deep personal misgivings about his position in a world both socially and spiritually barbarous, he had sought an image for his emotion, and had found it in the sea—a natural phenomenon still obscured by the drapings of conventional beauty and used by all manner of poets to express all manner of feelings. "Dover Beach" would always remain notable, Professor Dewing decided, as an expression of Victorian sensibility. It contained lines of ever memorable poetic skill. But it could not, he felt, be accepted as a uniformly satisfactory example of poetic art.

III

It was occasionally a source of wonder to those about him just why Professor Oliver Twitchell spent so much time and eloquence urging that man's lower nature must be repressed, his animal instincts kept in bounds by the exertion of the higher will. To the casual observer, Professor Twitchell himself did not seem to possess much animal nature. It seemed incredible that a desperate struggle with powerful bestial passions might be going on at any moment within his own slight frame, behind his delicate white face in which the most prominent feature was the octagonal glasses that focused his eyes on the outside world. Professor Twitchell was a good deal given to discipleship but not much to friendship. He had himself been a disciple of the great Irving Babbitt, and he attracted a small number of disciples among his own more earnest students. But no one knew him well. Only one of his colleagues, who took a somewhat sardonic interest in the mysteries of human nature, possessed a possible clue to the origin of his efforts to repress man's lower nature and vindicate his higher. This colleague had wormed his way sufficiently into Oliver Twitchell's confidence to learn about his family, which he did not often mention. Professor Twitchell, it turned out, had come of decidedly unacademic stock. One of his brothers was the chief salesman for a company that made domestic fire-alarm appliances. At a moment's notice he would whip out a sample from his bag or pocket, plug it into the nearest electric outlet, and while the bystanders waited in terrified suspense, would explain that in the dead of night, if the house caught fire, the thing would go off with a whoop loud enough to warn the soundest sleeper. Lined up with his whole string of brothers and sisters, all older than he, all abounding in spirits, Professor Twitchell looked like the runt of the litter. His colleague decided that he must have had a very hard childhood, and that it was not his own animal nature that he needed so constantly to repress, but his family's.

Whatever the reasons, Professor Twitchell felt no reality in the teaching of literature except as he could extract from it definitions and illustrations of man's moral struggle in the world. For him recent history had been a history of intellectual confusion and degradation, and hence of social confusion and degradation. Western thought had fallen into a heresy. It had failed to maintain the fundamental grounds of a true humanism. It had blurred the distinction between man, God, and nature. Under the influence of the sciences, it had set up a monism in which the moral as well as the physical constitution of man was included within nature and the laws of nature. It had, therefore, exalted man as naturally good, and exalted the free expression of all his impulses. What were the results of this heresy? An age, complained Professor Twitchell bitterly, in which young women talked about sexual perversions at the dinner table, an age in which everyone agreed that society was in dissolution and insisted on the privilege of being dissolute, an age without any common standards of value in morals or art; an age, in short, without discipline, without self-restraint in private life or public.

Oliver Twitchell when he received Professor Chartly's envelope sat down with a strong favorable predisposition toward his task. He accepted wholeheartedly Arnold's attitude toward literature: the demand that poetry should be serious, that it should present us with a criticism of life, that it should be measured by standards not merely personal, but in some sense *real*.

"Dover Beach" had become Arnold's best-known poem, admired as his masterpiece. It would surely contain, therefore, a distillation of his attitude. Professor Twitchell pulled down his copy of Arnold and began to read; and as he read he felt himself overtaken by surprised misgiving. The poem began well enough. The allusion to Sophocles, who had heard the sound of the retreating tide by the Aegean centuries ago, admirably prepared the groundwork of high seriousness for a poem which would culminate in a real criticism of human experience. But did the poem so culminate? It was true that the world

Hath really neither joy, nor love, nor light, . . .
Nor certitude, nor peace, nor help for pain

if one meant the world as the worlding knows it, the man who conducts his life by unreflective natural impulse. Such a man will soon enough encounter the disappointments of ambition, the instability of all bonds and ties founded on nothing firmer than passion or self-interest. But this incertitude of the world, to a true disciple of culture, should become a means of self-discipline. It should lead him to ask how life may be purified and ennobled, how we may by wisdom and self-restraint oppose to the accidents of the world a true human culture based on the exertion of a higher will. No call to such a positive moral will, Professor Twitchell reluctantly discovered, can be heard in "Dover Beach."

Man is an ignorant soldier struggling confusedly in a blind battle. Was this the culminating truth that Arnold the poet had given men in his masterpiece? Professor Twitchell sadly revised his value-judgment of the poem. He could not feel that in his most widely admired performance Arnold had seen life steadily or seen it whole; rather he had seen it only on its worldly side, and seen it under an aspect of terror. "Dover Beach" would always be justly respected for its poetic art, but the famous lines on Sophocles better exemplified the poet as a critic of life.

IV

As a novelist still referred to in his late thirties as "young" and "promising," Rudolph Mole found himself in a curious relation toward his academic colleagues. He wrote for the public, not for the learned journals; hence he was spared the necessity of becoming a pedant. At the same time the more lucrative fruits of pedantry were denied to him by his quiet exclusion from the guild. Younger men sweating for promotion, living in shabby genteel poverty on yearly appointments, their childless wives mimicking their academic shoptalk in bluestocking phrases, would look up from the stacks of five-by-three cards on which they were constantly accumulating notes and references, and would say to him, "You don't realize how lucky you are, teaching composition. You aren't expected to know anything." Sometimes an older colleague, who had passed through several stages of the mysteries of preferment, would belittle professional scholarship to him with an elaborate show of graciousness and envy. "We are all just pedants," he would say. "You teach the students what they really want and need." Rudolph noticed that the self-confessed pedant went busily on publishing monographs and being promoted, while he himself remained, year by year, the English Department's most eminent poor relation.

He was not embittered. His dealings with students were pleasant and interesting. There was a sense of reality and purpose in trying to elicit from them a better expression of their thoughts, trying to increase their understanding of the literary crafts. He could attack their minds on any front he chose, and he could follow his intellectual hobbies as freely as he liked, without being confined to the artificial boundaries of a professional field of learning.

Freud, for example. When Professor Chartly and his accomplices decided that a teacher of creative writing should be included in their scheme and chose Rudolph Mole for the post, they happened to catch him at the height of his enthusiasm for Freud. Not that he expected to psychoanalyze authors through their works; that, he avowed, was not his purpose. You can't deduce the specific secrets of a man's life, he would cheerfully admit, by trying to fit his works into the text-book patterns of complexes and psychoses. The critic, in any case, is interested only in the man to the extent that he is involved in his work. But everyone agrees, Rudolph maintained, that the man is involved in his work. Some part of the psychic constitution of the author finds expression in every line that he writes. We can't understand the work unless we can understand the psychic traits that have gained expression in it. We may never be able to trace back these traits to their ultimate sources and causes, probably buried deep in the author's childhood. But we need to gain as much light on them as we can, since they appear in the work we are trying to apprehend, and determine its character. This is what criticism has always sought to do. Freud simply brings new light to the old task.

Rudolph was fortunate enough at the outset to pick up at the college bookstore a copy of Mr. Lionel Trilling's recent study of Matthew Arnold. In this volume he found much of his work already done for him. A footnote to Mr. Trilling's text, citing evidence from Professors Tinker and Lowry, made it clear that "Dover Beach" may well have been written in 1850, some seventeen years before it was first published. This, for Rudolph's purposes, was a priceless discovery. It meant that all the traditional talk about the poem was largely null and void. The poem was not a repercussion of the bombshell that Darwin dropped on the religious sensibilities of the Victorians. It was far more deeply personal and individual than that. Perhaps when Arnold published it his own sense of what it expressed or how it would be understood had changed. But clearly the poem came into being as an expression of what Arnold felt to be the particular kind of affection and passion he needed from a woman. It was a love poem, and took its place with utmost naturalness, once the clue had been given, in the group of similar and related poems addressed to "Marguerite." Mr. Trilling summed up in a fine sentence one strain in these poems, and the principal strain in "Dover Beach," when he wrote that for Arnold "fidelity is a word relevant only to those lovers who see the world as a place of sorrow and in their common suffering require the comfort of constancy."

> Ah, love, let us be true
> To one another! for the world . . .
> Hath really neither joy, nor love, nor light . . .

The point was unmistakable. And from the whole group of poems to which "Dover Beach" belonged, a sketch of Arnold as an erotic personality could be derived. The question whether a "real Marguerite" existed was an idle one, for the traits that found expression in the poems were at least "real" enough to produce the poems and to determine their character.

And what an odd spectacle it made, the self-expressed character of Arnold as a lover! The ordinary degree of aggressiveness, the normal joy of conquest and possession, seemed to be wholly absent from him. The love he asked for was essentially a protective love, sisterly or motherly; in its unavoidable ingredient of passion he felt a constant danger, which repelled and unsettled him. He addressed Marguerite as "My sister!" He avowed and deplored his own womanish fits of instability:

> I too have wish'd, no woman more,
> This starting, feverish heart, away.

He emphasized his nervous anguish and contrary impulses. He was a "teas'd o'erlabour'd heart," "an aimless unallay'd Desire." He could not break through his fundamental isolation and submerge himself in another human soul, and he believed that all men shared this plight:

> Yes: in the sea of life enisl'd
> With echoing straits between us thrown,
> Dotting the shoreless watery wild,
> We mortal millions live *alone*.

He never "without remorse" allowed himself

To haunt the place where passions reign,

yet it was clear that whether he had ever succeeded in giving himself up wholeheartedly to a passion, he had wanted to. There could hardly be a more telltale phrase than "Once-long'd-for storms of love."

In short much more illumination fell on "Dover Beach" from certain other verses of Arnold's than from Darwin and all his commentators:

> Truth—what is truth? Two bleeding hearts
> Wounded by men, by Fortune tried,
> Outwearied with their lonely parts,
> Vow to beat henceforth side by side.
>
> The world to them was stern and drear;
> Their lot was but to weep and moan.
> Ah, let them keep their faith sincere,
> For neither could subsist alone!

Here was the nub. "Dover Beach" grew directly from and repeated the same emotion, but no doubt generalized and enlarged this emotion, sweeping into one intense and far-reaching conviction of insecurity not only Arnold's personal fortunes in love, but the social and religious faith of the world he lived in. That much could be said for the traditional interpretation.

Of course, as Mr. Trilling did not fail to mention, anguished love affairs, harassed by mysterious inner incompatibilities, formed a well-established literary convention. But the fundamental scene of insecurity in "Dover Beach" was too genuine, too often repeated in other works, to be written off altogether to that account. The same sense of insecurity, the same need for some rock of protection, cried out again and again, not merely in Arnold's love poems but in his elegies, reflective pieces, and fragments of epic as well. Whenever Arnold produced a genuine and striking burst of poetry, with the stamp of true self-expression on it, he seemed always to be in the dumps. Everywhere dejection, confusion, weakness, contention of soul. No adequate cause could be found in the events of Arnold's life for such an acute sense of incertitude; it must have been of psychic origin. Only in one line of effort this fundamental insecurity did not hamper, sadden, or depress him, and that was in the free play of his intelligence as a critic of letters and society. Even there, if it did not hamper his efforts, it directed them. Arnold valiantly tried to erect a barrier of culture against the chaos and squalor of society, against the contentiousness of men. What was this barrier but an elaborate protective devise?

The origin of the psychic pattern that expressed itself in Arnold's poems could probably never be discovered. No doubt the influence that Arnold's father exercised over his emotions and his thinking even though Arnold rebelled to the extent at least of casting off his father's religious beliefs, was of great importance. But much more would have to be known to give a definite clue—more than ever could be known. Arnold was secure from any attempt to spy out the heart of his mystery. But if criticism could not discover the cause, it could assess the result, and could do so (thought Rudolph Mole) with greater understanding by an attempt, with up-to-date psychological aid, to delve a little deeper into the essential traits that manifested themselves in that result.

V

In 1917 Reuben Hale, a young instructor in a western college, had lost his job and done time in the penitentiary for speaking against conscription and for organizing pacifist demonstrations. In the twenties he had lost two more academic posts for his sympathies with Soviet Russia and his inability to forget his Marxist principles while teaching literature. His contentious, eager, lovable, exasperating temperament tried the patience of one college administration after another. As he advanced into middle age, and his growing family suffered repeated upheavals, his friends began to fear that his robust quarrels with established order would leave him a penniless outcast at fifty. Then he was invited to take a flattering post at a girls' college known for its liberality of views. The connection proved surprisingly durable; in fact it became Professor Hale's turn to be apprehensive. He began to be morally alarmed at his own security, to fear that the bourgeois system which he had attacked so valiantly had somehow outwitted him and betrayed him into allegiance. When the C.I.O. made its initial drive and seemed to be carrying everything before it, he did his best to unseat himself again by rushing joyfully to the nearest picket lines and getting himself photographed by an alert press. Even this expedient failed, and he reconciled himself, not without wonder, to apparent academic permanence.

On winter afternoons his voice could be heard booming out through the closed door of his study to girls who came to consult him on all manner of subjects, from the merits of Plekhanov as a Marxist critic to their own most personal dilemmas. They called him Ben; he called them Smith, Jones, and Robinson. He never relaxed his cheerful bombardment of the milieu into which they were born, and of the larger social structure which made bourgeois wealth, bourgeois art, morals, and religion possible. But when a sophomore found herself pregnant it was to Professor Hale that she came for advice. Should she have an abortion or go through with it and heroically bear the social stigma? And it was Professor Hale who kept the affair from the Dean's office and the newspapers, sought out the boy, persuaded the young couple that they were desperately in love with each other, and that pending the revolution a respectable marriage would be the most prudent course, not to say the happiest.

James Joyce remarks of one of his characters that she dealt with moral problems as a cleaver deals with meat. Professor Hale's critical methods were comparably simple and direct. Literature, like the other arts, is in form and substance a product of society, and reflects the structure of society. The structure of society is a class structure: it is conditioned by the mode of production of goods, and by the legal conventions of ownership and control by which the ruling class keeps itself in power and endows itself with the necessary freedom to exploit men and materials for profit. A healthy literature, in a society so constituted, can exist only if writers perceive the essential economic problem and ally themselves firmly with the working class.

Anyone could see the trouble with Arnold. His intelligence revealed to him the chaos that disrupted the society about him; the selfishness and brutality of the ruling class; the ugliness of the world which the industrial revolution had created, and which imperialism and "liberalism" were extending. Arnold was at his best in his critical satire of this world and of the ignorance of those who governed it. But his intelligence far outran his will, and his defect of will finally blinded his intelligence. He was too much a child of his class to disown it and fight his way to a workable remedy for social injustice. He caught a true vision of himself and of his times as standing between "two worlds, one dead, one powerless to be born." But he had not courage or stomach enough to lend his own powers to the birth struggle. Had he thrown in his sympathies unreservedly with the working class, and labored for the inescapable revolution, "Dover Beach" would not have ended in pessimism and confusion. It would have ended in a cheerful, strenuous, and hopeful call to action. But Arnold could not divorce himself from the world of polite letters, of education, of culture, into which he had been born. He did his best to purify them, to make them into an instrument for the reform of society. But instinctively he knew that "culture" as he understood the term was not a social force in the world around him. Instinctively he knew that what he loved was doomed to defeat. And so "Dover Beach" ended in a futile plea for protection against the hideousness of the darkling plain and the confused alarms of struggle and flight.

Professor Chartly's envelope brought Reuben Hale his best opportunity since the first C.I.O. picket lines to vindicate his critical and social principles. He plunged into his answer with complete zest.

VI

When Peter Lee Prampton agreed to act as moderator in Professor Chartly's experiment he congratulated himself that this would be his last great academic chore. He had enjoyed his career of scholarship and teaching, no man ever more keenly. But now it was drawing to an end. He was loaded with honors from two continents. The universities of Germany, France, and Britain had first laid their formative hands on his learning and cultivation, then given their most coveted recognition to its fruits. But the honor and the glory seemed a little vague on the June morning when the expressman brought into his library the sizable package of papers which Professor Chartly had boxed and shipped to him. He had kept all his life a certain simplicity of heart. At seventy-four he could still tote a pack with an easy endurance that humiliated men of forty. Now he found himself giving in more and more completely to a lust for trout. Half a century of hastily snatched vacations in Cape Breton or the Scottish Highlands had never allowed him really to fill up that hollow craving to find a wild stream and fish it which would sometimes rise in his throat even in the midst of a lecture.

Well, there would be time left before he died. And meanwhile here was this business of "Dover Beach." Matthew Arnold during one of his American lecture tours had been entertained by neighbors of the Pramptons. Peter Lee Prampton's father had dined with the great man, and had repeated his conversation and imitated his accent at the family table. Peter himself, as a boy of nineteen or so, had gone to hear Arnold lecture. That, he thought with a smile, was probably a good deal more than could be said for any of these poor hacks who had taken Professor Chartly's bait.

At the thought of Arnold he could still hear the carriage wheels grate on the pebbly road as he had driven, fifty odd years ago, to the lecture in town, the prospective Mrs. Prampton beside him. His fishing rod lay under the seat. He chuckled out loud as he remembered how a pound-and-a-half trout had jumped in the pool under the clattering planks of a bridge, and how he had pulled up the horse, jumped out, and tried a cast while Miss Osgood sat scolding in the carriage and shivering in the autumn air. They had been just a little late reaching the lecture, but the trout, wrapped in damp leaves, lay safely beside the road.

It was queer that "Dover Beach" had not come more recently into his mind. Now that he turned his thoughts in that direction the poem was there in its entirety, waiting to be put on again like a coat that one has worn many times with pleasure and accidentally neglected for a while.

The sea of faith was once, too, at the full.

How these old Victorian battles had raged about the Prampton table when he was a boy! How the names of Arnold, Huxley, Darwin, Carlyle, Morris, Ruskin had been pelted back and forth by the excited disputants! *Literature and Dogma, God and the Bible, Culture and Anarchy.* The familiar titles brought an odd image into his mind: the tall figure of his father stretching up to turn on the gas lamps in the evening as the family sat down to dinner; the terrific pop of the pilot light as it exploded into a net of white flame, shaped like a little beehive; the buzz and whine of a jet turned up too high.

Ah, love, let us be true
To one another! for the world, which seems
To lie before us like a land of dreams,
So various, so beautiful, so new,
Hath really neither joy, nor love, nor light,
Nor certitude, nor peace, nor help for pain . . .

Peter Lee Prampton shivered in the warmth of his sunny library, shivered with that flash of perception into the past which sometimes enables a man to see how all that has happened in his life, for good or ill, turned on the narrowest edge of chance. He lived again in the world of dreams that his own youth had spread before him, a world truly various, beautiful, and new; full of promise, adventure, and liberty of choice, based on the opportunities which his father's wealth provided, and holding out the prospect of a smooth advance into a distinguished career. Then, within six months, a lavish demonstration that the world has neither certitude, nor peace, nor help for pain; his mother's death by cancer, his father's financial overthrow and suicide, the ruin of his own smooth hopes and the prospect instead of a long, hampered, and obscure fight toward his perhaps impossible ambition. He lived again through the night hours when he had tramped out with himself the youthful question whether he could hold Miss Osgood to her promise in the face of such reversals. And he did not forget how she took his long-sleepless face between her hands, kissed him, and smiled away his anxiety with unsteady lips. Surely everyone discovers at some time or other that the world is not a place of certitude; surely everyone cries out to some other human being for the fidelity which alone can make it so. What more could be asked of a poet than to take so profound and universal an experience and turn it into lines that could still speak long after he and his age were dead?

The best of it was that no one could miss the human feeling, the cry from the heart, in "Dover Beach"; it spoke so clearly and eloquently, in a language everyone could understand, in a form classically pure and simple. Or did it? Who could tell what any job-lot of academicians might be trusted to see or fail to see? And this assortment in Chartly's package might be a queer kettle of fish! Peter Lee Prampton had lived through the *Yellow Book* days of Art for Art's sake; he had read the muckrakers, and watched the rise of the Marxists and the Freudians. Could "Dover Beach" be condemned as unsympathetic with labor? Could a neurosis or a complex be discovered in it? His heart sank at the sharp sudden conviction that indeed these and worse discoveries about the poem might be seriously advanced. Well, he had always tried to go on the principle that every school of criticism should be free to exercise any sincere claim on men's interest and attention which it could win for itself. When he actually applied himself to the contents of Professor Chartly's bale he would be as charitable as he could, as receptive to light from any quarter as he could bring himself to be.

But the task could wait. He felt the need of a period of adjustment before he could approach it with reasonable equanimity. And in the meanwhile he could indulge himself in some long-needed editorial work on his dry-fly book.

CRITICAL APPROACHES AS METHODS OF INQUIRY

The previous exercises ask you to consider the possibilities of understanding and learning from others whose experiences, methods, and conclusions may differ from your own. Our predispositions lead us to see significance in different features, elements, facts. But in sharing our observations, we all see more. Seeing more possibilities, our conclusions about probable significance can be richer and more satisfying. When we identify questions we want to answer, it helps to know that others may have considered those questions from various **critical approaches**. In Morrison's essay, the perspectives include formalist, which looks at the features of a work to determine the way they work together to form a satisfyingly unified artistic composition; ethical, which looks at the way a work addresses moral imperatives thought to be shared by the human community; biographical/psychoanalytic, a combined perspective which relates information about authors and the emotional content of a work to paradigms for analyzing psychological states; and Marxist, which studies the presentation of power, especially economic power, in literary representations of social conditions. These are not the only ways of looking at texts, nor are these methods of reading mutually exclusive, though Morrison's article may make them seem so. Each method of reading offers us information about a literary work that can help us express, make more specific, or clarify our answers to our questions at issue.

EXERCISE 6.4. QUESTIONS AT ISSUE

The following questions were raised by a class studying "Dover Beach." Read the descriptions of **critical approaches** in Part B of the Appendix, the glossary of literary terms, and see if you can identify a school of criticism to which each question might belong. For each question, speculate about what information from outside the work itself might be necessary or helpful evidence in supporting an answer.

1. What techniques has the poet used to "bring/The eternal note of sadness in"?

2. What "ignorant armies" might he be talking about? Why this particular setting? What could be the particular causes of his feelings of doubt and despair?

3. What happens to the sea as the poem progresses?

4. How does the mention of Sophocles relate to the rest of the poem?

5. What is the woman in the poem supposed to represent? How is she a part of his "answer" to his despair?

6. Is this an anti-war poem?

7. What is the narrator's spiritual state of mind in relation to the "Sea of Faith"?

KINDS OF CRITICAL QUESTIONS EXPERIENCED READERS ASK

Your questions, like those which motivate the scholarship and criticism of experienced readers, concern the reader's relationship to the work, relationships among the elements and structures of the work itself, and the relationships between the work and information from other fields of inquiry. The following generic questions may help you reflect on and express your own questions at issue.

The Work as Experienced by Readers

In Chapter 3, you worked with questions that assume responsible readers will reflect on their own experience, will relate that to features of the work, and will bring to their observations their knowledge of and experience with other literary works. They are concerned with the relationship of the work to the reader or readers, with what is being said and how it is being understood.

1. How does this literary work affect readers? How does it accomplish this? What techniques contribute to this effect?

2. How does my own background and experience offer insight into my reading of this work? How does this work influence my understanding of my background and experience? What does my resistance to this work tell me about myself, the work, or the world of ideas in which the work is read or constructed?

The Work as Art

In Chapter 4 you practiced working with questions that allow you to examine the features of the work in the context of our knowledge about style's relationship to meaning. These questions focus your attention on the work as a work of art and help you discover how the parts fit the whole.

3. How does this work exemplify, modify, or reject the conventions of a particular **genre**, or describable literary form?

4. How do the elements of this individual literary work combine to form a satisfyingly unified artistic composition?

5. What underlying systems or structures of ideas are implicit in the work? How are these structures or systems fulfilled or undermined in the work?

The Work as Event

Literary works can be viewed as events taking place in time and space, involving writers and readers with lives and personalities. The next three questions assume that we can enlarge our understanding of a literary work by reflecting on how it emerged from a particular person in a particular time and place, and how it may fit into a particular literary tradition.

6. How does this work relate to a particular historical or cultural moment? What concerns of that historical or cultural moment might be reflected in the work?

7. What can we know about the writer that might help us understand the creation of or impulse for the work?

8. What literary traditions can we see this work as emerging from or contributing to? How do those traditions help us understand the origin or composition of the work?

The Work and Other Works

When we examine literary works in light of other works, we are looking for ways in which one work offers insight into another, or for connections between them that suggest some evolution of an idea, some give and take between writers in response to each others' words. When we tell stories to one another, each relates to the preceding one in some way, often developing, contradicting, or modifying what came before. In the same way, written works sometimes offer evidence of complicated and significant relationships with each other, whether those works are by the same author, by authors who share an acquaintance or a moment in history, or by authors distant in time and space, one of whom has influenced the other through the experience of reading. The following questions about **influence** or intertextuality, the technical term for relationships between works, invite various comparisons.

9. What else has the author written that might help us interpret his or her choices of word, image, and idea?

10. What other works, literary or non-literary, seem to address these concerns? How are they alike? How different?

11. What other works seem to have influenced the creation of this one? What allusions to other works can be identified, and what do they suggest about the work's meanings?

The Work and Other Ideas

Literary critics frequently ask questions that relate a work to ideas outside literature, putting literary studies in the context of other disciplines and fields of study and showing us how, despite our separate ways of looking at the world, we all share common concerns. The following interdisciplinary questions refer to specific subject areas, but the questions that relate literature to knowledge from other fields are as various as the fields themselves.

12. What does the work say about the concerns of or roles of women in the world? What does the work say about the relationships, especially power relationships, between men and women?

13. What can we learn by reading this work in terms of a particular psychological theory?

14. What assumptions about morals, ethics, or religious beliefs emerge from my reading of this work?

15. What questions or concerns from the field of politics, sociology, or law are being examined through the social and individual dynamics among characters, settings, and events of the work?

16. In what ways does the work challenge or affirm traditional assumptions about cultural privilege, race, and class? How does it raise issues about oppression, resistance, or cultural stereotypes?

Now, after you've considered the possible types of questions, we want to remind you that reading or writing critical research on literature is not a simple matter of discovering or choosing and applying a method of inquiry. Expert readers learn from each other. Though they bring different strategies to bear, they share the features of the work, and they build on each others' observations, verifying, extending, modifying, and challenging other readings.

The generic questions above aren't meant to classify arguments about literature, but they can help us probe a work for questions at issue, questions that may be hovering around the edges of our response but are difficult to call to the surface. In addition, they can help us articulate an issue that is more complicated than any one generic question can encompass, or see what expert readers are trying to accomplish when they combine different kinds of questions, which they almost always do.

Exercise 6.5. Questions Researchers Answer

The following articles on "Dover Beach" are listed in the *Modern Language Association Bibliography*. What do the titles suggest about the kinds of critical questions addressed in the articles?

Bell, Bill. "Arnoldian Culture in Transition: An Early Socialist Reading." *English Literature in Transition (1880–1920)* 35, no. 2 (1992): 141–161.

Gibson, Mary Ellis. "Dialogue on the Darkling Plain: Genre, Gender and Audience in Matthew Arnold's Lyrics." In *Gender and Discourse in Victorian Literature and Art*, ed. Antony H. Harrison and Beverly Taylor. De Kalb: Northern Illinois University Press, 1992, 30–48.

Holland, Norman N. "Psychological Depths and 'Dover Beach'." *Victorian Studies* 9 (1965), Supp., 5–28. Rejoinder by Wendell V. Harris, *Victorian Studies* 10, 70–76; reply by Holland, 76–82.

Roberts, Robin. "Matthew Arnold's 'Dover Beach,' Gender, and Science Fiction. *Extrapolation* 33, no. 3 (1992): 245–258.

Sharp, Ronald A. "A Note on Allusion in 'Dover Beach'." *English Language Notes* 21, no. 1 (Sept. 1983): 52–55.

Smidt, Kristian. "The Beaches of Calais and Dover: Arnold's Counterstatement to Wordsworth's Confession of Faith." *Victorian Poetry* 14 (1976): 256–257.

Mediating Critical Questions through Dialogue

We must not forget what seems to be an important matter for Morrison: **critical approaches** should help us answer *our* questions; they should not impede or displace our own engagement with or response to the work. In the following article, Gerald Graff argues that hearing the conversation among literary critics can enlarge and enrich the dialogue among students, indeed that the best place to mediate the various critical possibilities is in the literature classroom. This way, the assumptions and experiences that lead critics—other experienced readers beyond the class—to ask and answer questions in particular ways will be exposed, examined, and evaluated in terms of our own reading experience, which occurs within a unique historical, cultural, and personal context.

Exercise 6.6. Critical Dialogues

1. As you read the following article by Gerald Graff, note your own reactions and responses in your reading notebook. What is Graff's concern? What does he want us to

do, think, feel, and know about the relationship between literature and criticism? About how we assign value to works? About the relationship between ourselves as readers and our ways of seeing? About the literary curriculum in university courses?

2. For each of Graff's professors, note the following: What is the purpose of literature? Of literary criticism? What are the criteria that identify literary significance? What kinds of information does each professor see as important to making a judgment? What *are* their judgments about the value of "Dover Beach" as literature?

3. Describe each professor's position on the poem's value, and try to construct a thesis statement that would reveal both the criteria for the judgment and the judgment itself.

4. With the YFP's judgment in mind, reread the poem and locate evidence for her resistance to it and her interpretation of it. Imagine you are the woman student in the class who cried as she read it. Write or stage an imaginary dialogue between these two women.

GERALD GRAFF

Debate the Canon in Class

In the faculty lounge the other day, a dispute arose between a couple of my colleagues that typifies the warfare currently agitating the educational world. It began when one of our older male professors complained that he had just come from teaching Matthew Arnold's "Dover Beach" and had been appalled to discover that the poem was virtually incomprehensible to his class. Why, can you believe it, said the older male professor (let us call him OMP for short), my students were at a loss as to what to make of Arnold's famous concluding lines, which he proceeded to recite with slightly self-mocking grandiloquence:

Ah, love, let us be true
To one another! For the world, which seems
To lie before us like a land of dreams,
So various, so beautiful, so new,
Hath really neither joy, nor love, nor light,
Nor certitude, nor peace, nor help for pain;
And we are here as on a darkling plain
Swept with confused alarms of struggle and flight
Where ignorant armies clash by night.

My other colleague, a young woman who has just recently joined our department (let us call her YFP), replied that she could appreciate the students' reaction. She recalled that she had been forced to study "Dover Beach" in high school and had consequently formed a dislike for poetry that had taken her years to overcome. Why teach "Dover Beach" anyway? YFP asked.

Furiously stirring his Coffee-mate, OMP replied that in *his* humble opinion—reactionary though he supposed it now was—"Dover Beach" was one of the great masterpieces of the Western tradition, a work that, until recently at least, every seriously educated person took for granted as part of the cultural heritage. YFP retorted that while it might be so, it was not altogether to the credit of the cultural heritage. Take those lines addressed to the woman by the speaker, she said: "Ah love, let us be true/To one another . . . ," and so on. In other words, protect and console me, my dear—as we know it's the function of your naturally more spiritual sex to do—from the "struggle and flight" of politics and history that we men have regrettably been assigned the unpleasant duty of dealing with. YFP added that she would have a hard time finding a better example of what feminists mean when they speak of the ideological construction of the feminine as by nature private and domestic and therefore justly disqualified from sharing male power. Here, however, she paused and corrected herself: "Actually," she said, "we *should* teach 'Dover Beach'. We should teach it as the example of phallocentric discourse that it is."

OMP responded that YFP seemed to be treating "Dover Beach" as if it were a piece of political propaganda rather than a work of art. To take Arnold's poem as if it were a species of "phallocentric discourse," whatever that is, misses the whole point of poetry, OMP said, which is to rise above such local and transitory problems by transmuting them into universal structures of language and image. Arnold's poem is no more about gender politics, declared OMP, than *Macbeth* is about the Stuart monarchical succession.

But *Macbeth is* about the Stuart monarchical succession, retorted YFP—or so its original audience may well have thought. It's about gender politics too—why else does Lady Macbeth need to "unsex" herself before she can participate in murdering Duncan? Not to mention all the business about men born of women and from their mother's womb untimely ripped. The fact is, Professor OMP, that what you presume to be the universal human experience in Arnold and Shakespeare is male experience presented as if it were universal. You don't need to notice the politics of sexuality because for you patriarchy is the normal state of affairs. You can afford to ignore the sexual politics of literature, or so "transmute" them, as you put it, onto a universal plane, but that's a luxury I don't enjoy.

There are many possible ways to describe what happened here, but one of them would be to say that "theory" had broken out. What we have come to call "theory," I would suggest, is the kind of reflective discourse about practices that is generated when a consensus that was once taken for granted in a community breaks down. When this happens, assumptions that previously had gone without saying as the "normal state of affairs"—in this case the OMP's assumption that literature is above sexual politics—have to be explicitly formulated and argued about.

OMP would probably complain that this trend diverts attention from literature itself. But YFP could reply that literature itself was not being ignored in their debate but discussed in a new way. It was not that she and OMP stopped talking about poetry and started talking about theory. It was rather that, because their conflicting theoretical assumptions differed about how to talk about poetry, they had to talk about it in a way that highlighted those theories.

The recent prominence of theory, then, is a result of a climate of radical disagreement, and the complaint that theory is pervasive finally reduces to the complaint that literature and criticism have become too controversial. Yet the complaint only has the effect of generating more theory and more of the theoretical disagreement being deplored. Forced by the disagreement to articulate his principles, OMP, the traditional humanist, was "doing theory" just as much as was YFP, articulating assumptions that previously he could have taken as given. For this reason, the belief that the theory trend is a mere passing fad is likely to be wishful thinking.

The question is: Who and what are hurt by this situation? Who and what are damaged by conflicts like the one in the faculty lounge? The obvious answer would seem to be "Dover Beach." But just how well was "Dover Beach" doing in college (and high school) literature classes before radical teachers like YFP came along? We need only look at the complaint by OMP that triggered the lounge debate to be reminded that such classics have often inspired deep apathy in students even when taught in the most reverential fashion—perhaps especially when taught in that fashion.

Considered in this light, one might argue that "Dover Beach" has little to lose from the debate between OMP and YFP and a good deal to gain. In an odd way, YFP is doing "Dover Beach" a favor: In treating Arnold's poem as a significant instance of ideological mystification, her critique does more to make the poem a live issue in the culture again than does the respectful treatment of traditionalist teachers like OMP, which, as he himself complains, fails to arouse his class.

What the debate between OMP and YFP really threatens is not "Dover Beach," I think, but OMP's conception of "Dover Beach" as a repository of universal values that transcend the circumstances of its creation and reception. Whereas this decontextualized concept of culture was once axiomatic in humanistic education, it has now become one theory among others, a proposition that has to be argued for rather than taken as given. What is threatened by the canon controversy, in other words, is not the classics but their unquestioned status. But again, when the classics enjoyed that unquestioned status there is little evidence that it made them seem more compelling to students than they seem now. In short, from an educational point of view, the classics have less to fear from newfangled ideological hostility than from old-fashioned indifference.

What is most unfortunate about the conflict between OMP and YFP is not *that* it is taking place but *where* it is taking place, behind the educational scenes where students cannot learn anything from it. My thought as I watched OMP and YFP go back and forth in the faculty lounge was that if OMP's students could witness this debate they would be more likely to get worked up over "Dover Beach" than they are now. They might even find it easier to gain access to the poem, for the controversy over it might give them a context for reading it that they do not now possess.

Then again, it might not. The controversy would have to be presented in a way that avoids pedantry, obscurity, and technicality, and this is difficult to do. And even when it is done, many students will still have as much trouble seeing why they should take an interest in critical debates over "Dover Beach" as they do in seeing why they should take an interest in "Dover Beach" itself. The alienation of students from academic culture runs deep, and it may deepen further as the terms of that culture become more confusingly in dispute than in the past.

In such a situation, helping students gain access to academic discourse means clarifying conflicts like the one between OMP and YFP (and numerous others not so neatly polarized). If the goal is to help students become interested participants in the present cultural conversation instead of puzzled and alienated spectators, the aim should be to organize such conflicts of principle in the curriculum itself. They are, after all, only an extension of the real-life conflicts that students experience every day.

Just opening reading lists to noncanonical works—necessary as the step is—will not itself solve the problem. Replacing "Dover Beach" with *The Color Purple* does not necessarily help the student who has difficulty with the intellectual vocabularies in which both texts are discussed in the academic environment. What makes reading and interpretation difficult for many students is not the kind of text being read, whether canonical or noncanonical, highbrow or popular, but the heavily thematic and symbolic ways in which all texts, irrespective of status, are discussed in the academic setting. (The student phrase for it is "looking for 'hidden meaning.'") If the practice of looking for hidden meaning seems strange to you, it will seem no less strange to look for it in *The Color Purple* than in *Hamlet*.

This last point needs underscoring, because educational progressives have been too quick to blame student alienation from academic literacy on the elitist or conservative aspects of that literacy. But students can be as alienated from democratized forms of academic literacy as from conservative forms. What alienates these students is academic literacy *as such*, with its unavoidably abstract and analytical ways of talking and writing, regardless of whether that literacy is traditional or populist.

There is no question of occupying a neutral position here: In my view, the shift from the traditionalist to the revisionist view of culture is very much a change for the better. But from the vantage point of students who feel estranged from the intellectual life as such, revisionist culture can easily seem like the same old stuff in a new guise. To such students a feminist theorist and an Allan Bloom would seem far more similar to each other than to people like themselves, their parents, and friends. In the students' eyes, the feminist and Bloom would be just a couple of intellectuals speaking a very different language from their own about problems the students have a hard time regarding as problems.

The new climate of ideological contention in the university seems to me a sign of democratic vitality rather than a symptom of "disarray," relativism, and declining standards that the critics on the Right take it to be. But so far the university has failed to make a focused curriculum out of its contentiousness. For this reason, it is failing to tap its full potential for drawing students into its culture.

The best way to do this is to make the conflicts themselves part of the object of study. There are worse things that could happen to literature than having a passionate controversy erupt over it.

EXERCISE 6.7. JOINING A CRITICAL CONVERSATION

1. Graff says the problem with the debate between the YFP and the OMP is that it happens in the faculty lounge rather than the classroom. He speaks for student readers, saying that the debate about what's worth reading should include you because it is good for you. Imagine that you enter the lounge during the conversation. What do you say to the OMP? To the YFP? To Graff? Does Graff really speak for you, or would you argue the issue in another way?

2. Discuss your responses in your reading group, and then try to write an account of the group's conversation.

CRITICAL RESISTANCES: THE SIGNIFICANCE OF DIFFERENCES

It's often easier to find motivation and substance for constructing an argument about a literary work when you find it compelling, when you engage with and inquire about a work because it moves you, but you can learn a great deal about yourself, the work, and the world by reading past your resistances. You may have to overcome distances of space and time, accommodate unfamiliar language or language forms, or discover and bridge differences in **culture** or perspective. You will in some cases have to come to terms with characters or world views you initially find mystifying or even repugnant. All of this bridging allows you to practice the arts of interpretation—understanding differences, perceiving patterns, assigning significance, creating meaning where once there was incomprehension.

The YFP in Graff's article resisted the poem "Dover Beach." Why? Possibly because her most obvious way of identifying with the poem was by imagining herself in it, and when she tried to do that, she discovered that the role of the woman in the poem is not one she could easily accept. It's apparent that she rejected the role offered her by the **persona** of the poem. Literature reflects, through its assumptions and **characterizations**, a version of reality. The way we understand a literary work is, in a sense, to experience its version of reality. To do so, we must assent to its assumptions enough to imagine ourselves within that world. Once we have done so, we can identify the way the world is, or is not, validated or challenged by our own experiences and knowledge. The point of writing out your resistances is not to prove a work wrong or right, but to identify differences that are significant, differences that tell us something about what we value, whom we value, what we assume, whom we believe, whose vision is privileged over what other possibilities.

In the series of exercises that follow, you will be thinking about resistances. First, you will see how some literary works are written in response to others, and thus are themselves literary and critical works. Looking at works in relation to each other can help you learn to think about the alternative worlds literature presents and can help you understand which assumptions are easier, or more difficult, for you to accommodate. Second, you will be invited to practice examining your own resistances.

EXERCISE 6.8. LITERARY DIALOGUES

The following poem was written by Anthony Hecht as a resistant response to "Dover Beach." In it, the **persona** sees the narrator of "Dover Beach" as Matthew Arnold, and then identifies with the narrator, extending the scene and changing the role of the woman. As you read, note your responses, and watch for conflicts, relationships, and changes inside the poem. Then reread Hecht's poem, considering its relationship with Arnold's poem. What in Arnold's poem is Hecht responding to? What does he resist? What alternate vision does he offer?

ANTHONY HECHT
The Dover Bitch
A Criticism of Life

So there stood Matthew Arnold and this girl
With the cliffs of England crumbling away behind them,
And he said to her, "Try to be true to me,
And I'll do the same for you, for things are bad
All over, etc., etc."
Well now, I know this girl. It's true she had read
Sophocles in a fairly good translation
And caught that bitter allusion to the sea,
But all the time he was talking she had in mind
The notion of what his whiskers would feel like
On the back of her neck. She told me later on
That after a while she got to looking out
At the lights across the channel, and really felt sad,
Thinking of all the wine and enormous beds
And blandishments in French and the perfumes.
And then she got really angry. To have been brought
All the way down from London, and then to be addressed
As sort of a mournful cosmic last resort
Is really tough on a girl, and she was pretty.
Anyway, she watched him pace the room
And finger his watch chain and seem to sweat a bit,
And then she said one or two unprintable things.
But you mustn't judge her by that. What I meant to say is,
She's really all right. I still see her once in a while
And she always treats me right. We have a drink
And I give her a good time, and perhaps it's a year
Before I see her again, but there she is,
Running to fat, but dependable as they come,
And sometimes I bring her a bottle of Nuit d' Amour.

EXERCISE 6.9. JOINING A LITERARY CONVERSATION

1. Imagine a dialogue between the narrator and the anonymous woman. What do you learn about her, and about him, as you listen in on their conversation? Now imagine a dialogue between the narrator of Hecht's poem and the narrator of Arnold's. How is this poem a response to "Dover Beach"?

2. Go back to your notes about the poem. What, if anything, did you like? What, if anything, did you resist? Is there humor? How does Hecht give the woman in the poem a stronger voice? What role does the woman play in shaping the narrator's ideas about the world? What might Gerald Graff's YFP think about the role of the woman in this poem? Don't forget to consider the title: who or what is a bitch? What "criticism of life" is Hecht presenting?

3. Can you learn from a literary work that you resist? If so, how?

4. Is resistance a component of critical reading? Is it important to your reading of critical research? If so, why?

KINDS OF CRITICAL RESEARCH: PRIMARY AND SECONDARY

Usually we think of research as further study beyond the details of the work that increases our understanding of the work and the concerns of its writer. However, the close reading and analysis of the work we are studying is our first stage of research. When we read responsibly, we are researching the way the poem, play, or story works, what details it contains, and how it is organized. Because we are attempting to find all the information that will allow us to formulate an answer to our question at issue, we are conducting research. The critic may gather information about the historical period and society in which the work was written, the geography of the place in which the work was set, the psychological profile of the writer or a particular **character**, biographical details of a writer's life, the religious beliefs of the writer or the times, the way narratives were structured in different times and places and societies, and so forth. Like our study of the details of the work itself, the research that these critics have conducted is *primary research*, or the original investigation of materials.

You may think you will only be able to conduct primary research when you are analyzing the work you are studying, but there are many ways you can begin doing primary research beyond the work. One place to begin is with other writings by the same author, or you could read letters the writer wrote in which he or she discussed the issues addressed in the work. Scholars have compiled many collections of the letters of well-known writers. After reading in a critical essay that your author was experimenting with narrative structures based on the visual arts, you might find a book containing illustrations of the art work your author admired, and you might then examine the details of the forms. If **setting** is important to the work you are reading, you might find maps of the geographical area. If your author writes a story about a miller, you might read documents from the time period that explain what rank millers had in their society. If the writer is Roman Catholic and the work deals with religious issues, you might use the *Catholic Encyclopedia* to find a reference the writer includes. Because the meanings of words change over time, you might need to use the *Oxford English Dictionary*, which contains all the words in the English language and meanings from every time period since the year 1000. Any good library will offer access to such documents. In any case, remember that your purpose in conducting research is finding information that will help you draw conclusions to the questions you have about the work you are studying. When you conduct such research, you will be asking the kinds of questions literary critics ask and employing methods of inquiry that parallel those of published writers.

When we read each others' studies, what we are doing is *secondary research* or learning about the investigations conducted by others. When critics write essays, one of their reasons for doing so is to share their research in addition to presenting positions justified by their studies on questions at issue for the community of readers. Knowledge generated through one kind of inquiry can lead to new questions and discoveries by a reader practicing a different kind of inquiry. The following readings, a play and some critical comments reflecting on its significance, offer you the opportunity to see how critical readers of the work "see" significance and meaning differently and how their differences may echo the way the **characters** inside a literary work "see" significance and meaning differently.

As you read *Trifles*, a one-act drama by Susan Glaspell, think about what assumptions the **characters** make as they investigate the crime. What seems important to each of them? Then read the excerpts of critical essays about the play which follow. What assumptions does each critic make which guide their investigations of the work? What has significance for each of them?

SUSAN GLASPELL

Trifles

SCENE: *The kitchen in the now abandoned farmhouse of* JOHN WRIGHT, *a gloomy kitchen, and left without having been put in order—unwashed pans under the sink, a loaf of bread outside the breadbox, a dish towel on the table—other signs of incompleted work. At the rear the outer door opens, and the* SHERIFF *comes in, followed by the* COUNTY ATTORNEY *and* HALE. *The* SHERIFF *and* HALE *are men in middle life, the* COUNTY ATTORNEY *is a young man; all are much bundled up and go at once to the stove. They are followed by the two women—the* SHERIFF'S WIFE *first; she is a slight wiry woman, a thin nervous face.* MRS. HALE *is larger and would ordinarily be called more comfortable look- ing, but she is disturbed now and looks fearfully about as she enters. The women have come in slowly and stand close together near the door.*

COUNTY ATTORNEY (*rubbing his hands*): This feels good. Come up to the fire, ladies.

MRS. PETERS (*after taking a step forward*):   I'm not—cold.

SHERIFF (*unbuttoning his overcoat and stepping away from the stove as if to mark the beginning of official business*): Now, Mr. Hale, before we move things about, you explain to Mr. Henderson just what you saw when you came here yesterday morning.

COUNTY ATTORNEY: By the way, has anything been moved? Are things just as you left them yesterday?

SHERIFF (*looking about*): It's just the same. When it dropped below zero last night, I thought I'd better send Frank out this morning to make a fire for us—no use getting pneumonia with a big case on; but I told him not to touch anything except the stove—and you know Frank.

COUNTY ATTORNEY: Somebody should have been left here yesterday.

SHERIFF: Oh—yesterday. When I had to send Frank to Morris Center for that man who went crazy—I want you to know I had my hands full yester- day. I knew you could get back from Omaha by today, and as long as I went over everything here myself—

COUNTY ATTORNEY: Well, Mr. Hale, tell just what happened when you came here yesterday morning.

HALE: Harry and I had started to town with a load of potatoes. We came along the road from my place; and as I got here, I said, "I'm going to see if I can't get John Wright to go in with me on a party telephone." I spoke to Wright about it once before, and he put me off, saying folks talked too much anyway, and all he asked was peace and quiet—I guess you know about how much he talked himself; but I thought maybe if I went to the house and talked about it before his wife, though I said to Harry that I didn't know as what his wife wanted made much difference to John—

COUNTY ATTORNEY: Let's talk about that later, Mr. Hale. I do want to talk about that, but tell now just what happened when you got to the house.

HALE: I didn't hear or see anything; I knocked at the door, and still it was all quiet inside. I knew they must be up, it was past eight o'clock. So I knocked again, and I thought I heard somebody say, "Come in." I wasn't sure, I'm not sure yet, but I opened the door—this door (*indicating the door by which the two women are still standing*), and there in that rocker—(*pointing to it*) sat Mrs. Wright. (*They all looked at the rocker*).

COUNTY ATTORNEY: What—was she doing?

HALE: She was rockin' back and forth. She had her apron in her hand and was kind of—pleating it.

COUNTY ATTORNEY: And how did she—look?

HALE: Well, she looked queer.

COUNTY ATTORNEY: How do you mean—queer?

HALE: Well, as if she didn't know what she was going to do next. And kind of done up.

COUNTY ATTORNEY: How did she seem to feel about your coming?

HALE: Why, I don't think she minded—one way or other. She didn't pay much attention. I said, "How do, Mrs. Wright, it's cold, ain't it?" And she said, "Is it?"—and went on kind of pleating at her apron. Well, I was surprised; she didn't ask me to come up to the stove, or set down, but just sat there, not even looking at me, so I said, "I want to see John." And then she—laughed. I guess you would call it a laugh. I thought of Harry and the team outside, so I said a little sharp: "Can't I see John?" "No," she says, kind o' dull like. "Ain't he home?" says I. "Yes," says she, "he's home." "Then why can't I see him?" I asked her, out of patience. "'Cause he's dead," says she. "*Dead?* says I. She just nodded her head, not getting a bit excited, but rockin' back and forth. "Why—where is he?" says I, not knowing what to say. She just pointed upstairs—like that (*himself pointing to the room above*). I got up, with the idea of going up there. I walked from there to here—then I says, "Why, what did he die of?" "He died of a rope around his neck," says she, and just went on pleatin' at her apron. Well, I went out and called Harry. I thought I might—need help. We went upstairs, and there he was lyin'—

COUNTY ATTORNEY: I think I'd rather have you go into that upstairs, where you can point it all out. Just go on now with the rest of the story.

HALE: Well, my first thought was to get that rope off. It looked . . . (*Stops, his face twitches*) . . . but Harry, he went up to him, and he said, "No, he's dead all right, and we'd better not touch anything." So we went back downstairs. She was still sitting that same way. "Has anybody been notified?" I asked. "No," she says, unconcerned. "Who did this, Mrs. Wright?" said Harry. He said it businesslike—and she stopped pleatin' of her apron.

"I don't know," she says. "You don't *know*?" says Harry. "No," says she. "Weren't you sleepin' in the bed with him?" says Harry. "Yes," says she, "but I was on the inside." "Somebody slipped a rope round his neck and strangled him and you didn't wake up?" says Harry. "I didn't wake up," she said after him. We must 'a looked as if we didn't see how that could be, for after a minute she said, "I sleep sound." Harry was going to ask her more questions, but I said maybe we ought to let her tell her story first to the coroner, or the sheriff, so Harry went fast as he could to Rivers' place, where there's a telephone.

COUNTY ATTORNEY: And what did Mrs. Wright do when she knew that you had gone for the coroner?

HALE: She moved from that chair to this over here . . . (*Pointing to a small chair in the corner*) . . . and just sat there with her hands held together and looking down. I got a feeling that I ought to make some conversation, so I said I had come in to see if John wanted to put in a telephone, and at that she started to laugh, and then she stopped and looked at me—scared. (*The* COUNTY ATTORNEY, *who has had his notebook out, makes a note.*) I dunno, maybe it wasn't scared. I wouldn't like to say it was. Soon Harry got back, and then Dr. Lloyd came, and you, Mr. Peters, and so I guess that's all I know that you don't.

COUNTY ATTORNEY (*looking around*): I guess we'll go upstairs first—and then out to the barn and around there. (*to the* SHERIFF) You're convinced that there was nothing important here—nothing that would point to any motive?

SHERIFF: Nothing here but kitchen things.

The COUNTY ATTORNEY, *after again looking around the kitchen, opens the door of a cupboard closet. He gets up on a chair and looks on a shelf. Pulls his hand away, sticky.*

COUNTY ATTORNEY: Here's a nice mess.

The women draw nearer.

MRS. PETERS (*to the other woman*): Oh, her fruit; it did freeze. (*to the* COUNTY ATTORNEY) She worried about that when it turned so cold. She said the fire'd go out and her jars would break.

SHERIFF: Well, can you beat the women! Held for murder and worryin' about her preserves.

COUNTY ATTORNEY: I guess before we're through she may have something more serious than preserves to worry about.

HALE: Well, women are used to worrying over trifles.

The two women move a little closer together.

COUNTY ATTORNEY (*with the gallantry of a young politician*): And yet, for all their worries, what would we do without the ladies? (*The women do not unbend. He goes to the sink, takes a dipperful of water from the pail and, pouring it into a basin, washes his hands. Starts to wipe them on the roller towel, turns it for a cleaner place.*) Dirty towels! (*Kicks his foot against the pans under the sink.*) Not much of a housekeeper, would you say, ladies?

MRS. HALE (*stiffly*): There's a great deal of work to be done on a farm.

COUNTY ATTORNEY: To be sure, and yet . . . (*with a little bow to her*) . . . I know there are some Dickson county farmhouses which do not have such roller towels.

He gives it *a pull to expose its full length again.*

MRS. HALE: Those towels get dirty awful quick. Men's hands aren't always as clean as they might be.

COUNTY ATTORNEY: Ah, loyal to your sex, I see. But you and Mrs. Wright were neighbors. I suppose you were friends, too.

MRS. HALE (*shaking her head*): I've not seen much of her of late years. I've not been in this house—it's more than a year.

COUNTY ATTORNEY: And why was that? You didn't like her?

MRS. HALE: I liked her all well enough. Farmers' wives have their hands full, Mr. Henderson. And then—

COUNTY ATTORNEY: Yes—?

MRS. HALE (*looking about*): It never seemed a very cheerful place.

COUNTY ATTORNEY: No—it's not cheerful. I shouldn't say she had the homemaking instinct.

MRS. HALE: Well, I don't know as Wright had, either.

COUNTY ATTORNEY: You mean that they didn't get on very well?

MRS. HALE: No, I don't mean anything. But I don't think a place'd be any cheerfuller for John Wright's being in it.

COUNTY ATTORNEY: I'd like to talk more of that a little later. I want to get the lay of things upstairs now.

He goes to the left, where three steps lead to a stair door.

SHERIFF: I suppose anything Mrs. Peters does'll be all right. She was to take in some clothes for her, you know, and a few little things. We left in such a hurry yesterday.

COUNTY ATTORNEY: Yes, but I would like to see what you take, Mrs. Peters, and keep an eye out for anything that might be of use to us.

MRS. PETERS: Yes, Mr. Henderson.

The women listen to the men's steps on the stairs, *then look about the kitchen.*

MRS. HALE: I'd hate to have men coming into my kitchen, snooping around and criticizing.

She arranges the pans under the sink which the COUNTY ATTORNEY *had shoved out of place.*

MRS. PETERS: Of course it's no more than their duty.

MRS. HALE: Duty's all right, but I guess that deputy sheriff that came out to make the fire might have got a little of this on. (*gives the roller towel a pull*) Wish I'd thought of that sooner. Seems mean to talk about her for not having things slicked up when she had to come away in such a hurry.

MRS. PETERS (*Who has gone to a small table in the left rear corner of the room, and lifted one end of a towel that covers a pan*): She had bread set.

Stands still.

MRS. HALE (*eyes fixed on a loaf of bread beside the breadbox, which is on a low shelf at the other side of the room. Moves slowly toward it.*): She was going to put this in there. (*Picks up loaf, then abruptly drops it. In a manner of returning to familiar things.*) It's a shame about her fruit. I wonder if it's all gone. (*gets up on the chair and looks*) I think there's some here that's all right, Mrs. Peters. Yes—here; (*holding it toward the window*) this is cherries, too. (*looking again*) I declare I believe that's the only one. (*Gets down, bottle in her hand. Goes to the sink and wipes it off on the outside.*) She'll feel awful bad after all her hard work in the hot weather. I remember the afternoon I put up my cherries last summer.

She puts the bottle on the big kitchen table, center of the room. With a sigh, is about to sit down in the rocking-chair. Before she is seated realizes what chair it is; with a slow look at it, steps back. The chair which she has touched rocks back and forth.

MRS. PETERS: Well, I must get those things from the front room closet. (*She goes to the door at the right, but after looking into the other room, steps back.*) You coming with me, Mrs. Hale? You could help me carry them.

They go in the other room; reappear, MRS. PETERS *carrying a dress and skirt,* MRS. HALE *following with a pair of shoes.*

MRS. PETERS: My, it's cold in there.

She puts the clothes on the big table, and hurries to the stove.

MRS. HALE (*examining the skirt*): Wright was close. I think maybe that's why she kept so much to herself. She didn't even belong to the Ladies' Aid. I suppose she couldn't do her part, and then you don't enjoy things when you feel shabby. She used to wear pretty clothes and be lively, when she was Minnie Foster, one of the town girls singing in the choir. But that—oh, that was thirty years ago. This all you was to take in?

MRS. PETERS: She said she wanted an apron. Funny thing to want, for there isn't much to get you dirty in jail, goodness knows. But I suppose just to make her feel more natural. She said they was in the top drawer in this cupboard. Yes, here. And then her little shawl that always hung behind the door. (*opens stair door and looks*) Yes, here it is.

Quickly shuts door leading upstairs.

MRS. HALE (*abruptly moving toward her*): Mrs. Peters?

MRS. PETERS: Yes, Mrs. Hale?

MRS. HALE: Do you think she did it?

MRS. PETERS (*in a frightened voice*): Oh, I don't know.

MRS. HALE: Well, I don't think she did. Asking for an apron and her little shawl. Worrying about her fruit.

MRS. PETERS (*starts to speak, glances up, where footsteps are heard in the room above. In a low voice.*): Mr. Peters says it looks bad for her. Mr. Henderson is awful sarcastic in a speech, and he'll make fun of her sayin' she didn't wake up.

MRS. HALE: Well, I guess John Wright didn't wake when they was slipping that rope under his neck.

MRS. PETERS: No, it's strange. It must have been done awful crafty and still. They say it was such a—funny way to kill a man, rigging it all up like that.

MRS. HALE: That's just what Mr. Hale said. There was a gun in the house. He says that's what he can't understand.

MRS. PETERS: Mr. Henderson said coming out that what was needed for the case was a motive, something to show anger, or—sudden feeling.

MRS. HALE (*who is standing by the table*): Well, I don't see any signs of anger around here. (*She puts her hand on the dish towel which lies on the table, stands looking down at the table, one half of which is clean, the other half messy.*) It's wiped to here. (*Makes a move as if to finish work, then turns and looks at a loaf of bread outside the breadbox. Drops towel. In that voice of coming back to familiar things.*) Wonder how they are finding things upstairs? I hope she had it a little more redd-up up there. You know, it seems kind of *sneaking.* Locking her up in town and then coming out here and trying to get her own house to turn against her.

MRS. PETERS: But Mrs. Hale, the law is the law.

MRS. HALE: I s'pose 'tis. (*unbuttoning her coat*) Better loosen up your things, Mrs. Peters. You won't feel them when you go out.

MRS. PETERS *takes off her fur tippet, goes to hang it on hook at back of room, stands looking at the under part of the small corner table.*

MRS. PETERS: She was piecing a quilt.

She brings the large sewing basket and they look at the bright pieces.

MRS. HALE: It's log cabin pattern. Pretty, isn't it? I wonder if she was goin' to quilt it or just knot it?

Footsteps have been heard coming down the stairs. The SHERIFF *enters, followed by* HALE *and the* COUNTY ATTORNEY.

SHERIFF: They wonder if she was going to quilt it or just knot it!

The men laugh; the women look abashed.

COUNTY ATTORNEY (*rubbing his hands over the stove*): Frank's fire didn't do much up there, did it? Well, let's go out to the barn and get that cleared up.

The men go outside.

MRS. HALE (*resentfully*): I don't know as there's anything so strange, our takin' up our time with little things while we're waiting for them to get the evidence. (*She sits down at the big table, smoothing out a block with decision.*) I don't see as it's anything to laugh about.

MRS. PETERS (*apologetically*): Of course they've got awful important things on their minds.

Pulls up a chair and joins MRS. HALE *at the table.*

MRS. HALE (*examining another block*): Mrs. Peters, look at this one. Here, this is the one she was working on, and look at the sewing! All the rest of it has been so nice and even. And look at this! It's all over the place! Why, it looks as if she didn't know what she was about! (*After she has said this, they look at each other, then start to glance back at the door. After an instant* MRS. HALE *has pulled at a knot and ripped the sewing.*)

MRS. PETERS: Oh, what are you doing, Mrs. Hale?

MRS. HALE (*mildly*): Just pulling out a stitch or two that's not sewed very good. (*threading a needle*) Bad sewing always made me fidgety.

MRS. PETERS (*nervously*): I don't think we ought to touch things.

MRS. HALE: I'll just finish up this end. (*suddenly stopping and leaning forward*) Mrs. Peters?

MRS. PETERS: Yes, Mrs. Hale?

MRS. HALE: What do you suppose she was so nervous about?

MRS. PETERS: Oh—I don't know. I don't know as she was nervous. I sometimes sew awful queer when I'm just tired. (MRS. HALE *starts to say something, looks at* MRS. PETERS, *then goes on sewing.*) Well, I must get these things wrapped up. They may be through sooner than we think. (*putting apron and other things together*) I wonder where l can find a piece of paper, and string.

MRS. HALE: In that cupboard, maybe.

MRS. PETERS (*looking in cupboard*): Why, here's a birdcage. (*holds it up*) Did she have a bird, Mrs. Hale?

MRS. HALE: Why, I don't know whether she did or not—I've not been here for so long. There was a man around last year selling canaries cheap, but I don't know as she took one; maybe she did. She used to sing real pretty herself.

MRS. PETERS (*glancing around*): Seems funny to think of a bird here. But she must have had one or why should she have a cage? I wonder what happened to it?

MRS. HALE: I s'pose maybe the cat got it.

MRS. PETERS: No, she didn't have a cat. She's got that feeling some people have about cats—being afraid of them. My cat got in her room and she was real upset and asked me to take it out.

MRS. HALE: My sister Bessie was like that. Queer, ain't it?

MRS. PETERS (*examining the cage*): Why, look at this door. It's broke. One hinge is pulled apart.

MRS. HALE (*looking, too*): Looks as if someone must have been rough with it.

MRS. PETERS: Why, yes.

She brings the cage forward and puts it on the table.

MRS. HALE: I wish if they're going to find any evidence they'd be about it. I don't like this place.

MRS. PETERS: But I'm glad you came with me, Mrs. Hale. It would be lonesome for me sitting here alone.

MRS. HALE: It would, wouldn't it? (*dropping her sewing*) But I tell you what I do wish, Mrs. Peters. I wish I had come over sometimes when she was here. I—(*looking around the room*)—wish I had.

MRS. PETERS: But of course you were awful busy, Mrs. Hale—your house and your children.

MRS. HALE: I could've come. I stayed away because it weren't cheerful—and that's why I ought to have come. I—I've never liked this place. Maybe because it's down in a hollow and you don't see the road. I dunno what it is, but it's a lonesome place and always was. I wish I had come over to see Minnie Foster sometimes. I can see now—

Shakes her head.

MRS. PETERS: Well, you mustn't reproach yourself, Mrs. Hale. Somehow we just don't see how it is with other folks until—something comes up.

MRS. HALE: Not having children makes less work—but it makes a quiet house, and Wright out to work all day, and no company when he did come in. Did you know John Wright, Mrs. Peters?

MRS. PETERS: Not to know him; I've seen him in town. They say he was a good man.

MRS. HALE: Yes—good; he didn't drink, and kept his word as well as most, I guess, and paid his debts. But he was a hard man, Mrs. Peters. Just to pass the time of day with him—(*shivers*) Like a raw wind that gets to the bone. (*pauses, her eye falling on the cage*) I should think she would 'a wanted a bird. But what do you suppose went with it?

MRS. PETERS: I don't know, unless it got sick and died.

She reaches over and swings the broken door, swings it again. Both women watch it.

MRS. HALE: You weren't raised round here, were you? (MRS. PETERS *shakes her head.*) You didn't know—her?

MRS. PETERS: Not till they brought her yesterday.

MRS. HALE: She—come to think of it, she was kind of like a bird her-self—real sweet and pretty, but kind of timid and—fluttery. How—she—did—change. (*silence; then as if struck by a happy thought and relieved to get back to everyday things*) Tell you what, Mrs. Peters, why don't you take the quilt in with you? It might take up her mind.

MRS. PETERS: Why, I think that's a real nice idea, Mrs. Hale. There could-n't possibly be any objection to it, could there? Now, just what would I take? I wonder if her patches are in here—and her things.

They look in the sewing basket.

MRS. HALE: Here's some red. I expect this has got sewing things in it. (*brings out a fancy box*) What a pretty box. Looks like something somebody would give you. Maybe her scissors are in here. (*Opens box. Suddenly puts her hand to her nose.*) Why—(MRS. PETERS *bends nearer, then turns her face away.*) There's something wrapped up in this piece of silk.

MRS. PETERS: Why, this isn't her scissors.

MRS. HALE (*lifting the silk*): Oh, Mrs. Peters—it's—

MRS. PETERS *bends closer.*

MRS. PETERS: It's the bird.

MRS. HALE (*jumping up*): But Mrs. Peters—look at it. Its neck! Look at its neck! It's all—other side *to.*

MRS. PETERS: Somebody—wrung—its—neck.

Their eyes meet. A look of growing comprehension, of horror. Steps are heard out-side. MRS. HALE *slips box under quilt pieces, and sinks into her chair. Enter* SHERIFF *and* COUNTY ATTORNEY. MRS. PETERS *rises.*

COUNTY ATTORNEY (*as one turning from serious things to little pleas-antries*): Well, ladies, have you decided whether she was going to quilt it or knot it?

MRS. PETERS: We think she was going to—knot it.

COUNTY ATTORNEY: Well, that's interesting, I'm sure. (*seeing the birdcage*) Has the bird flown?

MRS. HALE (*putting more quilt pieces over the box*): We think the—cat got it.

COUNTY ATTORNEY (*preoccupied*): Is there a cat?

MRS. HALE *glances in a quick covert way at* MRS. PETERS.

MRS. PETERS: Well, not *now*. They're superstitious, you know. They leave.

COUNTY ATTORNEY (*to* SHERIFF PETERS, *continuing an interrupted conversation*): No sign at all of anyone having come from the outside. Their own rope. Now let's go up again and go over it piece by piece. (*They start upstairs.*) It would have to have been someone who knew just the—

MRS. PETERS *sits down. The two women sit there not looking at one another, but as if peering into something and at the same time holding back. When they talk now, it is in the manner of finding their way over strange ground, as if afraid of what they are saying, but as it they cannot help saying it.*

MRS. HALE: She liked the bird. She was going to bury it in that pretty box.

MRS. PETERS (*in a whisper*): When I was a girl—my kitten—there was a boy took a hatchet, and before my eyes—and before I could get there— (*covers her face an instant*) If they hadn't held me back, I would have— (*catches herself, looks upstairs where steps are heard, falters weakly*)—hurt him.

MRS. HALE (*with a slow look around her*): I wonder how it would seem never to have had any children around. (*pause*) No, Wright wouldn't like the bird—a thing that sang. She used to sing. He killed that, too.

MRS. PETERS (*moving uneasily*): We don't know who killed the bird.

MRS. HALE: I knew John Wright.

MRS. PETERS: It was an awful thing was done in this house that night, Mrs. Hale. Killing a man while he slept, slipping a rope around his neck that choked the life out of him.

MRS. HALE: His neck. Choked the life out of him.

Her hand goes out and rests on the birdcage.

MRS. PETERS (*with rising voice*): We don't know who killed him. We don't know.

MRS. HALE (*her own feeling not interrupted*): If there'd been years and years of nothing, then a bird to sing to you, it would be awful—still, after the bird was still.

MRS. PETERS (*something within her speaking*): I know what stillness is. When we homesteaded in Dakota, and my first baby died—after he was two years old, and me with no other then—

MRS. HALE (*moving*): How soon do you suppose they'll be through, looking for the evidence?

MRS. PETERS: I know what stillness is. (*pulling herself back*) The law has got to punish crime, Mrs. Hale.

MRS. HALE (*not as if answering that*): I wish you'd seen Minnie Foster when she wore a white dress with blue ribbons and stood up there in the choir and sang. (*a look around the room*) Oh, I *wish* I'd come over here once in a while! That was a crime! That was a crime! Who's going to punish that?

MRS. PETERS (*looking upstairs*): We mustn't—take on.

MRS. HALE: I might have known she needed help! I know how things can be—for women. I tell you, it's queer, Mrs. Peters. We live close together, and we live far apart. We all go through the same things—it's all just a different kind of the same thing. (*brushes her eyes; noticing the bottle of fruit, reaches out for it*) If I was you, I wouldn't tell her her fruit was gone. Tell her it *ain't*. Tell her it's all right. Take this in to prove it to her. She—she may never know whether it was broke or not.

MRS. PETERS (*takes the bottle, looks about for something to wrap it in; takes petticoat from the clothes brought from the other room, very nervously begins winding this around the bottle. In a false voice.*): My, it's a good thing the men couldn't hear us. Wouldn't they just laugh! Getting all stirred up over a little thing like a—dead canary. As if that could have anything to do with—with—wouldn't they *laugh!*

The men are heard coming downstairs.

MRS. HALE (under her breath): Maybe they would—maybe they wouldn't.

COUNTY ATTORNEY: No, Peters, it's all perfectly clear except a reason for doing it. But you know juries when it comes to women. If there was some definite thing. Something to show—something to make a story about—a thing that would connect up with this strange way of doing it.

The women's eyes meet for an instant. Enter HALE from outer door.

HALE: Well, I've got the team around. Pretty cold out there.

COUNTY ATTORNEY: I'm going to stay here a while by myself. (*to the* SHERIFF) You can send Frank out for me, can't you? I want to go over everything. I'm not satisfied that we can't do better.

SHERIFF: Do you want to see what Mrs. Peters is going to take in?

The COUNTY ATTORNEY *goes to the table, picks up the apron, laughs.*

COUNTY ATTORNEY: Oh, I guess they're not very dangerous things the ladies have picked up. (*Moves a few things about, disturbing the quilt pieces which cover the box. Steps back.*) No, Mrs. Peters doesn't need supervising. For that matter, a sheriff's wife is married to the law. Ever think of it that way, Mrs. Peters?

MRS. PETERS: Not—just that way.

SHERIFF (*chuckling*): Married to the law. (*moves toward the other room*) I just want you to come in here a minute, George. We ought to take a look at these windows.

COUNTY ATTORNEY (*scoffingly*): Oh, windows!

SHERIFF: We'll be right out, Mr. Hale.

HALE *goes outside. The* SHERIFF *follows the* COUNTY ATTORNEY *into the other room. Then* MRS. HALE *rises, hands tight together, looking intensely at* MRS. PETERS, *whose eyes take a slow turn, finally meeting* MRS. HALE'S. *A moment* MRS. HALE *holds her, then her own eyes point the way to where the box is concealed. Suddenly* MRS. PETERS *throws back quilt pieces and tries to put the box in the bag she is wearing. It is too big. She opens box, starts to take bird out, cannot touch it, goes to pieces, stands there helpless. Sound of a knob turning in the other room.* MRS. HALE *snatches the box and puts it in the pocket of her big coat. Enter* COUNTY ATTORNEY *and* SHERIFF.

COUNTY ATTORNEY (*facetiously*): Well, Henry, at least we found out that she was not going to quilt it. She was going to—what is it you call it, ladies?

MRS. HALE (*her hand against her pocket*): We call it—knot it, Mr. Henderson.

CURTAIN

READING THE RESEARCH: LISTENING TO DIVERSE CRITICAL VOICES

As experienced readers find and create meaning in response to Glaspell's play, they observe, analyze, and argue for the **value** of a particular reading. The insight each offers may come from close examination of the play's effects, language, historical origins, or relationship to other ideas or disciplines. Included in the critical excerpts which follow are references to a short story, "A Jury of Her Peers," which Glaspell wrote after the play and which includes all of the same **plot** events and **characters**. Although critics have argued that with the translation from the dramatic to the fictional form, shifts in theme and emphasis occur, the readers quoted here are concerned with the shared elements. Judith Fetterley and Elaine Hedges in fact discuss the story rather than the play, but their arguments are frequently cited in discussions of the play.

EXERCISE 6.10. ANALYZING RESEARCH ARGUMENTS

Read the following excerpts, thinking about the types of questions raised by each passage. In your reading notebook, identify the central critical questions you think each writer is asking. Then list the other types of questions they ask or answer in the process of exploring their issues. (Use the list of critical questions that appears earlier in this chapter to help you find and identify the questions explored in the passages.) Finally, compose or locate a thesis statement, either stated or implied, that you perceive to be guiding their observations and analyses. Share these questions and statements with your reading group. How similar are they? Which statement did you find most compelling?

LINDA BEN-ZVI

Excerpt 1

In the process of completing research for a bibliography of Susan Glaspell, I discovered the historical source upon which *Trifles* and "Jury" are based: the murder of a sixty-year-old farmer named John Hossack on December 2, 1900, in Indianola, Iowa. Glaspell covered the case and the subsequent trial when she was a reporter for the Des Moines *Daily News*, a position she began full time the day after she graduated from Drake University in June 1900, a twenty-four-year-old woman with a Ph.D. in philosophy and several years of newspaper work in Davenport and Des Moines behind her. Although her general beat was the Iowa statehouse, and she would later say that the experiences there provided her with sufficient material to quit her job a year later and turn to fiction, it was the Hossack murder case that was the central story of her brief journalistic career. . . .

[T]he Hossack killing . . . focuses on a woman accused of murder. The investigation and subsequent trial offers one more example of . . . the process by which juridical attitudes toward, and prosecution of, women are shaped by societal concepts of female behavior, the same concepts that may have motivated the act of murder. . . . Glaspell was actually a primary contributor to the shaping of public opinion about the woman being tried. The news accounts, therefore, offer more than an important contextual basis for approaching the fictional works. They also provide important biographical information about the author and her own personal and artistic evolution, and document the cultural shifts which took place between 1900 when the murder took place and 1916 when Glaspell wrote her play.

JUDITH FETTERLEY

Excerpt 2

The reason for the striking display of masculine incompetence in an arena where men are assumed to be competent derives from the fact that the men in question cannot imagine the story behind the case. They enter the situation bound by a set of powerful assumptions. Prime among these is the equation of textuality with masculine subject and masculine point of view. Thus, it is not simply that the men cannot read the text that is placed before them. Rather, they literally cannot recognize it as a text because they cannot imagine that women have stories. . . . . Minnie Foster Wright's kitchen is not a text to them, and so they cannot read it. . . .

Just as the women in the story have the capacity to read as men or as women, having learned by necessity how to recognize and interpret male texts, so are the men in the story presumably educable. Though initially they might not recognize a clue if they saw it, they could be taught its significance, they could be taught to recognize women's texts and to read as women. If this were not the case, the women in the text could leave the text as they find it; but they don't. Instead, they erase the text as they read it. Martha Hale undoes the threads of the quilt that, like the weaving of Philomel, tells the story of Minnie Wright's violation and thus provides the clue to her revenge; Mrs. Peters instinctively creates an alternate story to explain the missing bird and then further fabricates to explain the absent cat; and Mrs. Hale, with the approval of Mrs. Peters, finally hides the dead bird. . . .

Thus, Glaspell's fiction is didactic in the sense that it is designed to educate the male reader in the recognition and interpretation of women's texts, while at the same time it provides the woman reader with the gratification of discovering, recovering, and validating her own experience.

ELAINE HEDGES

Excerpt 3

Glaspell's details work so effectively as a symbol system because they are carefully chosen reflectors of crucial realities in the lives of 19th and early 20th century midwestern and western women. . . .

Hard as the work was, that it went unacknowledged was often harder for women to bear. The first annual report of the Department of Agriculture in 1862 included a study of the situation of farm women which concluded that they worked harder than men but were neither treated with respect as a result nor given full authority within their domestic sphere. And Norton Juster's study of farm women between 1865 and 1895 leads him to assert that women's work was seen merely as "the anonymous background for someone else's meaningful activity," never attaining "a recognition or dignity of its own." Indeed, he concludes, women's work was not only ignored; it was ridiculed, "often the subject of derision." Mr. Hale's remark about the preserves, that "women are used to worrying over trifles," is a mild example of this ridicule, as is the attorney's comment, intended to deflect that ridicule but itself patronizing—"yet what would we do without the ladies." It is this ridicule to which Mrs. Hale and Mrs. Peters especially react. When Mr. Hale belittles women's work we are told that "the two women moved a little closer together"; and when the attorney makes his seemingly conciliatory remark the women, we are further told, "did not speak, did not unbend." Mrs. Hale and Mrs. Peters, who at the beginning of the story are comparative strangers to each other, here begin to establish their common bond with each other and with Minnie. Their slight physical movement towards each other visually embodies that psychological and emotional separation from men that was encouraged by the nineteenth century doctrine of separate spheres, a separation underscored throughout the story by the women's confinement to the kitchen, while the men range freely, upstairs and outside, bedroom to barn, in search of the "real" clues to the crime.

EXERCISE 6.11. EVALUATING RESEARCH ARGUMENTS

Having read and analyzed the critical excerpts, discuss their arguments in your reading group. What is similar in their readings? What is different? Who offers you information that validates, extends, modifies, or challenges your own response? What kind of evidence do they offer? Is your mind changed about anything? If so, why?

WRITING AND CRITICAL RESEARCH: ANSWERING YOUR QUESTION

The best way, we believe, to enter the parlor of literary studies is to identify a question of interest, one that came to you as you reflected on your reading, and then to go exploring. Who may have asked it before? What did they decide? Why? How do their answers support, modify, or challenge your reading experience? What kinds of evidence do they offer? Imagine you are in a room with these experienced readers, and that they are talking to each other. When do you enter the conversation? What do you say? How do they respond?

Such reflective reading requires that you manage to find and surround yourself with possibilities, a task that has in recent decades been made much less daunting. Because of computers, many of us can now walk up to a monitor, enter the name of—and even narrow—our subject, and see before us the resources in print, our library's holdings, and even the current status (on the shelves, due in soon) of the resources we want. The task can also, however, become labor intensive if we look first at volumes listing writing done, then at catalogs listing the resources available, then at records indicating availability. But research can be as exciting as reading a mystery novel, as clues lead to clues unpredicted and surprising.

Here is how one of our students describes the process:

Let's say you have a paper to write on a work you responded to, but your notion of how to focus your ideas is not very clear and the time for conversations with friends is pretty well gone. Rather than staring at the surface of your desk until you've memorized the pattern in the wood grain, go to the library.

It was hard for me to get through the library turnstile the first time I was assigned the task. There were so many things to check on, so many possibilities to explore, so much I didn't know. Now I know that research is part system, part persistence, and part accident or serendipity. It requires that I trust my reactions, give myself permission to change my mind, and trust that the pieces will come together.

Here's what I recommend: on a rainy or quiet day, with an unexpectedly free hour or two, go scope out the terrain. Walk in with a writer's name or a favorite work in hand. Go to the card catalog, where the works are listed by title or author, followed by critical writing *about* those works or authors. Note interesting titles, but most of all note the first two lines of the call number for most of the books, which indicate where the collection on your subject will be found in the building. (I'm a hands-on kind of researcher. I want to stand in the middle of the stacks.)

Go there. Browse. Look for interesting perspectives or chapter titles. Look for repeated or surprising ideas. As you survey the possibilities, formulate questions, allowing your own response to the subject to be strengthened or pushed around by these other readers.

Now go to the reference section. Look for the *bibliographies*, a word meaning, basically, writings about books. As examples, check out Robert Spiller's *Literary History of the United States*, which has a bibliography volume, if your subject is American; or try George Watson's *The New Cambridge Bibliography of English Literature* if your subject is British. These are general listings and are not the most current references; your library will have more specialized materials which you will locate as you really get motivated by your search. Then check out the indexes related to literature and language. For example, the *Humanities Index* includes descriptions of critical writings listed by author and subject. The *Essay and General Literature Index* lists articles and essays which are printed in books rather than journals.

The next part is, for me, the most fun, most absorbing and usually most quickly rewarding. Find the *MLA Bibliography* collection in the reference section. Take with you a copy of the library's list of their periodical holdings on language and literature. (If they don't have one, ask them if they would consider making one up. Get your friends to support your request.) Pick out a Subject Volume, 1981 or after, and locate the listings on your subject. The number at the end of each listing corresponds to a citation in the Author Volume for the same year, and these are listed in numerical order. (If you get lost or things look unfamiliar, read the directions at the front, which are different for volumes before 1981.) The periodical and journal titles, abbreviated in the citations, are identified in a list in the front of all Author volumes. By comparing your discoveries to the list of library holdings, you will soon become familiar with what journals are readily accessible, and you will discover more than you thought possible about who's writing about what.

At this point, instead of not being able to think of a question to investigate, your only problem will be that you will have thought of dozens. Now you have to make up your mind, and I have no more advice.

Here's a second student's thoughts about research, written after transferring to a university that has computerized its holdings.

I've decided to stick with English as a major. Computers have made this choice possible for me. Now I walk up to a monitor, select as my database the library's holdings, and enter my subject. The screen shows me 1) what's available, 2) where on campus it's located, 3) what form it's in, 4) whether it's available or checked out, and if checked out, 5) when it's due. In addition, I can check on what's available anywhere else through databases such as Infotrack and ERIC or those accessed through the Internet.

The limitations? Most of the information available is contemporary; for historical work, you'll have to go back to "pre-electronic tools." The benefits? Computers eliminate much of the "footwork" of research, leaving more time for reading and writing. I will admit, though, that the computer lists made sense because I already had experience with the research tools they were indexing. Without prior research experience of the "labor intensive" kind, it's difficult to know how to use the information computers give you. Nonetheless, I'm a believer, and I advise researchers to use all the tools available to them.

You might expect at this point a comprehensive list of reference tools with detailed instruction in their use, but as the two students describing their research make clear, the information and assistance available will vary from library to library. We like the advice the students offer. The most important tasks for you are to venture in, get oriented, immerse yourself in information, and see what reference tools become valuable to you. Our own explorations and our students' accounts of their research experiences have persuaded us that active, hands-on interaction with research tools is far more effective for encouraging confidence and success than any lists or instructions we could provide in this chapter. If this interaction with literary research is, as Kenneth

Burke suggests, like a parlor gathering, then we encourage you to join the party. The longer you hang around, the more comfort and familiarity you will achieve.

Summary

As you explore critical possibilities and questions, as you become aware of ongoing conversations about literature and contribute to their progress, as you come to understand that your voice, your experience, your resistance to or identification with other readings are essential to the continuity and vigor of the discussion, you will be able to extend your confidence with literary interpretation beyond your current readings and reading companions. We want you to be able, alone or with others, to consider and evaluate other readings in terms of your own experience with the work.

An Invitation to Write: The Research Essay

We have separated one kind of essay from another to help you practice the art of interpretation; however, the critical research essay, as is true of the other essays described in this text, includes response, analysis, and reasoned argument. Practicing those forms of reading will help you find a place for literary criticism within your own reading experience.

To write a research essay, you will have to respond, reflect, analyze, and reason your way to a tentative answer to a question at issue, and this answer will continue to evolve as you consult relevant research material. As you write your essay, you should remember to include references to sources only when you have a specific reason to include them, when they serve your purpose. You can get support from them, let them help you explain, argue with them, use their insights to help you fit your observations into a pattern or context, or borrow their words when theirs offer clarity or vividness to your argument. You are obliged, as an effective reader and writer, to integrate your response and expose your assumptions as you develop your answer to your question at issue; the research essay obligates you further to use other voices accurately, responsibly, and purposefully in addressing your question.

There are three general strategies for incorporating source material: summarizing, paraphrasing, and quoting. Use summary when you wish to represent the general direction and key points of an argument but are not concerned with the specific support for or expression of those points. Use paraphrase when you need to link specific points to your argument, but when rephrasing the points in your own words would make your paper more cogent, concise, or readable. Quotation may be your best choice when language itself is the focus, when you wish to take issue with an argument or observation a writer is making, or when the expression of a point is more vivid or concrete than any restatement you could devise.

You are obligated in a research essay to document your sources fully and accurately whether you are summarizing, paraphrasing, or quoting. The student paper at the end of this chapter provides examples of how to cite authors of books and articles in the context of the paper and how to list their works in a bibliography. However, you will sometimes want to use materials that require more specific or complicated documentation; look to writing handbooks or your instructor's guidelines for documentation requirements and preferences. Keep good records as you browse and take notes so you will not have to retrace your steps as you finish your paper and complete your documentation.

Writing Group Activity

Write a draft of a research essay on works in this text or works of your choice, and bring your draft to your writing group. As you present your paper, ask your readers to watch for your question at issue and your answer to your question. Then have them examine each place where you have summarized, paraphrased, or quoted an experienced reader; ask them how the information contributes to the development of the paper by clarifying, supporting, or complicating the argument. Are the other voices necessary? Effective? Persuasive? Challenging?

Sample Writing: The Research Essay

Read the following paper on *Trifles*. What question at issue is the writer asking? How does he answer it? Identify where and why other readings have been incorporated into the interpretation. Where has the writer used summary, paraphrase, and quotation? Is the additional information useful? Is it necessary?

TRIAL BY TRIFLES: WHY DIDN'T THEY TELL?

The scene of Susan Glaspell's play *Trifles* is set in the disordered, gloomy farm kitchen of John Wright, who has been murdered, and his wife Minnie, who is accused of the crime. The people in the scene include three men, a sheriff, a district attorney, and a neighbor who discovered the crime; and two women, Mrs. Peters, the sheriff's wife, and Mrs. Hale, Minnie's neighbor and childhood friend. Those in charge of the investigation, County Attorney Henderson and Sheriff Peters, are there to look for clues and evidence which could provide "a motive; something to show anger or—sudden feeling" or could explain the way that John Wright was murdered, "rigging it all up like that." While the men roam the house and property searching for answers, the women keep each other company in the kitchen, noticing, one by one, details, or "trifles" of Minnie's life which to them, although not to the men, carry meaning and significance.

As they notice and reflect on the "trifles," which include such everyday items as a dirty roller towel, a broken stove, a cracked jar of preserves, a half-wiped table, and a less-than-perfectly stitched quilt block, they begin to put together the pieces of Minnie's existence. Like blocks of a quilt, the pieces show a pattern: a harsh, lonely life, and a marriage to a difficult man. They recognize in these "trifles" evidence of disturbance or anger. Thus when they discover a bird with its neck wrung, they (and we) have no trouble imagining a motive: John Wright has killed the bird, which may have been one of his wife's only comforts. Standing in the kitchen and reflecting on the "trifles" of Minnie's life, the two women solve the crime in a way the men didn't, and couldn't. Though this is a murder mystery, the shock at the end is not that Minnie did it; it is that the women, who knew this, did not tell. Why didn't they? Why the conspiracy of silence?

One answer is that the two women empathized with Minnie's life. In the details of her existence they see reflected the harshness and isolation which characterized the days of many farm women. As critic Elaine Hedges explains, the work of 19th century farm women was almost endless, and the division of labor exploited women by assigning them a great many invisible jobs which went unnoticed and received little credit. Hedges cites from one farm woman's journal a list of the "routine" work of the "women folk" as including "water carrying, cooking, churning, sausage making, berry picking, vegetable drying, sugar and soap boiling, hominy hulling, medicine brewing, washing, nursing, weaving, sewing, straw platting, wool picking, spinning, quilting, knitting, gardening and various other tasks." It was not uncommon that the workday, Hedges tells us, "began at 4:30 a.m., and didn't end until 11:30 p.m." (95).

The life's harshness made social connection and mutual support absolutely essential for women, and as the two women realized, Minnie Wright was alone. As Sharon Friedman suggests, "[g]iven the significance of home and family in women's lives, and the female network through which women formed close and supportive relationships in the sparsely populated prairie, the women in *Trifles* understand the stillness of Minnie Wright's childless existence, and the psychological repercussions of her enforced isolation from other women" (74). Isolation could be both dangerous and damaging.

The descriptions of the setting reinforce our sense that by geography, as well as because her husband required it, Minnie Wright was isolated: the house was set "down in a hollow and you don't see the road." "I don't like this place," Mrs. Hale remarks to Mrs. Peters, who answers "I'm glad you came. It would be lonesome for me sitting here alone." John Wright refuses to have a telephone, and we learn that he has denied Minnie the connections to town life that may have made her life bearable, such as singing in the church choir. As Hedges puts it, "Minnie Wright's emotional and spiritual loneliness, the result of her isolation, is, in the final analysis, the reason for the murder of her husband" (94). Mrs. Hale and Mrs. Peters seem to conclude that the combined effects of the harshness of existence and the damage of isolation could be not just motives for murder, but also conditions which might justify it.

Another explanation for their silence may be that, as Mrs. Peters and Mrs. Hale reflect on the conditions of Minnie's life, they also seem to take on some responsibility for the murder. Each comes to see herself as potentially having contributed to the tragedy, or as capable of committing it. Mrs. Hale sees herself in Minnie's house, identifies with her situation, and concludes that she might have come to Minnie's aid. "I wish I had come over sometimes when she was here. . . . I could have come. I stayed away because it weren't cheerful—and that's why I ought to have come." Mrs. Peters does not confess feelings of complicity but does, nonetheless, identify with the feelings that might have resulted in the murder. When she discovers the bird cage and the dead canary, she sees in her own past that helplessness and grief and even violence are understandable reactions to brutality: "When I was a girl—my kitten—there was a boy took a hatchet, and before my eyes—and before I could get there—(*covers her face for an instant*) If they hadn't held me back I would have . . . hurt him." By coming to see circumstances which would explain Minnie's act or would make it seem an acceptable response, Mrs. Wright and Mrs. Hale join forces with Minnie and each other, redefining what is "criminal" in terms the three of them, but not the men, can understand.

Even so, how is it that the women's views of right and wrong would differ so significantly from the men's? Critic Phyllis Mael points out what recent psychological theory has documented—that women and men seem to have different ways of going about making moral decisions. If that is true, then Mrs. Hale and Mrs. Peters may not have revealed their knowledge because they understood that traditional law would apply the wrong criteria to Minnie's situation; they may have realized that they were Minnie's true "peers," and must decide her case. Mrs. Peters, who is the sheriff's wife and "married to the law," comments that "the law is the law"; Mrs. Hale responds with "I s'pose 'tis." Yet both women seem to feel, as Mael notes, "the need to reinterpret abstract law within a particular context." Mrs. Peters shows this need as she remembers her

kitten, and again as she recalls the powerful, disturbing stillness she experienced after the death of her first baby. Then, when
Mrs. Hale reflects on her own complicity, she compares her failure
to help Minnie to the murder, redefining the rules about what is
criminal: "Oh, I wish I'd come over here once in a while! That was
a crime! That was a crime! Who's going to punish that!" Thus the
two women both come to understand that there is more than one way
to judge guilt, and that their way, in this case, may be more
appropriate.

The fact that their concerns and abilities were taunted and
"trivialized" in the play may have increased the likelihood that
they would keep their story to themselves. The County Attorney
inquires about what the sheriff has seen in the kitchen that would
point to a motive, and the sheriff responds, "Nothing here but
kitchen things." The sheriff also wonders at Minnie's concern over
her responsibilities: "Well, can you beat the women! Held for murder and worryin' about her preserves." Mr. Hale concludes, "Well,
women are used to worrying over trifles." These trifles, however,
hold the answers to the mystery, and the women who could interpret
such details were denied a voice by the men who could not believe
they would have anything of value to say.

They may have known that their language and their stories would
not be understood in any case. As Hedges tells us, "Any symbol
system . . . is a shorthand, a script to which the reader must
bring a great deal of knowledge not contained in the text. . . . In
Glaspell's story, Mrs. Hale and Mrs. Peters comprise an ideal (if
small) community of readers precisely because they are able to
bring to the 'trivia' of Minnie Wright's life . . . a 'unique and
informing context'" (90–91). Accepting that they, having lived
similar lives, *could* understand the evidence, and the men, who
could never have access to that context, *could not*, the women do
not attempt to explain their knowledge. Calling the kitchen a
"text" to be read, Judith Fetterley elaborates on the separate
languages evident in the story:

> [I]t is not simply that the men cannot read the text
> that is placed before them. Rather, they literally can-
> not recognize it as a text because they cannot imagine
> that women have stories. This preconception is so power-
> ful that, even though, in effect, they know Minnie
> Wright has killed her husband, they spend time trying
> to discover their own story, the story they are famil-
> iar with, can recognize as a text, and know how to
> read. They go to the barn; they check for evidence of
> violent entry from the outside; they think about guns.
> In their story, men, not women, are violent, and men
> use guns. . . . Minnie Foster Wright's kitchen is not a
> text to them, and so they cannot read it (115).

So the women remain silent because the men would not understand their evidence; but by keeping the evidence to themselves, they also take control of the story away from the men. As Fetterley reminds us,

> Martha Hale undoes the threads of the quilt that, like the weaving of Philomel, tells the story of Minnie Wright's violation and thus provides the clue to her revenge; Mrs. Peters instinctively creates an alternate story to explain the missing bird and then further fabricates to explain the absent cat; and Mrs. Hale, with the approval of Mrs. Peters, finally hides the dead bird. (162)

If the women didn't believe the men were capable of interpreting the "trifles" in the kitchen, they would not have altered the evidence.

Finally, the women may have remained silent because the traditional justice system denied them their stories and a voice with which to speak. As Linda Ben-Zvi argues in her article which ties the play to the social and legal realities of the time, women had no voice on juries; they had no say in court. So Susan Glaspell, in *Trifles*, gives them a voice in art:

> By having the women assume the central positions and conduct the investigation and the trial, she actualizes an empowerment that suggests there are options short of murder which can be imagined for women. Mrs. Peters and Mrs. Hale may seem to conduct their trial sub rosa, because they do not actively confront the men; but in Mrs. Hale's final words, "We call it—knot it, Mr. Henderson," ostensibly referring to a form of quilting but clearly addressed to the actions the women have taken, they become both actors and namers. Even if the men don't understand the pun . . . the audience certainly does. (158)

Thus their silence becomes, in art, a powerful form of speech. By their shared understanding of the pun at the end, we see that the two women may not tell because they realize the powers *and* limits of their own capacity to decide, and name, justice. Although they cannot vote or serve on juries, they can control the outcome of this case.

Because they interpret the significance of the trifles of Minnie's life, trifles the men ignore, Mrs. Hale and Mrs. Peters not only solve the murder mystery, but develop a sense of their common identity as women. This common identity is established through their empathy with the conditions of Minnie's life, their identifi-

cation with her circumstances and her responses, their shared way
of making moral decisions, their common subjection to trivializa-
tion and powerlessness, and their recognition of the fact that
they have a language the men do not share—a language men cannot,
and in the social and historical context, would not, hear. In
their silence, their refusal to share their knowledge with the
traditional justice system, they demonstrate their awareness of an
alternative to the legal and justice system which excludes them.

Bibliography

Ben-Zvi, Linda. "Murder, She Wrote: The Genesis of Susan Glaspell's
    Trifles." *Theatre Journal* 44, no. 2 (May 1992): 141–153.

Fetterley, Judith. "Reading about Reading: 'A Jury of Her Peers,' 'Murder
    in the Rue Morgue,' and 'The Yellow Wallpaper.'" In *Gender and Reading:
    Essays on Readers, Texts and Contexts*, ed. Elizabeth A. Flynn and
    Patrocinio P. Schweikart, 147–164. Baltimore, Md.: Johns Hopkins Univer-
    sity Press, 1986.

Friedman, Sharon. "Feminism as Theme in Twentieth-Century American Women's
    Drama." *American Studies* 25, no. 1 (Spring 1984): 69–89.

Hedges, Elaine. "Small Things Reconsidered: Susan Glaspell's 'A Jury of
    Her Peers'," *Women's Studies* 12, no. 1 (1986) 89–110.

Mael, Phyllis. "*Trifles*: A Path to Sisterhood." *Literature Film Quarterly*
    17, no. 4 (Oct. 1989): 281–285.

Extra Practice: Additional Writing Invitations

1. Go back to your own questions at issue that you noted as you read
   Trifles. Construct a thesis statement that could provide the structure
   for a paper about the play, one that might lead you to examine
   other critical readings. Test it. What kind of question are you asking? What kind of information from outside the play might help
   you with your inquiry? Check the list of ways research can be
   incorporated into your interpretations. Which of these ways might
   be relevant to your paper?

2. Conduct some independent research on a literary work of your
   choice. Articulate your question at issue, read the work carefully
   with your question in mind to challenge and clarify your response,
   and formulate a tentative thesis. Investigate the resources described
   in the chapter: browse the critical works and collections of essays in
   the stacks, and locate titles of articles in periodicals in bibliographies and indexes. Skim abstracts or first paragraphs to get an idea

of the argument the writer is making, and select a few pieces for careful study.

Read your selections to relate them to each other. What assumptions do they share? Where and how do they disagree? What evidence does each use? Is one an example of another? Then, taking your observations into account, compose an imaginary panel discussion the writers would conduct based on *your* question at issue. Put yourself on the panel. What do you add?

3. Reread John Keats's "When I Have Fears," in Chapter 5. Identify any words whose meanings might have changed since the early nineteenth century. Read the word's entry in the *Oxford English Dictionary* and then write a paragraph explaining how an understanding of the nineteenth-century meaning is important in interpreting the poem.

A p p e n d i x

Coming to Terms
Literary Language
and Its Uses

Every discipline is defined and redefined through the conversations of informed, responsible participants. As these conversations evolve, participants find and make new knowledge through observing, generalizing, and interpreting. To talk about discoveries and insights, to build on old ideas and test new ones, those who have chosen a particular field of study must find ways to fit words to ideas, names to observations. In the history of our literary conversation, a language has evolved that strengthens our skills in literary analysis in three ways:

1. When we make an observation, it helps to have a specific, precise word to name what we see.

2. Each time we learn to use one of these discipline-specific words, we learn to look for, to observe, something that we may not have seen before.

3. Each new observation becomes the basis of new insight, new generalizations, new interpretive possibilities that can help us find value and significance in a literary work.

Practice in looking for the kinds of language features described here helps you become a more observant reader. Part A of this appendix illustrates the significance of related features by organizing them into categories and by associating these categories with questions readers can ask. Part B defines and exemplifies the terms in an alphabetical glossary. So that you can examine the terms in context, we provide examples from literary works included in this book and from widely anthologized works.

One way to exercise your observing and generalizing skills is to pick one or two literary works you would like to investigate. Then, read Part A: Categories of Terms and Questions to Ask. Go through the four sections asking the questions you see posed for each category and noting your observations. Finally, ask how your observations are *related to* or *in conflict with* each other, and how features *change* as the work progresses. Observing and reflecting on features of literary language are different activities from interpreting literature, in the same way that practicing scales on a musical instrument differs from playing music, or bouncing a ball on a racket differs from playing tennis. But as you know from learning other things, such exercise can increase confidence, fluency, and satisfaction.

PART A: CATEGORIES OF TERMS AND QUESTIONS TO ASK

Our four categories—shape, language, participants, and situation—can help you focus the kind of literary question you are asking; recognizing the questions underlying these four categories can allow you to see more fully and generalize more responsibly about literary works. With our discussions of each category, we have included generic questions to help you generate interesting, specific issues to research. We suggest that you read Part A before using Part B, the glossary. The questions will help you find what you need, and the categorized lists will help you understand how related terms are defined together, in the same entries, so that you will have an understanding of their context and use.

Attempts to categorize ideas can sometimes expose ambiguous terms, ideas that cross categories or defy them altogether. For example, **irony** can result from a discrepancy between the audience's knowledge and the protagonist's awareness, between the audience's expectations and what happens, between characters' attempts to control their life and the larger forces that shape their fate, or between a statement and its intended meaning. In each case the effect is ironic, though the particular kind of irony may be included in our discussions of language, participants, or situation. To help you locate the idea or term you are interested in, we have listed the terms related to each category so that you can find them alphabetically in the glossary, Part B of the Appendix.

Shape: Design and Development

What choices of form and order does the author make?

How do these choices help to establish and fulfill expectations?

How are choices of form and order related to your response, to each other, and to other elements of the work?

Design

How is the work divided? How are the parts related?

Literary works are almost always divided, or can be divided, into parts. Sometimes divisions are dictated by the form, sometimes by considerations external to the form. Authors divide their works in many ways, including sections, chapters, acts, scenes, pages, paragraphs, stanzas, sentences, and lines. Sometimes no explicit divisions are indicated, but it's possible to see and name changes in language or perspective that allow us to identify distinct parts. All divisions are purposeful. To analyze design, ask: Why did the author divide the work this way? How do the divisions complicate or support the other elements of the work? How do the parts relate to each other? How would changing the divisions modify the effect?

Looking at the design of literary works and asking how the parts are related helps you to see the works as unified wholes. The parts don't simply lead to each other, but usually complicate, challenge, reflect, or complete each other. Reading a poem or story or seeing a play for the first time can leave you confused because you have not yet "composed" the parts of the work into a complete artistic statement or discovered the way the separate elements work meaningfully together. Paying attention to your responses, to the way you are being asked to identify with the experience offered by the text, can help you perceive and analyze the relationship of the parts to the whole.

When you observe design in literary works, be aware that writers have chosen a specific design to lend support to their vision. Some of the designs and design elements that have been recognized as typical or traditional by experienced readers are listed below and are defined and exemplified in Part B.

ballad	lyric
elegy	monologue
epic	novel
essay	ode
frame story	plot
free verse.open form	short story
genre	sonnet
	stanza

Development

What propels the progression of events?

What sustains and motivates your interest as a reader?

When you look at elements of design, you are concerned with the literary work as a whole. When you look at elements of development, you watch for the ways in which the work progresses through time, in a sequence. Of course, design and development are difficult to separate. For example, plot includes not only the events that occur but their order; plot events necessarily happen in a sequence. Nonetheless, there are two reasons to be concerned with developmental progressions through time. First, the design elements, the parts of the work, are sometimes made evident by structural clues like indentations and spacing, but more often they are marked by emotional curves of intensity, risings and fallings caused, as Kenneth Burke tells us, by the arousing and fulfillment of desires. Second, especially in reading modern literature, time is often manipulated: the writer takes us through dimensions of present, future, and past as if they were all contained in any single moment. The choices of order and sequence made by the writer call attention to themselves, inviting us to ask why something comes first, second, and third in the presentation of the work.

What does Kenneth Burke mean by the arousal and fulfillment of desires? As we state in the definition of plot, an expectation combined with concern can result in suspense: we are led to anticipate, and to care about, an outcome. We also may be moved to engage with the progression of a work by an incongruity or a paradox resulting in what is called "cognitive dissonance," a gap between what is familiar and what is unfamiliar; we are motivated to fill the gap by finding a way to comprehend the unfamiliar in terms of the familiar, finding coherence or resolving the paradox. In addition, we may be aroused by an image or idea that is repeated, with variation, through the work, and that seems to promise with each new rendering a sense of the significance of the experience. Finally, we may be led, through the writer's subtle rendering of the mood of the work, from one state of mind to another that seems appropriately to follow. In all of these ways, the writer's choices are made to engage us with and then propel us through the work, experiencing it in a kind of literary time that is created and sustained within the work. Following are the terms in Part B that clarify modes or elements of development.

conventional form	**qualitative progression**
foreshadowing	**repetition**
incongruity	**syllogistic progression**

Language

> How do the author's choices of words, sentences, sounds, silences, rhythms, and figures of speech relate to your response and to other elements of the work?

As you read and respond to literature, you learn to be attentive to language. Much of interpretation, inside and outside literature classes, is guided by the assumption that looking at language brings meaning into focus. The process of observing will lead us beyond what the words say to what they suggest, to what—collectively—they mean, and through this attentiveness to words, sentences, punctuation, sound, and figurative language. We are involved in composing that meaning as we perceive possibilities and patterns, form generalizations, and construct interpretations.

It's important to remember that language, even figurative language, is not poetic window dressing. Language represents values, and understanding the power of language is an essential skill in a diverse, changing world. A casual metaphor, for example, can carry with it judgments and even prescriptions for human behavior: when someone calls a woman a "chick" or a "babe," the language brings with it assessments of brainlessness and vulnerability and thus an implicit assumption of the superiority of the speaker. An attentiveness to language makes it more likely that we will reflect on the power of our statements, recognizing the way that control over language also can become control over other aspects of life. Thus reading language responsibly makes us capable of using language, and the power that comes with it, responsibly.

The following terms listed in Part B help readers focus on the significance of language features related to style, words and phrases, lines and sentences, sound and rhyme, and figurative language.

abstract language	**meter**
allegory	**metonymy**
alliteration	**onomatopoiea**
archaic language	**personification**
concrete language	**rhyme**
connotation	**rhyme scheme**
diction	**similie**
figurative language	**style**
hyperbole	**symbol**
imagery	**syntax**
line breaks	**verbal irony**
metaphor	

Participants

> What relationships, conflicts, and changes can be observed among or within the characters?
>
> What perspectives, attitudes, and assumptions can be observed within the work?
>
> What perspectives, attitudes, and assumptions of the author toward the subject or reader can be observed or inferred?

The premise of this text is that literary interpretation is like conversation, and although we clearly mean to emphasize the benefits of reading with other readers, we also intend to clarify ways in which your interactions with the voices in the texts themselves are conversational. This section, then, categorizes terms and perspectives that are helpful in taking inventory of, distinguishing, and analyzing the interaction among the voices in the work and your reactions to the various voices you hear as you read.

These voices include, of course, characters in the story, whose actions or changes can motivate the development, whose interactions can set up the conflicts and relationships that are being mediated both literally and figuratively in the work, or whose presence can add a dimension or complication to our understanding of other characters and events. Another participant in the conversation is the writer, with whom we can engage through all of the choices he or she has made in constructing the work, and sometimes through interpretive suggestions as often appear in stage directions for plays or in critical commentaries the writer provides. Other voices emerge from within the text as the writer crafts a persona or speaking voice that takes its character from the role assigned it within the context of the work.

One of the pitfalls of becoming attentive to the voices within the text is mistaking the persona or speaking voice for the author, attributing a world view evident in the text to the writer of the work. It is possible to inquire about a writer's assumptions and biases by studying biographical and historical documents that give accounts of the writer's opinions and ideas or by examining carefully and critically the characteristic style choices the writer makes. It is also important to recognize the writer's artfulness in crafting a role for the storyteller, even when the story told is autobiography.

The following terms are useful in conversations about these participants, those telling and those told about, as you take into account what information you have in shaping your interpretive response. As you read about them in Part B, classify them according to whether they concern relationships between or among characters, between characters and readers, or between writer and reader.

antagonist
archetype
character
characterization
chorus

dramatic irony
identification and empathy
persona, speaker, or narrator
point of view
protagonist

Situation

What is the relationship of setting to meaning?

How might the work's location in space, time, and cultural circumstance influence the assumptions, actions, behaviors, and events within the work?

How might these same factors have influenced the inception and creation of the work?

What behaviors, values, and social understandings does the work seem to presume? Are there differences between those in the work and those of the reader?

What emotional or psychological atmosphere is evoked by the work?

By what criteria might the work be judged? What assumptions about value underlie the criteria?

What influences—other ideas, other voices, other texts—can be perceived within the work?

The conversation at work in this set of terms is contextual: how do we relate to participants whose reality—in time, space, and culture—differs from our own? This question is more problematic, and thus more interesting, than it may at first seem. Many people believe that we are capable of seeing and understanding only what we have seen and understood before, or that our own personal experience and cultural background limit our ability to perceive and accommodate difference. Regardless of the degree to which we believe those ideas about perception, we also believe that through responsible study of literature, readers can expand their own cultural framework by imagining themselves into—identifying with—works that challenge their boundaries of understanding. Cultures other than your own are not puzzles to be mastered but complex networks of paths to be explored. The more wandering you do, the more familiar and less foreign the terrain will seem. Writers of literature are artful at giving directional signs even when you are not their intended audience.

Interpreting setting in any work gives us the skills we need to interpret culture. The traditional notion of setting, limited to the background of the action in the work itself, helps us understand the kinds of connections between place and person, context and culture within the work. Having examined these connections, we can go beyond them to explore the relationships between the work and the world, ours or that of its origin. The following terms related to the way the text, the author, or the reader are situated in time and space are included in Part B.

atmosphere	**setting**
canon	**situational irony**
critical approaches	**tone**
culture	**value**
influence	

PART B: AN ALPHABETIZED GLOSSARY

abstract language: See **concrete language**.

allegory: A story with two parallel and consistent levels of meaning, one literal and one figurative, in which the figurative level offers a moral or political lesson. In Chapter 3, one of the readers of "Where Are You Going, Where Have You Been?" says that Arnold Friend is the devil, and then offers evidence that his two roles, as Friend and devil, are parallel and consistent. People who read Arnold Friend as an allegorical figure will then attempt to define the moral lesson Connie learned, or the one we learn as we read the story.

alliteration: Repetition of sound. When a sound or set of sounds is repeated in close proximity, the repetition calls attention to itself. The repetition may be used for emphasis or to link related words, or the purpose of repeating the sound may have something to do with the sound itself, as in the opening paragraph of "Home," where the "l's" of "looked at the late afternoon light on the lawn" seem to reinforce the lulling effect of rocking in a chair on a warm day. Another example of this is in "Filling Station," where as one reader noted in Chapter 2, the "s" sounds of "several quick and saucy and greasy sons assist him" have a sharp edge, as if the speaker is "hissing" her resistance to the scene. Later in the poem, however, the "s's" reinforce a different mood, as "rows of cans . . . softly say: ESSO—SO—SO—SO / to high-strung automobiles." As the speaker's attitude toward the setting has changed, so the effect of a sound has evolved, reinforcing the development of the work.

When the sounds of final consonants are repeated, the pattern is called *consonance*. One example of this is in Arnold's poem "Dover Beach" in Chapter 6. The speaker is telling how "The Sea of Faith" once lay "round earth's shore . . . like the folds of a bright girdle furled." In these lines the "l's," "f's," and "d's" layer over each other reinforcing the furling and folding of the image. When the repeated sounds are vowels, the pattern is called *assonance*. In the same poem, as the speaker laments his loss of the "Sea of Faith," he says "But now I only hear/Its melancholy, long, withdrawing roar. " The "ah" sounds of melancholy, long, and withdrawing extend the line and reinforce the depth of the speaker's sadness, making his faith and former certainty seem agonizingly distant.

antagonist: A person or persons in conflict with or opposing the **protagonist**, though a force or a circumstance can also function as antagonist. Our most obvious example of an antagonist is Arnold Friend, who terrorizes Connie in "Where Are You Going, Where Have You Been?"

archaic language: Words that were, but are no longer, in common use. Inexperienced readers may find that archaic terms distance them from a literary work, but experienced readers take into account that in the context of works written in earlier times archaic language offers us a glimpse of that historical moment. In contemporary works, archaic words may be used to connote past ideas, attitudes, or circumstances.

archetype: Generally, archetypes are what we perceive to be original patterns, models of being and behaving we recognize from the collective unconscious we all share; for example, we recognize the stories, personalities, emotions, and situations of the Olympian gods and goddesses as familiar models in literature. We also refer to a perfect example of a type or group as an archetype. Referring to a character, an archetype is a figure so seemingly familiar that it registers imaginatively as universal—for example, the hero who sacrifices his own life for the betterment of humanity (e.g., Prometheus), or the scapegoat, or the sorceress.

atmosphere, mood, or ambiance: These terms refer to the emotional or psychological climate of a work. Although subjective, the way works register with readers is important and predictable enough to be a part of most literary discussions. One reader of "Where Are You Going, Where Have You Been?" said it was "scary"; *Trifles* might be seen as anxious or conspiratorial. In either case, the atmosphere generates reader expectations about the progression of events in the work. Sustained or changing, it is usually communicated through details of setting. Reading for atmosphere, particularly with other readers, helps foster an ability to recognize and name complex emotional responses to experience and to become aware of the way a prevailing mood can influence events and behaviors.

ballad: A story poem that usually comes out of an oral or song tradition and is arranged in four-line stanzas rhyming "abab." Usually a refrain, or repeating part, contains a line that advances the story. The formula and repetition enhance the emotional effect and help the singer remember the words.

canon: A term that has come to denote "works worth reading," as determined by a broad consensus of scholars with diverse critical viewpoints and over the passage of time. Words like "masterpieces" and "classics" and "great books" also refer to canonical works. The ongoing critical conversation about what is worth reading is called "canon formation," and as the group involved in that process evolves from its rather homogeneous composition to include women and ethnic minorities, it has become obvious that the criteria used to judge literary merit are contextual and negotiable. For example, knowing about a writer's culture or the culture represented in the text can help you see how the language choices are effective within that cultural context and may allow you to make an evaluation that is relevant to the cultural origins of the work.

character: The representation of a person in an imaginative work whom we come to know from the words on the page. When characters are one dimensional, stereotypical, predictable, or simple we refer to them as *flat*. Flat characters usually act as foils or backdrops, offering motivation for or an interpretive clue about the main characters. When characters seem real, are fully developed, are unpredictable and difficult to pin down, we refer to them as *round*. Round characters usually are aligned with the central conflicts or questions at issue in the work; it is their dilemmas which concern us and their interests with which we identify. In Flannery O'Connor's short story "A Good Man Is Hard to Find," the grandmother and the Misfit are round characters, whereas the other characters are flat, providing characterization, motivation, and suspense. In "Where Are You Going, Where Have You Been?" we know almost nothing about the strange, silent Ellie, yet his presence lends palpable density to the threatening atmosphere.

When characters grow and change in the course of the action, they are said to be *dynamic*; remaining unchanged, they are *static*. Sometimes the change occurs not in the protagonist but in someone watching, as the reader or another character becomes aware that the protagonist is more complicated than was first realized. The old waiter in "A Clean, Well-Lighted

Place" generates this kind of realization on the part of readers. These classifications of characters are important when we are reflecting on the way the work progresses, what happens or what changes, which usually requires us to align our understanding of plot or circumstance with our understanding of character.

characterization: How would you describe an old friend to a new one? You might use physical description—green teeth, Brillo pad hair—which is called *exposition*. But you also would show what he or she is like through characterization—with stories and anecdotes about what the person does or has done, with indirect presentation through objects or details or the reactions of others, with the words of others about your friend. This is precisely how writers control characterization in literature. Observing the various kinds of information the writer has given you about a character, you form generalizations the same way you might in your everyday interactions. This is one of the most valuable kinds of practice literary interpretation offers: how to take stock of others, taking into account everything you can and in the process recognizing human complexity, rather than making hasty judgments based on little information or preconceived notions and biases.

Plot and character are interdependent; one evokes the other. For example, in *Trifles*, the character Mrs. Peters changes over the course of the play; in the beginning, she is "married to the law," and in the end, she subverts it. But we had to believe she would do it, or we wouldn't find the plot credible. This is one of our requirements for good characterization: characters must register as believable; their actions must seem probable. They also must be consistent, or we must be able to infer reasons for changes. When we perceive changes, we must understand possible motives for those changes. Although the characters may stretch our credulity, and although their motivations may not be obvious, a writer's artful choices will give us some basis for speculation and generalization.

chorus: In classical Greek drama, a group of actors stood together alongside the action, commenting on it, offering opinions, and often advising the hero. We have come to think of them as the voice of public response, formally representing a dialogic relationship between the work and the audience. The importance of this idea goes beyond the study of ancient theater, however, because often characters in literary works still fill this role, not as participants in the action but as commentators, a reflective voice. Some readers have seen the men in *Trifles* acting as a chorus, voicing the accepted perspective of the status quo, the traditional way of seeing attributed to the institutions of law.

concrete language: Because literature communicates imaginatively and emotionally as well as intellectually, it is particularly dependent on concrete language. Concrete words are specific, vivid, graphic, and appeal to the senses. Abstract language on the other hand is general or without material references and appeals primarily to the intellect. Grief, love, fatherhood, and evil are abstract; teeth, oil can, a hand on my wrist, and Arnold Friend are concrete.

Concrete language appears in literature as **imagery**, which is often called "mental pictures" experienced by readers through the senses. Imagery engages the reader's imagination, thereby aiding identification with the experience, through words that appeal to our senses of sight, hearing, smell, touch, and taste directly through description or metaphorically through comparisons. In "Home," Brooks helps us identify with the abstraction in the title by offering us a series of sense images that place us with the characters on the porch: talking softly, rocking slowly, surrounded by a snake plant, a magnificent Michigan fern, the late afternoon light on the lawn, the poplar tree, and the emphatic iron of the fence, "They sat, making their plans."

connotation: The associations, feelings, and attitudes that a word suggests or implies, as opposed to the denotation, which is a word's primary meaning. While the word "home" denotes one's place of residence, it connotes familiarity, privacy, and intimacy. While one reader thought of grease monkeys when she read the phrase "monkey suit" in Bishop's poem "Filling Station," another thought of tuxedos. Sharing connotations brings richness to poetic language; relating the various connotations promotes a fuller understanding.

conventional form: As you discovered in the descriptions of designs, specific combinations of design elements can become traditional or conventional through their application and recognition. With conventional forms, you come to desire and expect certain kinds of progressions, such as the way a **sonnet** often raises a question in the first eight lines and addresses it in the last six. These anticipations are raised by the design itself, and thus conventional expectations connect design to development. Because the design is familiar, or conventional, it leads you to expect a related sequence, or development.

When you reflect on the progression in terms of its conventions, ask yourself whether the story seemed similar to other works you have read: a mystery, a tale of growing up, a journey of discovery, an adventure tale. Then ask yourself if, in the middle of reading, you had expectations of how the work would end. Are these two observations related? Did the kind of work you perceived it to be influence your expectations of the progression or the outcome? "Where Are You Going, Where Have You Been?" is an example of a short story that uses categorical expectations to move the story forward (see **short story** and **plot**). In contrast, in the story "Home," Gwendolyn Brooks deliberately reshapes her story to challenge us to suspend those expectations of closure or fulfillment, preparing us to accept as fitting an ending that resolves the immediate crisis but results in no reduction of the intensity of the first line: the characters continue rocking, holding onto the moment, and the house, with a stubborn if vulnerable obstinacy.

critical approaches: When your reading group discusses literature, you are engaging in literary criticism. As this text shows in every chapter, conversation about literature naturally elicits critical questions. When critics formulate general principles that characterize a particular method of inquiry, a particular way of investigating a work, we call it a critical approach, or a critical school. Although the six brief descriptions that follow do not cover the spectrum of critical approaches, they represent ways of reading that will be a part of most programs of literary study. We list them separately, but as you discovered in Chapter 6, critics often combine the approaches to explain and develop their readings.

> *Formalist criticism*: The formalist critic regards the literary work as a unified artistic object. To a formalist, the key interpretive information is in a work's intrinsic features, or the elements found in the work itself: the form, diction, syntax, sound, or genre. Formalists are not concerned with social, biographical, or historical information; they ask instead, how do all of the parts of the work fit together to create a particular effect. The "close reading" strategy employed by the formalist critic is a careful, step-by-step analysis involving observation, generalization, and interpretation.

> *Historical criticism*: Historical critics place a literary work in the historical context from which it emerged. Some reconstruct the world that existed at the time the text was written in order to understand it the way it might have been understood by the people of the time, or to investigate how the conditions of its creation may have affected its meaning. Others gather historical data that can lend significance to elements of the text for which modern readers have no specific context. Still others examine the ways particular works have been interpreted over the passing of time to understand something about the interpreters' view of the world.

> *Feminist criticism*: Feminist critics ask how works represent and relate issues of sexuality and power. They are concerned with how works were created and how they are interpreted and valued. Feminist critics are concerned with the ways in which male-oriented assumptions have permeated literary culture and

given privilege to the ideas and works that matched those assumptions. Others look at how a writer's gender influences his or her writing, or how sexual orientation influences literary creation and interpretation.

Biographical criticism: Critics interested in biography focus on the fact that literary works emerge from the experiences of real people, and believe that information about writers can help us understand the meanings of their writings. As our experiences shape our readings of literary works, so the experiences of writers shape their creations. Knowing specific facts about an author's life often deepens our appreciation of or engagement with a work. Biographical critics explain literary works in terms of their knowledge of an author's life.

Psychoanalytic criticism: Psychoanalytic critics ask how particular theories of psychology can explain the human behavior and motivation of writers and/or their characters. Typically, they look at what a work suggests about what is operating at unconscious levels, treating the literary work as a psychoanalyst might regard a dream. The systems for finding significance in scenes, events, feelings, and behaviors vary according to the psychological or psychoanalytic theory being applied. However, in specific works of psychoanalytic criticism, these theories are usually summarized in the body of the work, to help the reader make the same assumptions as the critic.

Cultural criticism: Cultural critics regard literary works as artifacts of a culture, or a set of beliefs, assumptions, and practices that connect a group of people. They prefer to describe rather than to evaluate. Literature, to cultural critics, is political and ideological, and should be read as a product of and as a means of revealing those agendas. They attempt to discover the criteria on the basis of which cultural phenomena are considered "high" or "low," and seek to dismantle the political hierarchies that are the basis of those judgments. They also consider the ways in which specific literary products perpetuate systems of cultural privilege among and between class, ethnic, and gender groups. Thus their reading strategy involves connecting works to a whole setting of other ideas, contexts, or issues within which the works make sense.

culture: In modern literary studies, culture has come to mean the whole milieu of ideas, morals, art, historical circumstances, customs, popular forms and figures, laws, and habits of a group of people. Lest you begin to believe that such a concept is too broad to be useful, remember that the readers of "Where Are You Going, Where Have You Been?" referred to the culture, or various cultures, of youth that could provide a context for comprehending and even judging Connie's behavior. The limits and extensions of a culture are evident in its prohibitions, its reward and punishment systems, the way adherence is promoted, and the consequences of violating the rules or norms of the culture.

When we read about a cultural moment, we can recover some of the conditions of existence that may have influenced the creation of, or the actions, events, and behaviors presented within, a work. Reading literature with an eye for what is praised, blamed, valued, or devalued by narrators and characters can help us imagine ourselves standing outside our own biases and assumptions and within a set of cultural boundaries unlike our own. Those boundaries may be ethnic, ideological, economic, or gender-marked, or they may exist between one neighborhood and another. Elizabeth Bishop finds foreignness in a filling station, and through conscious observation makes sense of, makes familiar, the unfamiliar culture.

diction: The vocabulary and phrasing in a literary work. Diction can be analyzed in a number of ways, but the best way to read for significance in diction is *substitution*: think of an alternative for a word or phrase and note meaningful differences between your choice and the writer's. Overall, we can read for whether the words are simple or complex, abstract or concrete, contemporary or archaic, familiar or formal. We can look at patterns in the way the writer uses particular parts of speech. We can look at denotations, or literal meanings, and connotations, or associations words have beyond their dictionary definitions. Finally, we can look at relationships between and among word choices within the text, observing patterns of meaning created by the writer's combinations and sequences. In Chapter 4, we look closely at the word choices, particularly the connotations and combinations, which appear in Roethke's poem "My Papa's Waltz." In Chapter 5, we note the way that the word "swerve" in the first stanza of Stafford's poem "Traveling through the Dark" has accumulated new meaning and significance when it reappears in the last.

dramatic irony: Irony is dramatic when it involves an incongruity between what the audience knows and what the character or characters have not yet realized. At the conclusion of *Trifles*, the county attorney, baffled by the circumstances of the crime, says facetiously to Mrs. Hale, "Well, at least we found out that she was not going to quilt it. She was going to—what is it you call it, ladies?" When Mrs. Hale replies, the audience, not the attorney, understands the relationship of her answer to the strangling: "We call it—knot it, Mr. Henderson."

elegy: A poem commemorating a death or loss, the style and form of which suggest a mournful reflection. Familiarity with this design would help you note quickly what William Dickey is up to in "A Poet's Farewell to His Teeth"; he enhances the humor by framing his loss in the form of an elegy.

epic: Epic poems celebrate the exploits of heroes. The stories are long, the subjects are the values and destinies of cultures, and the style is elevated. They usually begin by asking audiences and muses to listen (some variation of "hear ye, hear ye"), then open in the middle of the action (*in medias res*). Along the way, supernatural helpers often assist the hero.

essay: A form of prose, mainly in the form of persuasion, which makes an appeal to the reader's way of thinking about a subject. As Montaigne employed the form, it became a kind of intellectual, emotional, and imaginative exploration of a subject. Modern examples range from the formal essay, which is relatively impersonal, authoritative, and orderly, to the informal essay, which assumes a tone of familiarity, focuses on everyday experiences, and is self-revealing, relaxed, and often humorous. The essays in this volume represent neither pole but assume relative positions on the spectrum. Dillard's piece on muskrats is informal in tone but leads us to reflect on larger issues; Morrison's extended exploration of critical views deals with a serious disciplinary debate in an authoritative way, but his decision to make characters of critics and to develop them imaginatively lends informality and humor to the piece.

figurative language: When language is used to mean something other than the usual or standard meaning, it is being used "figuratively," that is, in order to achieve some special meaning or effect. These figures once were studied primarily as stylistic devices, but we know that they go beyond their classifications as elements of literary language to describing indispensable characteristics of all language. Imagine having to describe something unfamiliar to someone else without using comparisons like metaphors or similes to make your description comprehensible. Imagine having to express outrage without resorting to exaggeration or hyperbole. Imagine trying to raise children without telling stories that mean something to them now, but also include allegorical lessons for later reflection. Reading figuratively is an essential ability for literary interpretation, which requires that you see in multiple ways, perceiving possibilities that can reveal patterns of significance.

foreshadowing: Often events, characters, or details that at first seem insignificant acquire importance as a work progresses. Seeing these elements in a new way not only causes you to reflect back on the sequence, connecting and relating what came before to see the progression of the work, but also gives you a sense of recognition and familiarity that propels you further into the reading experience. You become a part of the work by becoming aware of connections between seemingly unrelated things. In the Hemingway story "A Clean, Well-Lighted Place," the beginning dialogue between the waiters illustrates foreshadowing: One waiter, told that the old man tried to commit suicide because he was in despair, asks "What about?"

The answer is "Nothing." Later the answer takes on significance as the story explores the idea of nothingness.

frame story: One story frames the events and discoveries of another story. Usually a narrator in the present tells a tale from the past that in some way explains the present. There are many contemporary examples, but the most familiar frame stories come to us from Boccaccio's *Decameron*, and from Chaucer, who developed the journey and the interactions among his story-tellers so fully that the frame of the *Canterbury Tales* itself includes elements of plot.

free verse/open form: Poetry that has no observable or strong pattern of rhyme or meter. Although it seems like a paradox, a "formless form" really is still a form; as the artist Ben Shahn tells us, form is "the shape of content." Look to free verse for explorations of open questions, surprises, questions unresolved but worth asking, experiences unpredictable but worth the risk, or challenges to assumptions. You have an example here in Leslie Marmon Silko's poem "In Cold Storm Light."

genre: Genres are classes of literary works. There are many genres, and the criteria used to distinguish these classes are varied. In fact, one group of literary critics has focused on "genre theory," or the study of the classification of literary works—what makes them one thing rather than another. When you figure out what a group of works has in common, you are defining a genre. We asked you to do that when, in Chapter 3, we invited you to reflect on your expectations for and assumptions about several genres, including novels, poems, and folktales. Understanding that genres carry with them traditional elements can help you see how writers are choosing to use, or to manipulate, those elements to support their vision.

hyperbole: Intentional overstatement, which Dickey uses with humorous effect in "A Poet's Farewell to His Teeth," when he describes how he and his teeth drove west, "spitting in all the branches of the Missouri."

identification and empathy: Identifying with a person or situation in a literary work involves feeling the experience being evoked by the language. When we identify, we find the common ground in ourselves, sometimes involuntarily, that we share with the character, the situation, or even the inanimate objects we are reading about. We are asked by Joyce Carol Oates to find a way to connect with Connie in "Where Are You Going, Where Have You Been?," and although some of the readers in the conversation about the story found that identification difficult, they all recognized that the text was inviting them to try. During the course of discoveries in the play *Trifles*, the women discovered that their identification with the accused was strong enough to supplant their prior identification with the "law." Writers are so confident of our willingness to identify, to participate in the experience the text offers, that they can ask of us what William Dickey does in "A Poet's Farewell to His Teeth," in which we are invited to identify with his teeth.

imagery: A term often used to refer to the ways writers compose mental images in writing, typically evoking visual pictures, but sometimes appealing to the other senses such as hearing, touch, smell, taste, or even movement. Elizabeth Bishop's poem "Filling Station" appeals to the reader's sense of sight with images such as the station's black translucency, the father's oil-soaked monkey suit, the dim doily, and the hirsute begonia. William Stafford's poem "Traveling through the Dark," on the other hand, appeals more to the reader's tactile sense with his description of the doe stiffened, almost cold but with her side still warm. Much of our response to a literary work depends upon the extent to which we identify with the work's imagery.

incongruity: A quality of a literary work produced when the reader perceives inconsistency or discord among elements of the work. While some inexperienced readers find literary incongruities intimidating, experienced readers understand that they raise questions worth asking about form, language, participants, and situations, and invite answers that complicate the work in interesting ways. Dramatic irony is a kind of incongruity between the audience and the protagonist: we know something the character has not yet realized, and we read for the moment of discovery. A *paradox* is another kind of incongruity, an apparent contradiction which, on reflection, makes a new kind of sense. In Roethke's poem "My Papa's Waltz," the speaker's experience with his father includes simultaneous, and seemingly paradoxical, elements of affection and of fear—complicating both responses in a way that helps us rethink father-son relationships. This play of opposites against each other is also called a *polarity*, and out of the incongruity caused by the pairing comes a new understanding of both terms.

influence: Informed readers talk about influence when their focus is the conversations between and among past and present literary texts and/or authors. The more you read, the more you will become accustomed to seeing connections between texts. Sometimes these are called *allusions*, which are direct or indirect references in one text to another. A newer term, *intertextuality*, refers to the way that the evolution of many works can be traced through historical antecedents, the concept being that all literature is in some way a reworking or revision of earlier writings. Tracing influences is scholarly work, involving immersion in the writings of various times and authors in order to establish not just reflections but conscious or unconscious connections. Such scholarship can be rewarding in our effort to perceive the work in a historical or cultural network that includes not just events and circumstances but authors and ideas.

lines, line breaks: In verse, many lines don't stop where sentences do. Thus line breaks become another meaningful division of syntactical parts that sometimes reinforce but more often skew or manipulate grammar for effect. To analyze line breaks, ask "why here, why not there?" and note differences that change the meaning or add significance. When line breaks coincide with ends of sentences, they are called *end-stopped lines*. When sentences continue beyond the end of a line, the strategy is called *enjambment*.

lyric: Any poem that, rather than telling a story, presents a speaker's state of mind or thought or feeling. It may include observation, reflection, recollection, thought, and feeling, and may be a short, simple expression of a moment, or a longer exploration of a mood or mindset, as in an elegy or an ode. Matthew Arnold's "Dover Beach," in Chapter 6, is a lyric poem.

metaphor: An implied comparison between one thing and something distinctly different. In Stafford's poem "Traveling through the Dark," the speaker observes that "The car aimed ahead its lowered parking lights;/under the hood purred the steady engine," comparing his car to an animal to complicate the easy separation of the human and natural worlds. Sometimes we call the object of the comparison the tenor, and that thing to which the subject is compared the vehicle. In the example from "Traveling through the Dark," the tenor would be the car and the vehicle would be an animal.

meter: The background rhythm to which the vowel, consonant, and rhyming sounds are played out. We can all hear a rhythm to spoken language, a rhythm that emphasizes certain words or sentences, that makes use of repetition and phrasing to help listeners make sense of the words. Writers of poetry consciously employ meter to reinforce their vision. When we read for meter by analyzing the rhythm, we are practicing *scansion*, or are said to be scanning the work.

The meter of a line of verse is first determined by the *pattern of stresses*, or the way stressed (or accented) and unstressed (or unaccented) syllables are arranged, and second by the number of *feet* in the line. One stressed syllable plus one or more unstressed syllables makes up what is called a foot, or a rhythmic unit that is characteristically repeated. The words used to indicate the number of feet per line from one to eight are monometer, dimeter, trimeter, tetrameter, pentameter, hexameter, heptameter, and octameter.

There are four standard feet in English:

iamb: two syllables, one unstressed followed by one stressed.

That TIME / of YEAR / thou MAYST / in ME / beHOLD (Shakespeare)

anapest: three syllables, two unstressed followed by one stressed.

Like a CHILD / from the WOMB

Like a GHOST / from the TOMB

I aRISE / and unBUILD / it aGAIN (Percy Bysshe Shelley)

trochee: two syllables, one stressed followed by one unstressed.

TROchee / TRIPS from / LONG to / SHORT (Coleridge)

dactyl: three syllables, one stressed followed by two unstressed.

PICture your / SELF on a / BOAT in a / RIVer with . . . (John Lennon and Paul McCartney)

To name the meter of a piece, we identify the type of foot used most often in the work, then modify it with the typical number of feet in a line. In the examples above, Shakespeare's line is iambic pentameter; Shelley's first is anapestic dimeter; Coleridge's line is trochaic tetrameter; and the Beatles' line is dactylic tetrameter.

metonymy: One term is used for another to which it is closely related, as in referring to a ruler as "the crown."

monologue: One character talks to one or more listeners without interruption. In *dramatic monologues* such as "Dover Beach," speakers usually reveal much more about themselves than they appear to intend. In *internal monologues* (like that of the older waiter in "A Clean, Well-Lighted Place" contemplating nothingness), a character reflects privately on an issue or idea, usually a central concern of the work.

novel: Fictional prose works longer than short stories, novels can contain more characters and offer more complications, relationships, and changes than shorter fictional works. Traditional expectations include plot, chapter divisions, characterization, descriptions of setting and states of mind, and a frame of reference to facilitate our engagement with the world of the novel.

Although the novel form has experienced a long, complicated, and well-documented historical evolution, it has become in modern times a

class distinguished primarily by its length and popularity. For every historical precedent to the current novel form, there are modern examples. The
picaresque novel, which emerged in Spain in the sixteenth century and follows a character (a "rogue") through a series of adventures, has its modern
counterparts in novels such as Jack Kerouac's *On the Road*. The epistolary
novel, made up entirely of letters, is an eighteenth-century form made contemporary in novels such as *The Color Purple* by Alice Walker. There are, as
well, novels that examine the social, economic, and political conditions of
times and characters; historical novels, which borrow details and circumstances, as well as characters and events, from recorded history; nonfiction
novels, which use fictional techniques to invite imaginative involvement
with actual events; and "new novels," which forego the standard expectations in favor of a series of disparate impressions out of which we are to
construct, or infer, a narrative coherence.

Some literature scholars have focused their research attention on the
evolution and permutations of the novel form, believing that our formal
expectations for order, relationship, and closure (how books should end)
affect our comprehension and evaluation of the works.

ode: A long lyric poem on a serious subject. Traditionally, the ode's stanzas
were presented in groups of three: the strophe, the antistrophe, and the
epode (point, counterpoint, and thrust). Each kind of stanza had its own
form. In the seventeenth century, "irregular" odes began to appear; these
retained a serious purpose and elevated style but allowed for variation in
line lengths, numbers of lines, and rhyme scheme. If you need examples,
find a poem with "ode" in the title (there are many), or find a copy of one of
our modern favorites: Wallace Stevens's "The Idea of Order at Key West."

onomatopoeia: The use of a word that sounds like what it means, as "hiss"
or "buzz" or "twitter."

persona, speaker, or narrator: The person telling the story. The voices of
the persona or narrators may be in *first person*, recounting their experiences,
or they may be in *third person*, describing what happened to others. The
persona may be inside or outside the work, a *participant* or an *observer*.

When a writer uses a particular speaking voice in a work, a voice to
which we can attribute particular attitudes, values, and biases, it is helpful
to understand that voice as a character or a role "put on" for the purposes
of the telling. (The word persona first referred to a mask worn by actors in
plays in ancient Greece.) To mistake that voice for the author often leads us
to assume that the writer is advocating, rather than examining, the statements or actions of the work.

Whether the persona is seemingly close to or distant from the writer's own experience or world view, it is much more interesting to think of the persona as "constructed," because even in autobiography, what we learn about a person is what that person chooses for us to know in an order artificially arranged for best effect. Our questions, then, about persona include who tells the story? How can we describe the role the persona is assuming?

personification: Attributing human qualities to things that are not human. Our most extended example of this type of figurative language is in William Dickey's poem "A Poet's Farewell to His Teeth," in which he makes his teeth his companions, lamenting their leaving and wishing them well.

plot: The structure of events in a story, what is included and in what order, is designed to arouse expectations in readers about what will happen and how characters will respond. Uncertainty, plus a concern on the part of the reader, results in suspense. If we are led to expect one thing but another happens, we experience surprise or anxiety, and we are lead to reflect on the turns of plot to see if, in fact, the ending was evident, if not obvious, in the story's development.

Gustav Freytag first characterized typical plot development with what is called "Freytag's pyramid," which depicts, with a triangular shape, the rising action, climax, and falling action of many plot structures. After an *exposition*, or opening section that sets the stage for later events, the *rising action* continues by introducing various complications and conflicts that reach their emotional apex in the *climax* (where they are resolved, for better or worse), and the *catastrophe* (where the protagonist faces the outcome of the climax). Following the emotional high point of the story is the *denouement* (French for "unknotting"), during which the story reaches a new resolution or "status quo" as a result of the plot events.

This structure is more evident in some stories than in others but is a valuable tool for studying nearly all narratives, in that it makes us conscious of the changes in the emotional climate of the work. Often in modern tales the moment of climax is not as evident in an event as in a change of mood or atmosphere—nothing much seems to happen, but the characters, or our reactions to the events, have reached an emotional climax anyway, as in the story "Home" by Gwendolyn Brooks in Chapter 3.

Freytag's pyramid can help us track double or multiple plots and their relationships to each other, and it can help us make more obvious the progression of an *anti-plot*, a structure grounded not in external events but in the psychological development of a character.

point of view: The perspective from which the story is told. We answer this when we ask about the persona or narrator. Narrators can know everything, not just events and details but also the thoughts and feelings of the characters, in which case they are called *omniscient*. Or they can have *limited* understanding, observing and recounting but not necessarily comprehending fully or clearly the events and details around them. When narrators seem to be all-knowing, we need to ask about their world view: what beliefs do they seem to hold? Can they be trusted? Do they project an attitude toward characters or events, and if so, is it based on assumptions we can identify? When the narrators have limited perspective, we must ask: What are those limitations? How do they influence the action, or our perceptions of characters or events?

protagonist: The main character in a story, novel, or drama around whom the action centers. Connie in "Where Are You Going, Where Have You Been?" is a protagonist, as is Maud Martha in "Home."

qualitative progression: In this kind of form, feelings rather than events motivate the development. Another of Kenneth Burke's terms, qualitative progression focuses our attention on the ways in which the presence of one quality or state of mind prepares us for another that can then appropriately follow. In Brooks's story "Home," for example, "quality" words in the opening like "little hope," "hard," "obstinate," and "emphatic iron" are used to describe features and details, but they contribute to an atmosphere or feeling that enables us to identify with the characters' suspension (their rocking back and forth), understand their sequence of alternating feelings, and relate both to their relief and to their resumption of rocking. If read conventionally, the plot could be said to progress toward a climax marked by the father's return, but read qualitatively, there is a second kind of climax in the middle, where they express and come to accept the possibility of a negative answer from the bank, which is followed by a deep "sigh." If you are aware of the qualitative progression, you may be better able to reflect on how the work's sequence affects you as a reader. This awareness may help you understand the development of plots that are difficult to explain by an analysis of conventionally expected stages marked by events.

repetition: The repetition of an image, feeling, or detail can propel the reader through a work by setting up a point of reference from which to view the progression. In "Home," for example, several references are made to "eyes." "Eyes" that view "possessively" end the richly provocative first paragraph; later Maud Martha tries to "keep the fronts of her eyes dry" as she gazes at a robin. Thus when we get to the clause "She knew from the way they looked at her," we know that we are to pay attention to the way eyes look, that this piece is about looking, and seeing, in a particular way. In the last sentence, Helen, "rocking rapidly," wants her friends "to just casually see that we're homeowners." Thus repetition can move a reader forward through a sequence even when the logical or structural progression is ambiguous.

To read for repetition as a developmental principle, watch for words, images, or ideas that are repeated, even if they don't seem obviously related. Watch, too, for words or images that seem significant, that seem to crystallize the meaning in some way, and ask whether they help to focus or explain the writer's vision.

rhyme: The most frequent types of rhymes are *close rhymes*, in which the last stressed vowel and all the sounds that follow it are alike, and *end rhymes*, which come at the ends of lines. *Internal rhymes* occur within a line. *Masculine or single rhymes* pair one syllable, as in "hill" and "still"; *feminine or double rhymes* pair two syllables, as in "started" and "parted."

Modern poetry may not rely on rhyme to convey or support meaning but frequently incorporates *irregular rhymes*, which occur when words don't quite rhyme but their similarity gets our attention. Irregular rhymes are also called *slant, near,* or *off* rhymes. Although different authorities define these in slightly different ways, irregular rhymes work to complicate an established order or link words that the writer wants the reader to connect. In Chapter 3, we note how an irregular rhyme in the first stanza of "My Papa's Waltz" subtly undermines the orderliness of the shape: "The whiskey on your breath/Could make a small boy dizzy;/But I hung on like death/Such waltzing was not easy." Rhyming dizzy with easy helps us feel how the waltz is not as easy as it might be, linking rhyme to meaning.

rhyme scheme: Reading for rhyme is one way of reading for relationships. To inquire about rhyme scheme is to analyze one of the ways in which the writer may have chosen to reinforce meaning with sound. Rhyme schemes indicate the patterns of end rhymes alphabetically. Thus in the first stanza of an Italian sonnet, the pattern *abbaabba* indicates that the first, fourth, fifth, and eighth lines rhyme, as do the second, third, sixth, and seventh. The rhyme scheme of John Keats's sonnet "When I Have Fears" can be represented as *abab cdcd efef gg*.

setting: The settings of literary works are the specific times, places, and circumstances against which the actions and events take place. Any reference to the place, whether it be a description of the chair in which a character sits or the landscape that surrounds her community can be considered purposeful, as can any reference to time—day, year, historical period, or era. References to circumstances, too, create a part of the environment within which characters choose, act, and respond. Their economic situation, job status, political leanings within a particular political moment, or social affiliations or disaffiliations can all influence the possibilities for characters and events in the perpetual balance of individual action and external forces. Setting contributes to meaning in a variety of ways: it can aid characterization, advance plot, create expectations, externally represent an internal mood or conflict, or suggest an attitude toward or ironic contrast with actions, behaviors, or events. Developing your skill at observing setting will help you meet a literary work on its own terms, a habit of mind that serves you well when you explore works that challenge the limitations of your own cultural experience.

short story: When Edgar Allan Poe set out to describe the "prose tale," which he so diligently and artfully composed, he included the following characteristics: it could be read at one sitting of from half an hour to two hours and it is limited to a "certain unique or single effect" to which every detail contributes. His description still seems applicable to many works of short fiction; perhaps because of the formal constraints, writers have tended to economize, making the most of every event, detail, and spoken word. Because of this concentration, the stylistic choices, the artistry of the writing, is often more evident in the short story than in the novel. You have several examples in this text, all of which can be read for the kind of "unity of effect" that Poe saw as the short story's distinguishing characteristic.

simile: A direct comparison of two unlike things using the words "like" or "as." The speaker in "My Papa's Waltz" dances with his father, holding on "like death," reinforcing the fear underlying the playfulness of the dance.

situational irony: A discrepancy or incongruity created when the circumstances of setting lead us to expect one thing and we get another, or when a setting seems to contrast with rather than to mirror an event or action. In Jeremy Cronin's poem "A Person Is a Person Because of Other People," the speaker is in prison, but his mirror reflects a message from another prisoner—with his "free hand," the unseen prisoner forms a "black fist," a symbol of freedom and power within a situation of powerlessness and isolation.

sonnet: A lyric poem in fourteen lines linked by an intricate rhyme scheme. Usually composed of an octave and a sestet, or three quatrains and a couplet (see "stanza"). The Italian or Petrarchan sonnet is divided into an octave (eight lines) rhyming *abbaabba* and a sestet (six lines) rhyming *cdecde*.

The octave usually presents a problem or problematic situation; the sestet usually presents the solution or resolution.

The English or Shakespearean sonnet is divided into three quatrains (four lines each) rhyming *abab cdcd efef* and a couplet (two lines) rhyming *gg*. The English sonnet also used the eight-line problem, six-line solution format, but it frequently appears with the three quatrains presenting variations of the same situation or idea, followed by a concluding or answering couplet.

The importance of the sonnet form for the reader of poetry is the same as its significance for writers: it's just long enough to present a complex idea with some resonance, and its formal requirements challenge the writer's artistry.

stanza: Italian for "stopping place," a stanza is a group of lines separated from other groups. Although the number of lines per stanza is unlimited and can vary within a poem, some stanza forms are used so frequently that they have names which help us discuss the design of the works we read. A two-line rhymed stanza is a *couplet*. A *tercet*, or triplet, has three lines. *Quatrains*, with four lines, are the most commonly used and are found with various rhyme schemes.

Particular combinations of stanzaic forms and rhyme schemes have become familiar by their association with classic works: *Rime royal* is a seven-line, iambic pentameter stanza rhyming *ababbcc*, and forms the structure of Chaucer's *Troilus and Criseyde*. *Ottava rima*, an Italian form, has eight lines rhyming *abababcc*. It was the perfect stanza form for Byron, who used it to write his masterwork *Don Juan*, partly because the two rhyming lines at the end often produces a comic effect.

Knowing about variation in stanza form can help us read for combinations of design elements in order to observe their effects. For example, Dylan Thomas's complicated reflection on death, "Do not go gentle into that good night," is a *villanelle*, which consists of five tercets and a quatrain. The extra line in the last stanza gives urgency and power to his vision.

style: The summation of an author's characteristic and unmistakable choices of words, syntactic structures, diction, imagery, tone, and ideas. If you imagine that the field of rhetorical choices about shape, language, participants, situations, and ideas a writer can make is just that, a "field," then a writer's style is the place in that field where he or she likes to stand. Inexperienced readers often say someone has or doesn't have style; experienced readers know to ask whether the writer's stylistic choices are or are not effective in creating and sustaining a vision. A sense of style, or the ability to distinguish the characteristic styles of various authors, comes with reading experience. Sometimes it helps to consider the style of groups rather than authors: an *idiom* is the characteristic language style of a group of people, whether that group consists of people from a particular region, occupation, ethnic group, neighborhood, or other affiliation.

syllogistic progression: A syllogism, the basic structure of an argument, is composed of a major premise, a minor premise, and a conclusion. In Chapter 5, you learned to work with logical progressions as you crafted your critical essays about literature. Syllogistic progression in literature is similar; it tracks the logical progression of the argument implicit in the work. The writer is persuading us to accept a possibility, to change an assumption, to set aside a preconceived notion, or to trade a simple vision for a more complicated one. Given one thing, something must logically follow. Aristotle's contention that literary works must have beginnings, middles, and ends describes syllogistic progression, as does Freytag's definition of the five stages in dramatic plots (see **plot**). In this text, we invited you to examine the syllogistic progressions of the critical articles in Chapter 6 and Annie Dillard's piece "Stalking Muskrats" in Chapter 3, but Elizabeth Bishop's poem "Filling Station" also makes a syllogistic argument. Her implied major premise is that evidence of coherent arrangement is also evidence of love. She finds evidence of coherent, purposeful arrangement, and concludes that "Somebody loves us all."

symbol: When words acquire complex or culturally significant meanings beyond themselves, they become symbols of those meanings. The term is broad enough to be difficult to distinguish from connotation except in the degree and significance of its network of meanings. The notion of symbol includes such conventionally accepted equivalencies as flag and country, such universally recognized patterns as the journey to the underworld, and such specific symbolic connections as that of darkness in "A Clean, Well-Lighted Place" to death and despair. In addition to being conventional, symbolic significance is related to culture (red is the color lighting prostitutes' windows in Amsterdam and the color of bridal gowns in traditional Hawaii), and context (red can symbolize love, and it can symbolize blood). It is more helpful, in some ways, to think about symbolic *uses* of language or ways to read *symbolically* than it is to classify specific features under the heading of symbol.

syntax: Analyzing syntax means examining the choices the writer makes in organizing the sentences that constitute the work. Literature follows predictable grammatical patterns but also varies, subverts, and manipulates them for effect. Thus when we analyze syntax, we're not always looking at complete sentences or regular grammar patterns; instead, we are observing how words and phrases are organized into sentences in ways that support the artist's vision. We can look at whether the sentences are more often simple or complex. We can observe whether the writer tends to use or avoid certain kinds of modifiers or how those modifiers are characteristically placed within sentences. We can watch for patterns of placement of certain sentence types. Whatever we notice, we use our observations to form generalizations in support of interpretive statements about the ideas.

In Chapter 4, we illustrated how repetition and variation in syntax in the poem "I Sing of a Maiden" reinforces a central paradox. Elizabeth Bishop's poem in Chapter 2 consists of sentences that include, at strategic points, phrases in parentheses that call attention to changes in her way of responding to the setting; the parentheses mark syntactical relationships, but they also visually reinforce the internal, personal nature of her reflections. The first paragraph of Gwendolyn Brooks's story "Home" manipulates normal sentence order: "What had been wanted was this always, this always to last— . . . These things might soon be theirs no longer." The wrenched syntax reinforces the characters' fear of displacement, and presses the reader forward in time to anticipate the resolution of the problem.

tone: When you speak, you express attitudes as well as explicit meaning. Using various gestures and inflections, you convey a range of attitudes. For example, you can ask the person next to you to "move over" and also communicate irritation, affection, or bored indifference. Through their stylistic choices, writers attempt to convey implicit attitudes toward the subject, the circumstances, or the audience of a work. Although tone is a subjective quality and difficult to characterize, we use and respond to it all the time. When we are offended by a message, it is most often the tone rather than the words that offends us.

Although tone in literature, as in life, can be misunderstood, writers give us a system of signals and signs to help us determine the attitude that will help us interpret the characters and events in meaningful ways. We can't know whether our reading of a work corresponds to what an author intended, nor does it really matter. When we read tone we are looking at how the signs and signals work to establish particular attitudes, assumptions, and values, and then reflecting on the way the tone influences our response and interpretation. William Dickey, we know, does not want us to cry over his loss in "A Poet's Farewell to His Teeth." Ernest Hemingway, however, clearly wants us to join in the older waiter's reverie over his "copita" in "A Clean, Well-Lighted Place."

value: Although this may seem an odd term to include in a list of literary language, it is relevant to a consideration of situations in which we place literary works as we inquire about them. Values are assigned based on criteria. Characters seem interesting or uninteresting, significant or insignificant, engaging or distancing depending on what criteria we bring to bear. Issues of value tend to come up in most literary discussions, as they did in both the conversation about "Filling Station" and the one about "Where Are You Going, Where Have You Been?" They begin with comments about liking or disliking something and evolve into discussions of what should, or shouldn't be valued.

Some of the most heated debates in current literary study, in fact, concern what is worth reading. You remember that in Chapter 6, Gerald Graff's OMP and YFP disagreed about the value of "Dover Beach." Such disagreements do not just affect what works we read in particular courses and programs; they can also influence what works are published. Gwendolyn Brooks's novel *Maud Martha*, from which we excerpted the chapter "Home," was published in 1953, the same year that James Baldwin published *Go Tell It on the Mountain*. Both books follow African-American characters from youth to adulthood. Baldwin's novel became a classic; Brooks's quickly went out of print and was unavailable for years. Why? Possibly readers did not know how to value Brooks's novel. It was poetic; it was quiet; its concern was not racial conflict or stereotypical presentations of oppression but the rich texture of ordinary life. When we judge the value of literature, our judgments are influenced by expectations that function as implicit criteria.

Criteria are contexts on the basis of which judgments of value are made. It is important for readers of literature to attempt to identify their criteria for making judgments in order to get beyond discussions of personal preference. It is also important to know that such criteria are negotiable, and that as responsible readers, you are a part of the evolving conversations going on in institutions and cultures that assign value to works over time. In this text we have included works that are generally believed to have enduring value; we also have included works less representative of traditional criteria. Which are which? All can inspire meaningful transactions between reader and work; all employ strategies of language that stretch our imaginations and challenge or clarify our way of seeing. As readers of literature, considering questions of value can help us identify our own criteria for judgment, become aware of those criteria being used by others, and argue for criteria that seem relevant to an appreciation of a work's significance.

verbal irony: When words are chosen that deliberately say something other than what they mean, the result is verbal irony, which can take the form of sarcasm, understatement, or hyperbole.

Acknowledgments

Bishop, Elizabeth. "Filling Station" from *The Complete Poems 1927–1979*. Farrar, Straus & Giroux. © 1989, 1983 by Alice Helen Methfessel. Reprinted by permission of Farrar, Straus & Giroux, Inc.

Brooks, Gwendolyn. "Home" from *Maud Martha*. Third World Press. © 1971 by Gwendolyn Brooks. Reprinted by permission of the author.

Caul, Leslee. "Good, Evil, and Gender in Sonnet 144." Central Washington University, 1995. Reprinted by permission.

Cronin, Jeremy. "Motho Ke Motho Ka Batho Babang (A Person Is a Person Because of Other People)" from *Inside*. Ravan Press. © 1983 by Jeremy Cronin. Reprinted by permission of the author.

Dickey, William. "A Poet's Farewell to His Teeth" from *The Rainbow Grocery*. Amherst: University of Massachusetts Press, 1978. © 1972, 1973, 1974, 1975, 1976, 1977, 1978 by William Dickey. Reprinted by permission of Leonard Sanazaro, executor of the estate of William Dickey.

Dillard, Annie. "Stalking Muskrats" from *Pilgrim at Tinker Creek*. Harper Perennial. © 1974 by Annie Dillard. Reprinted by permission of the author.

Finn, Robert. "Review of the Cleveland Orchestra," *The Cleveland, Ohio, Plain Dealer*, March 13, 1992. Reprinted by permission.

Glaspell, Susan. *Trifles*. © 1951 by Walter H. Baker Company. Reprinted by permission of John B. Welch.

Graff, Gerald. "Debate the Canon in Class" from *Beyond the Culture Wars*. © 1991, 1992 by Gerald Graff. Reprinted by permission of W. W. Norton and the author.

Harris, Darryl. "Old Men." Central Washington University, 1995. Reprinted by permission.

Hecht, Anthony. "The Dover Bitch: A Criticism of Life" from *Collected Earlier Poems*. © 1990 by Anthony E. Hecht. Reprinted by permission of Alfred A. Knopf at Random House.

Hemingway, Ernest. "A Clean, Well-Lighted Place" from *Winner Take Nothing*. © 1933 by Charles Scribner's Sons; renewed 1961 by Mary Hemingway. Reprinted by permission of Scribner, an imprint of Simon & Schuster.

Kelly, Patrick. "Moving Inside." Central Washington University, 1995. Reprinted by permission.

Morrison, Theodore. "Dover Beach Revisited: A New Fable for Critics" from *Harper's Magazine*, February 1940. © 1940 by Harper's Magazine. Reprinted by permission.

Oates, Joyce Carol. "Where Are You Going, Where Have You Been?" from *Where Are You Going, Where Have You Been?* Ontario Review Press/Princeton, 1993. © 1970 by Joyce Carol Oates. Reprinted by permission of the author.

Poole, Erin C. "Connie, Where Are You Going Where Have You Been?" Central Washington University, 1994. Reprinted by permission.

Porter, James. "Seeing the Ordinary as Extraordinary." Central Washington University, 1995. Reprinted by permission.

Roethke, Theodore. "My Papa's Waltz" from *The Collected Poems of Thoedore Roethke*. © 1942 by Hearst Magazines. Used by permission of Doubleday, a division of Bantam Doubleday Dell Publishing Group.

Silko, Leslie Marmon. "In Cold Storm Light" from *Storyteller*. Seaver Books. © 1981 by Leslie Marmon Silko.

Stafford, William. "Traveling through the Dark" from *Stories That Could Be True*. Harper and Row. © 1960. Reprinted by permission of Kim R. Stafford, executor of the estate of William Stafford.

Index